The Writings of the Apostolic Fathers

The Writings of the Apostolic Fathers

Edited by

Paul Foster

t&t clark

Published by T&T Clark
A Continuum imprint
The Tower Building, 11 York Road, London SE1 7NX
80 Maiden Lane, Suite 704, New York, NY 10038

www.continuumbooks.com

British Library Cataloguing-in-Publication Data
A catalogue record for this book is available from the British Library.

Typeset by Data Standards Ltd, Frome, Somerset, UK.
Printed on acid-free paper in Great Britain by Cromwell Press Ltd,
Trowbridge, Wiltshire

ISBN-10 0-567-03105-5 (hardback)
         0-567-03106-3 (paperback)
ISBN-13 978-0-567-03105-1 (hardback)
         978-0-567-03106-8 (paperback)

CONTENTS

PREFACE

1. *The Collection of Texts*

As is noted by many of the contributors to this volume, the collection of writings that is known by the title of 'the Apostolic Fathers' is in fact an artificial corpus, and in its current form a modern construct. The eleven texts that are treated here reflect different genres and diverse theological outlooks. The range of forms embraces a Church rule, various epistles, an early Christian homily, statements of defence of the Christian faith (apologies), visionary texts, fragments concerning early Christian trad-itions, and an account of the martyrdom of the author of one of the texts included in this corpus. This may rightly seem to be an odd jumble of texts. Yet this very diversity reflects the creativity and the different ways in which nascent Christianity expressed various aspects of its message prior to the end of the second century. To read the writings of the Apostolic Fathers is to gain a greater sense of such pluriformity. Also these texts provide an understanding of the battles that were fought as attempts were made to unify disparate groups by transforming this spontaneous and charismatic religious phenomenon into a structured, sustainable and stable movement.

Although it is true that the collection of writings is in large part artificial, based upon similarities in dating and the perception that such writings were proto-orthodox, there was already a tendency prior to the modern age to group some of these writings together. The *First* and *Second Epistles of Clement* circulated together as early as the fifth century as part of the biblical Codex Alexandrinus. This seems to suggest that at least in some circles these writings were considered scriptural. It might be argued that it is unsurprising that these two writings were grouped together since they are the first and second epistles of a common author. But closer examination reveals that the second is not an epistle at all (unlike the first of these writings), and in fact neither text bears the name Clement – that is a later addition. So the mystery is how the name Clement became attached to both these writings – one an epistle, the other a homily, how they became grouped together, and why they were put on an equal footing by some early Christians with biblical texts. Similarly, two very different texts, the *Epistle of Barnabas* and the *Shepherd of Hermas*, are both included at the end of the fourth-century Codex

Sinaiticus, another great biblical manuscript. Here is a further example of the status afforded to some of these writings.

The next major piece of evidence in the formation of this evolving corpus dates to 1056 CE, when the so-called Jerusalem codex was written (also known by the Latin title, Codex Hierosolymitanus, and represented by the letter H). This manuscript contains the previously unidentified document known as the *Didache*, along with the *Epistle of Barnabas, 1 and 2 Clement*, and the longer recension of the Ignatian letters. It was discovered in 1873 in the library of the Jerusalem Monastery of the Holy Sepulchre at Constantinople by Philotheos Bryennios, the Metropolitan of Nicomedia.

In the modern era the first printed edition of texts that could be labelled as the Apostolic Fathers was produced by J.B. Cotelier in 1672. The two volumes he published were entitled *SS. Patrum qui temporibus apostolicis floruerunt . . . opera . . . vera et supposticia*. This collection included the writings of Barnabas, Clement, Hermas, Ignatius and Polycarp.[1] Over subsequent generations the collection was expanded to include the *Epistle to Diognetus*, the fragments of Papias, the fragment of the *Apology of Quadratus* and finally the *Didache*.

2. *The Discussions of the Texts in this Volume*

There has been a growing recognition of the significance of this collection of texts in recent years, as is evidenced by the ever-increasing body of research. This interest is in part stimulated by a desire to know what happened immediately after the close of the New Testament period. It should be noted, however, that some of the texts in the Apostolic Fathers are perhaps contemporary with, or even earlier than, the last writings of the New Testament. Also, many scholars have investigated these writings in their own right, since they provide a window into early second-century Christianity and the religio-social forces that shaped the various expressions of this movement during this period of rapid change and transformation.

The introductory essay is a contribution by Professor Helmut Koester, who has been writing on this topic for more than fifty years. His incisive survey here tackles much broader questions than his doctoral dissertation, which investigated the use of the New Testament in the Apostolic Fathers.[2] That initial research was carried out under the supervision of Professor Rudolf Bultmann, a colossus in the twentieth century in the

---

1. See M.W. Holmes, *The Apostolic Fathers: Greek Texts with English Translations* (Grand Rapids: Baker Academic, 1999), 3.

2. H. Koester, *Synoptische Überlieferung bei den Apostolischen Vätern*, Texte und Untersuchungen 65 (Berlin: Akademie-Verlag, 1957).

study of the New Testament and Christian origins. This pedigree produces a chain of tradition for this volume that characters like Quadratus and Papias would be happy to boast about! Koester's essay is a breath of fresh air, weaving together the insights he has gained from his fifty years of research. In many ways this is not a traditional introduction to the corpus – enough of those are available elsewhere. Instead it is a creative appreciation of the writings of the Apostolic Fathers as reflections of the forces that were at work in the second century reshaping Christianity. To read this essay is to enter into the vibrant and polemical struggles at work in the emergent movement.

Professor Jonathan Draper is an acknowledged world expert on the *Didache*.[3] Again his contribution is a rich source of fact and reflection upon the text. Readers may be surprised to learn that this text contains the earliest known Christian prohibitions against pederasty and abortion, but more significantly it gives a glimpse into the life of an early Jewish-Christian community, describing its baptismal and Eucharistic liturgy. Draper argues that the *Didache* is not dependent on Matthew's Gospel; rather, the dependence is reversed, and it is Matthew which is dependent on the *Didache*. The consequence of this, according to Draper, is that the *Didache* could be an extremely early Jewish-Christian text dating back as far as the mid-first century.

In the essay on *1 Clement*, Dr Andrew Gregory discusses the purpose of this occasional letter, which attempted to resolve a conflict in Corinth. He highlights the fact that there already existed a communication network between some of the early churches, and although the author of this epistle does not claim any intrinsic authority over the Corinthian congregation, he is extremely keen for harmony to return to this group. Gregory argues that *1 Clement* is very much a product of the Hellenistic world and utilizes the rhetorical conventions that existed in that context. The discussion of the use of the New Testament in *1 Clement* reflects his previous research into this text.[4]

The artistry with which Dr Paul Parvis writes his essay on *2 Clement* makes reading this piece a sheer pleasure. In fact, with due respect to the author of *2 Clement*, without this sympathetic and insightful introduction one could look upon this text in the Apostolic Fathers as dull and uninspiring. Yet the text is rescued by Parvis, who again and again produces perceptive pearls of wisdom about the nature and purpose of this earliest extant Christian homily. Parvis's forthcoming work on Justin

---

3. See for instance J.A. Draper (ed.), *The Didache in Modern Research* (Leiden: Brill, 1996).

4. A. Gregory, '*1 Clement* and the Writings that Became the New Testament', in A. Gregory and C.M. Tuckett (eds), *The Reception of the New Testament in the Apostolic Fathers* (Oxford: Oxford Universiry Press, 2005), 129–57.

Martyr is testimony to his ongoing contribution to research into Christianity in the second century.[5]

Fool, or faithful transmitter of tradition? That is the question that confronts those who wish to evaluate the contribution of the early Christian writer Papias of Hierapolis. What makes this question difficult is the fact that his writings are only preserved in fragmentary citations embedded in the works of others, primarily in the *Historia Ecclesiastica* of Eusebius of Caesarea. Professor Charles Hill takes a scholarly and sympathetic approach to assessing the contribution of this author. There are detailed discussions of some of the fragments from Papias' five-volume work *Expositions of the Dominical Logia*. Hill's wider interest in the Apostolic Fathers is apparent from his recent volume which identifies the author of the *Epistle to Diognetus* as none other than Polycarp of Smyrna.[6]

The single fragment of the *Apology of Quadratus* that is contained in the writings of Eusebius may provide the earliest preserved example of a Christian apology. Interestingly, the fragment offers a defence of the Christian faith based on the testimony of those who had experienced healing or resurrection from death directly from Jesus. Such an argument was only tenable while representatives of this first generation of the Jesus-movement were alive, or at least while people who had first-hand contact with them could pass on the accounts of their miraculous healing. It is perhaps for this reason that this argument is not reproduced by later apologists. This oft-neglected fragment is given equal acknowledgement in this volume alongside the other texts in the corpus, rather than being relegated to a learned footnote.

'Peculiar' is the adjective that Professor Joseph Verheyden uses to describe the text known as the *Shepherd of Hermas*, and it is debatable whether a more apt description could be found. Yet despite its apparently strange apocalyptic air, at least to modern tastes, it was remarkably popular in the early Church and is preserved in a number of manuscripts and cited by various Church Fathers. Verheyden characterizes the author as both a preacher and a prophet based in Rome, yet apparently without any official status. Thus it appears that the numerous house churches in Rome may have retained a loose confederacy, but that any form of structured episcopacy was late in coming to the imperial capital. Verheyden has written previously on second-century Christianity and

---

5. Parvis is currently producing a new critical edition of the *Apologies* of Justin Martyr with Dr Denis Minns of Blackfriars, Oxford.

6. C.E. Hill, *From the Lost Teaching of Polycarp: Identifying Irenaeus' Apostolic Presbyter and the Author of* Ad Diognetum (Tübingen: Mohr-Siebeck, 2006).

recently produced a study on the use of the New Testament in the *Shepherd of Hermas*.[7]

Dr James Carleton Paget skilfully leads readers through the problematic issues that surround the *Epistle of Barnabas*. Perhaps the most fascinating aspect of the discussion is the author's attitude towards Judaism and Jewish traditions. The *Epistle of Barnabas* appeals to the Old Testament repeatedly, but promotes non-literal interpretations which appear quite consciously to contrast with Jewish interpretations. While the author is happy to 'take over' the Jewish scriptures, he nonetheless adopts an extremely separatist stance towards Jews. Carleton Paget perceptively questions whether this indicates a situation where absolute division between the two communities has taken place, or rather reflects a complex form of interaction. Carleton Paget has previously made a major contribution to research on the *Epistle of Barnabas* in a monograph tackling a range of issues raised by this writing.[8]

Every critical issue surrounding the epistles written by Ignatius of Antioch appears to be contested. Although most scholars are happy to adopt the middle recension of the shorter forms of the seven epistles as representing the genuine Ignatian corpus, there are still dissenting voices – some of whom suggest that the entire corpus is a later fabrication. The dating of the epistles is extremely problematic, and linked to both the dating of Polycarp's *Epistle to the Philippians* and the accuracy of dating provided by Eusebius in his *Chronicon*. The theological issues contained in the epistles raise perennial questions about the emergence of ecclesiastical structures, the threefold pattern of ministry, monarchical episcopacy, the real presence in the Eucharist, and the theology of martyrdom. Despite one's predilections concerning such matters, it is hard not to have some glowing admiration for the way in which Ignatius heroically approaches his fate in the Roman arena.

Professor Michael Holmes's treatment of Polycarp's *Epistle to the Philippians* makes what may be the most significant rebuttal of theories which suggest that two separate fragments of previous epistles have been joined together to produce the current textual form. Holmes also highlights the centrality of the concept and language of 'righteousness' in this epistle. Holmes convincingly suggests that this is a unified perspective which sees 'right beliefs' and 'right behaviours' as intrinsically linked. According to Polycarp, if one of these is defective, the other is also likely to be deficient. This explains Polycarp's denounciation of Valens,

7. J. Verheyden, 'The *Shepherd of Hermas* and the Writings that Later Formed the New Testament', in Gregory and Tuckett (eds), *The Reception of the New Testament in the Apostolic Fathers*, 293–329.

8. J.C. Paget, *The Epistle of Barnabas: Outlook and Background*, WUNT 2.82 (Tübingen: Mohr-Siebeck, 1994).

since as Holmes states, 'Valens denies by his deeds what the "heretics" deny by their words.' Holmes is best known for his editions of the texts of the Apostolic Fathers,[9] and he is currently engaged in writing the Hermeneia commentary on this text.

The *Martyrdom of Polycarp* is one of those texts which emblazons itself on the mind of both pious and scholars alike. Apart from the graphic description of Polycarp's death, the text communicates much of the value-inverting attitudes of early Christians towards death. Martyrdom is the means of life, suffering is the path to exaltation, and dying for Jesus enables one to rise with him in glory. Dr Sara Parvis elucidates these aspects in the thought of this martyrdom account. Her earlier work focused on the Arian controversy, and in particular upon the role of Marcellus of Ancyra.[10] Here she examines a problematic and much-discussed text and produces fresh arguments for its authenticity and integrity. Of particular interest is the original discussion of Roman legal procedures and the way this impinges on understanding the irregularity of judicial conduct in sentencing Polycarp.

The *Epistle to Diognetus* comes to us as 'one untimely born' and unfortunately, also, as one with an untimely demise. Not cited by the Church Fathers, this text was discovered in a fishmonger's shop in the fifteenth century, and then destroyed by fire during the Franco–Prussian war in 1870. Fortunately a number of transcriptions were made which still survive. These transcriptions preserve various marginal notes from the original which make it clear that the work is a composite, with the final two chapters being attached at some stage to the initial ten (the larger section also being lacunose in at least one place). The first ten chapters are an apology addressed to a certain Diognetus, attempting to convince this figure of the claims of the Christian faith. The epistle is an intellectually muscular defence of the faith, which exudes a confidence in the superiority of the author's belief system in comparison to the beliefs held by the main competitors of the day, namely paganism and Judaism.

3. *The Value of the Apostolic Fathers*

The collection of texts of the Apostolic Fathers is of interest as a historical artefact reflecting Christianity during the second century. Yet, both individually and cumulatively, these texts offer much more than mere historical curiosity. They are a rich theological resource and explain many of the developments and trajectories that emerged in Christianity. The

9. M.W. Holmes, *The Apostolic Fathers in English*, 3rd edn (Grand Rapids: Baker Academic, 2006). For the Greek text consult LHH. (see Abbreviations, below).

10. S. Parvis, *Marcellus of Ancyra and the Lost Years of the Arian Controversy 325–345*, Oxford Early Christian Studies (Oxford: Oxford University Press, 2006).

thinking enshrined in these writings helps explain the initial stages of the transformation of a collection of individual communities loosely linked by their common belief in Jesus as God's Messiah to an organization with a structured hierarchy and empire-wide links. In short, one sees the beginning of the understanding of the Church as a universal entity.[11]

Paul Foster
The Feast of the Martyrdom of St Ignatius of Antioch
1 February 2006

---

11. The chapters contained in this volume are in the process of appearing in *Expository Times* 117:4 (January 2006) to 118:4 (January 2007).

Abbreviations

Strom.	Clement of Alexandria, *Stromateis*
Vit. Poly.	*Life of Polycarp*

Secondary Sources:

ABD	D.N. Freedman (ed.), *The Anchor Bible Dictionary* (New York: Doubleday, 1992)
AGAJU	Arbeiten zur Geschichte des antiken Judentums und des Urchristentums
ANRW	H. Temporini and W. Haase (eds), *Aufstieg und Niedergang der römischen Welt* (Berlin: W. de Gruyter, 1972–)
BR	*Biblical Research*
EDNT	H. Balz and G. Schneider (eds), *Exegetical Dictionary of the New Testament*, 3 vols ET (Grand Rapids: Eerdmans, 1990–3)
ESCJ	Studies in Christianity and Judaism/Études sur le christianisme et le judaïsme
ExpT	*Expository Times*
FRLANT	Forschungen zur Religion und Literatur des Atten und Neuen Testaments
HNT	Handbuch zum Neuen Testament
HTR	*Harvard Theological Review*
JECS	*Journal of Early Christian Studies*
JETS	*Journal of the Evangelical Theological Society*
JSNT	*Journal for the Study of the New Testament*
JSOTSup	*Journal for the Study of the Old Testament, Supplement Series*
JTS	*Journal of Theological Studies*
KAV	Kommentar zu den Apostolischen Vätern
LCL	Loeb Classical Library
LHH	J.B. Lightfoot, J.R. Harmer and M.W. Holmes (eds), *The Apostolic Fathers: Greek Texts and English Translations of their Writings*, 2nd edn (Grand Rapids: Baker Book House, 1999)
NovT	*Novum Testamentum*
NovTSup	*Novum Testamentum*, Supplements
NTS	*New Testament Studies*
PTS	Patristische Texte und Studien
RB	*Revue Biblique*
RSPhTh	*Revue des sciences philosophique et théologique*
RHR	*Revue de l'histoire des religions*
SC	Sources Chrétiennes
SecCent	*Second Century*

StPatr	*Studia Patristica*
ThZ	*Theologische Zeitschrift*
VC	*Vigiliae Christianae*
VCSupp	*Vigiliae Christianae*, Supplement Series
WUNT	Wissenschaftliche Untersuchungen zum Neuen Testament
ZAC	*Zeitschrift für antikes Christentum*
ZNW	*Zeitschrift für die neutestamentliche Wissenschaft*

LIST OF CONTRIBUTORS

Jonathan A. Draper is Professor of New Testament at the University of KwaZulu-Natal, South Africa.

Paul Foster is Lecturer in New Testament Language, Literature and Theology at the University of Edinburgh.

Andrew Gregory is Chaplain of University College and a member of the Faculty of Theology at the University of Oxford.

Charles E. Hill is Professor of New Testament at Reformed Theological Seminary, Orlando, Florida.

Michael Holmes is Professor of Biblical Studies and Early Christianity at Bethel University, St Paul, Minnesota.

Helmut Koester is John H. Morison Research Professor of Divinity and Winn Research Professor of Ecclesiastical History at Harvard Divinity School.

James Carleton Paget is Lecturer in New Testament at the University of Cambridge.

Paul Parvis was formerly Regent of Blackfriars, Oxford and is currently a private scholar based at the University of Edinburgh.

Sara Parvis is Lecturer in Patristics at the University of Edinburgh.

Joseph Verheyden is Professor of New Testament at Katholieke Universiteit Leuven, Netherlands.

Chapter 1

THE APOSTOLIC FATHERS AND THE STRUGGLE FOR CHRISTIAN IDENTITY

Helmut Koester

It does not have to be repeated here that the term 'Apostolic Fathers' is an artificial designation originating in the period of the Renaissance. But different from other writings produced around the turn of the first century CE and during the early decades of the second century CE – excluding those that were incorporated into the canon of the New Testament[1] – most of the documents included in this corpus enjoyed some reception among the Church Fathers of the following period and some were even considered as possible candidates for the canon of the New Testament. Dionysius of Corinth wrote to the Romans in the middle of the second century that they were still reading the letter that had been sent from Rome to Corinth by Clement.[2] The *Shepherd of Hermas* was widely used at an early time and debated later in the Canon Muratori with respect to its possible canonical status. The letters of Ignatius of Antioch played a significant role in the Trinitarian controversies in Antioch, where revised editions of these letters were produced in the fourth century. But already at the time of their writing early in the second century they served as instruments for admonishing and for ordering the life of churches; this is evident from the letter(s) of Polycarp of Smyrna, who distributed copies of Ignatius' letters to other churches.[3] The *Epistle of Barnabas* as well as *1 Clement* and the *Shepherd of Hermas* appeared early in biblical manuscripts.[4] The *Didache*, though not often copied in antiquity, was nevertheless very influential as its materials entered into several later church orders and liturgies. All these were therefore documents that the later church neither forgot nor rejected.

---

1. Namely, 1 Peter, Ephesians and the Pastoral Epistles.
2. Eusebius, *HE* 4.23.11.
3. Poly. *Phil.* 13.2.
4. The *Epistle of Barnabas* and the *Shepherd of Hermas* were found in the fourth-century Codex Sinaiticus, *1 Clement* in the fifth-century Codex Alexandrinus.

1. *The Formation of Christian Identity*

All these documents reflect the struggle for Christian identity that took place in the post-apostolic period, and all of them represent to various degrees a position that points to the preservation of the apostolic heritage for the founding of viable Christian communities. In order to understand this struggle other writings of this period should be studied together with the Apostolic Fathers, especially the Letter to the Ephesians, the First Epistle of Peter[5] and first and foremost the Pastoral Epistles[6] of the New Testament, and to a certain degree the Gospel of Matthew and the Acts of the Apostles. The Apostolic Fathers can no longer be separated from the contemporaneous documents that happened to be included in the canon of the New Testament. The purpose and intent of much of this literature has traditionally been described as an effort to establish order and ecclesiastical authority. While this is undeniably true, this effort is only a part of a larger struggle. In order to understand that struggle it is necessary to give a brief analysis of the very beginnings of the attempts to define the heritage of Jesus' message and fate.

The two earliest documents that provide some evidence for the very first developments after the death of Jesus are the genuine letters of Paul and the Synoptic Sayings Gospel (Q). Both were composed during the first generation after the death of Jesus[7] and both grasp the fact that Jesus' ministry was that of a prophet. As a prophet, Jesus called for a new obedience which is demanded in the recognition that no earthly ruler or Messiah but God is king. Furthermore, Jesus suffered the fate of the prophet in the conduct of his ministry, being despised and rejected and eventually killed. But the Sayings Gospel presents a very different interpretation of this prophetic heritage in comparison to the perspective contained in the writings of Paul.

The interpretation dominating the earliest form of the Sayings Gospel is highly religious and ultimately individualistic.[8] While it tries to preserve the eschatological aspects of Jesus' proclamation, it calls the individual into a special personal commitment, wisdom and conduct that is appropriate for the coming rule of God. In such conduct the presence of this divine rule is already realized. That, however, required a withdrawal from the ways of the existing society. The community of these followers of

---

5.   Both probably written at the very beginning of the second century.

6.   The Pastoral Epistles, in my opinion, may have been written as late as the middle of the first half of the second century.

7.   Although the final edition of the Synoptic Sayings Gospel should probably be dated after the year 70 CE, an earlier draft of this Gospel must have appeared at about the time of Paul's ministry.

8.   I am guided here by the analysis in J.S. Kloppenborg, *The Formation of Q*, Studies in Antiquity and Christianity (Philadelphia: Fortress Press, 1987).

Jesus was a 'sectarian' organization of those who had committed themselves to a life according to the commands of the divine rule that was present in Jesus' sayings. Perhaps the Eucharistic prayers of the *Didache* preserve the central community ritual for these circles of Jesus' followers. In the later stage of the development of the Sayings Gospel, the groups of followers of Jesus who were guided by this document apparently had to face a political decision: should they follow the call for a revolutionary uprising in Palestine against Roman occupation or should they distance themselves from such messianic propaganda? Prophets guiding these groups proclaimed that the future would not be fulfilled by a messianic war; rather, the Son of Man would appear suddenly and unexpectedly for judgement of the world and salvation of the faithful. This prophetic message shaped the later form of the Sayings Gospel that was adapted by Matthew and Luke into their writings.

But, at the same time, the interpretation by other followers, who also saw in the heritage of the words of Jesus the guiding principle of their religious commitment, thoroughly individualized the message of these sayings. This is visible in the development of the sayings tradition that is preserved in the *Gospel of Thomas*. Here, the sayings of Jesus call for a complete separation not only from the structures of the existing society but altogether from the earthly and material world. The 'single one' is the one who will not taste death but realizes the immortality of the imperishable ultimate self. It does not matter whether or not this interpretation of Jesus' sayings is labelled as 'Gnostic'. What is at stake here is the fact that the heritage of Jesus' message and ministry is understood in purely religious terms. 'Religion' for this interpretation is the singular concentration upon the concept of the salvation of the individual in the overcoming of death, unsullied by any political, social or other worldly concerns. The ideal of a new community of Christ in this world has disappeared completely.

On the other hand, for Paul and his work, as it is documented in his genuine letters, the prophetic heritage of Jesus' ministry is reduced to the concept of the suffering and death of the prophet as a result of the faithful conduct of his office. Here the office of the prophet is understood in political terms. The prophet is seen as the one who announces God's justice in the midst of the disobedience of the people. The prophet is not just sent to Israel but also to the nations. This understanding of the prophetic office had already been universalized in the tradition of Israel, as is most evident in the prophetic book of Second Isaiah.[9] As Jesus, the

9. See especially Isa. 49.6. The inspiration for this understanding of Deutero-Isaiah is due to K. Baltzer, *Deutero-Isaiah: A Commentary on Isaiah 40—55*, Hermeneia (Minneapolis: Fortress Press, 2001). See also my essay 'Suffering Servant and Royal Messiah: From Second Isaiah to Paul, Mark, and Matthew', *Theology Digest* 51 (2004), 103–24.

prophet, has atoned already for the disobedience and sinfulness of all people through his suffering and death, this event becomes for Paul the turning point in the course of the world which ushers in the possibility of the realization of God's rule of justice and equity for all people.

The task of the apostle therefore has uniquely political dimensions: he is commissioned to call all people into a new community of love, justice and equity, the *ecclesia*, that is, the assembly of all people of a new society authorized by the righteousness of God. Specific 'religious' values play no role here. Paul never speaks about conversion as an individualistic process, by which one achieves a new status of piety. He considers the exercise of special religious and spiritual gifts as highly problematic and possibly destructive.[10] The Eucharist should not be abused for the documentation of individual piety but is the realization of unity and respect for all in a new community; the poor should not be despised.[11] Spiritual gifts are useless as long as they demonstrate nothing but individual religious achievement; they are legitimately exercised solely for the building of the community, which is the body of Christ.[12]

There are, however, two problems with this political interpretation of the heritage of Jesus that confronted the post-apostolic generation. First, Paul's concept of the new community is framed by an eschatological perspective. It could be called utopian; in fact, the image of the body of Christ is spelled out by Paul in 1 Corinthians 12 in patterns that draw from the utopian Hellenistic vision of the ideal city. The new community, which is the body of Christ, is asked to create now in its own midst what will be realized fully in the future. Only in the future, at the return of Christ, will this political vision be fully realized. This future is expected to be very near. Second, while the ritual law is rejected because it would only perpetuate the division between Jews and Gentiles, the moral law of the tradition of Israel is radically reduced to the commandment of love.[13] As Paul spells out the demands of the new conduct, he does not seek guidance by returning to the moral law of Israel; rather, he details the various aspects of a loving conduct in which the good of the other is the foremost concern.[14] This does not imply that Paul condones transgressions of Jewish and Roman law, such as murder, theft and adultery; these are simply outside of the concerns for the building of the community.[15] But at the same time, the utopian elements of Paul's vision of justice and equity in the new community cast aside the established structures upon which the

10. Of particular significance are 1 Corinthians 8 and 14.
11. 1 Cor. 11.17–34.
12. 1 Cor. 13.1–3; 12.4–31.
13. Rom. 13.8–10 and elsewhere.
14. 1 Cor. 13.4–7; Gal. 5.22–4.
15. 1 Cor. 5.1–8; Rom. 13.1–7; and elsewhere.

piety and morality of the Roman world was established, especially the preservation of ethnic identities and the differentiations in gender and social status.[16] Because such distinctions would jeopardize the vision of the new community of justice and equality, Paul has no interest in accommodating Christian conduct to the piety and morality of the Roman world. Although this justice and equality for all, the righteousness of God, would be generally established only at the return of Christ in the near future, it is to be realized right now in anticipation of that return of Christ. The evident consequences of this interpretation of the heritage of Jesus are that the delay of the return of Christ would call for a new orientation of the concept of the building and preservation of the community.

In the post-apostolic period, the expectation of the eventual return of Christ for the establishment of a new world is indeed upheld. That this return of Christ would come soon, however, is no longer a functioning principle of the orientation of the churches and their conduct in this world. Indeed, talk of a return of Christ in the near future could even become a threat to the well-being of the Christian churches. That is clearly shown in the deutero-Pauline Second Letter to the Thessalonians, and it was to reappear a century later in the polemic of the anti-Montanist writers. It soon became evident that the Christian churches were here to stay in this world for the time being. That implied, however, that these churches had to adjust their moral conduct to the established moral and social norms of the Roman world in which they existed, unless they wanted to accept the alternative presented by the radical interpreters of the sayings of Jesus, which increasingly denied the relevance of all social and worldly structures in favour of the achievement of an individualistic religious concept of salvation as it is recommended in the *Gospel of Thomas*. That, however, would also have destroyed the possibility of defining Christian existence in the context of communal structures – Christian existence as bound into a community of love, support and respect.

2. *Roman Responses to the New Religious Movement*

An additional factor played a role in this struggle for the definition of Christian identity. The Romans, with their imperialistic ideals of a functioning society, had been extremely suspicious, ever since the Dionysiac crisis of the Hellenistic period, of any movements that did not respect the piety and morality of society at large. Rome was quick to prosecute any groups that did not adhere to these standards. For Rome,

16. Gal. 3.28.

what was at stake here was the maintaining of 'piety' against 'superstition'. The letter which Pliny the Younger as governor of Bithynia sent to
the emperor Trajan at the beginning of the second century, and Trajan's
rescript, illuminate the problem.[17] To be sure, both reveal that the
Christians did not do anything that was punishable by existing laws. On
the contrary, Pliny acknowledges that the Christians even took oaths that
they would not wrong anyone. But they not only met early in the morning,
in their stubbornness they also refused to demonstrate their piety by
sacrificing to the gods and the emperor and they had slave women who
were leaders (deacons) in their assemblies, which was considered an
offence against generally accepted moral standards.

Anonymous accusations, however, were not deemed acceptable, and
there was no incentive for the ruling authorities to seek out Christians. A
few decades later, Hadrian sent a *rescript* to Minucius Fundanus,
governor of the province of Asia, in which those bringing wrong
accusations against Christians were threatened with punishment.[18] The
implications of such policies are evident: as long as Christians did not do
anything that offended their neighbours they did not have to fear
persecutions. The questions of piety and morality did not have any place
in Paul's eschatological concept of the new community. But if Christian
communities wanted to continue living unscathed within the pious and
moral order of Rome's world, they evidently had to reflect upon orders of
piety and morality that did not offend the Roman order. It seems that
there was no possible compromise with respect to the worship of the
emperor as a god – not to speak of the worship of any pagan gods. These,
however, were not issues with which Christians, Jews or any others were
confronted in their daily life. There may have been occasional situations,
such as the building of the first neokorate temple of the city of Ephesus at
the time of the emperor Domitian, to which the prophet of the Revelation
of John responds. But on the whole, during most of the period from the
end of the first century to the times of Marcus Aurelius (after 160),
worship of the gods of the Roman people and the emperor seems not to
have been generally demanded by the authorities. In this respect,
Christians could rest in peace as long as they made it evident that they
respected political authority and prayed for the emperor, as 1 Peter,
the Pastoral Epistles and the epistle of Polycarp to the Philippians
recommend.[19]

17. See Pliny, *Letters of Pliny the Younger to Trajan*, 10.96.
18. Eusebius, *HE* 4.8.6—4.9.3.
19. 1 Pet. 2.13–14; 1 Tim. 2.2; Poly. *Phil.* 12.3.

3. *Ordering the New Community*

The other question, however, remained: how could the life of the Christian communities be ordered in such a way that no offence would be given to their non-Christian neighbours and friends? And could these communities, at the same time, maintain their vision of being a people that belonged to a kingdom that was not of this world? Attempts to respond to these questions characterize most of the writings of the Apostolic Fathers as well as other documents of the period and make them fascinating documents, which should be read with an empathy that rejects all modern approaches, which are only too eager to condemn these writings for their anti-feminism, their condoning the institution of slavery, and their submission to hierarchical structures. The wisdom, courage and prudence of the writers of these documents deserve to be investigated with all necessary humility.

Attempting to find resources for the ordering of churches in the new situation of the post-apostolic age, the Apostolic Fathers first turned to the heritage of Diaspora Judaism. This included, of course, the Septuagint, the Greek translation of Israel's scriptures. This marks a fundamental difference from those followers of Jesus who cherished the tradition of Jesus sayings as their guide; references to scripture are astoundingly rare in that branch of the early Christians. In Diaspora Judaism, however, these scriptures had already been transformed from being a guide to correct ritual into a resource for morality and piety. This had elevated the Decalogue to a distinguished position as the enshrinement of a supreme moral code that could be interpreted for the definition of whatever was good and beneficial for the individual and for the community. The description of the 'way of life' in the first chapters of the *Didache* (and in the *Epistle of Barnabas*), which was part of the heritage of Diaspora Judaism, is nothing but an interpretation of the Decalogue. Analogous arguments can be found in the *Mandates* of the *Shepherd of Hermas*. It was this understanding of the Decalogue that had enabled Diaspora Judaism to establish itself in the daily conduct of its members as a legitimate part of the required morality of the Roman world. On this basis the Jewish philosopher Philo of Alexandria had recommended the Decalogue as the foundation both of a perfect philosophical life and of the moral legislation of a perfect society.[20]

The second element of the heritage of the Jewish Diaspora and its Bible was the mining of this Bible for examples of good moral conduct and of the consequences of immorality. This process was guided by catalogues of virtues and vices that had been developed in popularized Stoic philosophy. Catalogues of vices could be used unaltered as a description of the

20. See Philo's treatise *De Decalogo*, which is part of his apologetic writings.

'Way of Death'[21] or expanded into admonitions for moral conduct.[22] But these catalogues were also turned into a tool for the search for fitting biblical examples. *1 Clement*, in chapters 3—23 and elsewhere, presents very well-structured examples of the teaching of moral conduct on the basis of corresponding biblical stories. First, a traditional catalogue of vices is quoted: 'jealousy and envy, strife and sedition, persecution and disorder, war and captivity'.[23] Then the first of these vices, jealousy, and its bad consequences are demonstrated with biblical examples: Jacob, Joseph, Moses, Aaron and Miriam, Dathan and Abeiron, etc.[24] The *Epistle of Barnabas*, on the other hand, utilizes methods of allegorical and typological exegesis that had been learned from the sages of the Jewish Diaspora.

For the liturgical requirements of gatherings of the community the Apostolic Fathers also made use of the tradition of Diaspora Judaism. The Eucharistic prayers of *Didache* 9—10 are well known as modifications of Jewish meal prayers.[25] The great prayer at the end of *1 Clement* (chaps 59—61) is based on prayers of the Jewish Diaspora. Psalms sung at the gatherings of the community are certainly the psalms of the Bible of Israel.[26] Prayers for the emperor also imitate the practice of the Jewish Diaspora. It can be argued that the Lord's Prayer which is quoted in *Didache* 8 derives ultimately from Jesus himself. But in the form in which it appears here, probably not dependent upon Matthew 6,[27] it has many parallels in Jewish prayers.

From the piety and morality of the established Graeco-Roman world in general the literature of this post-apostolic period inherited the tables of 'household duties'. They appear already in the Epistles to the Colossians and to the Ephesians and in 1 Peter. That *Did.* 4.9–11 utilizes these tables as part of the Two Ways suggests that these tables have also been inherited from the Jewish Diaspora, although they ultimately derive from Stoic teachings. The ideal of good citizenship closely follows Greek concepts. These ideals appear not only in the Pastoral Epistles but also in *1 Clement* and in the Letter of Polycarp. Requirements for leadership in the Church are spelled out according to Greek patterns in the Pastoral Epistles as well as in Ignatius' *Epistle to Polycarp*.

It is surprising that specifically Christian resources, such as Gospel

21. *Did.* 5; *Barn.* 20.
22. For example, Eph. 4.25–31 and elsewhere.
23. *1 Clem.* 3.2.
24. *1 Clem.* 3—6.
25. See K. Niederwimmer, *The Didache: A Commentary*. ET Hermeneia (Minneapolis: Fortress Press, 1998), 150–67.
26. Eph. 5.19.
27. H. Koester, *Synoptische Überlieferung bei den Apostolischen Vätern*, Texte und Untersuchungen 65 (Berlin: Akademie-Verlag, 1957), 203–9.

materials and the genuine letters of Paul, play a comparatively small role in these attempts of the post-apostolic churches to reorient themselves to a new situation that is no longer dominated by a utopian eschatological vision. To be sure, sayings of Jesus are occasionally quoted.[28] But where they appear, they have become moral and liturgical instruction, as in *1 Clem.*13.2; 46.8; *Did.* 8; 9.5. Ignatius can on occasion refer to sayings of Jesus, but he never quotes them explicitly. Written Gospels existed at the time, including several Gospels that were later not incorporated into the canon of the New Testament.[29] But whatever Gospel materials appear in the Apostolic Fathers are apparently not drawn from any of these Gospels but derive from the oral tradition of sayings of Jesus. Narrative materials of the Gospel tradition are not utilized. While the sayings of Jesus quoted in *2 Clement* reflect the existence of the Gospels of Matthew and Luke, the author seems to have drawn these sayings from a collection that was composed on the basis of these two Gospels and which also contained apocryphal materials. Polycarp of Smyrna must have been familiar with Matthew's and Luke's Gospel; once he quotes a saying of Jesus that is drawn from the Gethsemane narrative (Matt. 26.41).[30] But what matters for him is the fact that this was something 'the Lord said'.

Gospel materials are not understood here as the saving message but as instructions for moral conduct and for the building of community. This explains the concentration upon the sayings of Jesus, which here became part of the general instruction for piety and morality that was primarily inherited from the Jewish Diaspora. The insertion of sayings from the Sermon on the Mount into the opening chapter of the Jewish Two Ways (*Did.* 1.2–4) appears therefore as quite appropriate. On the other hand, the difference between this utilization of Jesus' sayings and their use in the tradition of the Synoptic Sayings Gospel and the *Gospel of Thomas* is striking.[31] In the Apostolic Fathers, sayings of Jesus are closely connected to the moral tradition of the Jewish Diaspora, while this particular Jewish heritage is completely absent in the development of the Sayings Gospel. At the same time, emphasis upon the creation of a piety and morality that builds up community makes it possible for these Christian communities to survive in the Roman world relatively, though not completely, free from persecution and rejection.

---

28. On Gospel materials in the Apostolic Fathers in general, see Koester, *Synoptische Überlieferung, passim.*

29. For example, the *Gospel of the Hebrews* that is mentioned by Papias of Hierapolis, the *Gospel of Thomas*, and possibly also the *Gospel of Peter* and the Unknown Gospel of Papyrus Egerton 2.

30. Poly. *Phil.* 7.2.

31. It is characteristic that Matt. 5.3–12 transforms the prophetic beatitudes of the Sayings Gospel (= Luke 6.20–1) into a catechism. The sayings of Jesus quoted in *1 Clem.* 13.2 also appear in the form of a moral catechism.

The use of Paul's letters is analogous. Where they are explicitly referred to, as once in *1 Clement* (47.1–2),[32] or used implicitly, as, for example, frequently in Ignatius of Antioch, Paul's words are primarily instructions for individual behaviour or for the edification of the community. Otherwise, Paul is primarily the prototype of the exemplary martyr.[33] 'Paul the theologian' does not make an appearance in the Apostolic Fathers. That is perhaps quite appropriate because Paul understood himself not as a 'theologian' but as a builder of communities. On the other hand, Paul wanted to build communities of believers on an eschatological model, whereas Christian communities are now built on a modified model of the piety and morality of the Roman world.

This development also implies that the eschatological expectation, wherever it is upheld, assumes a different role. In Paul's genuine letters, this expectation determined the structures of the building of the new community. In the post-apostolic period, this expectation is closely related to the morality of the individual believer. Most writings of the Apostolic Fathers adhere to the expectation of a return of Christ – although at some undetermined future date – but emphasize that Christ is coming for judgement, reward and punishment. The *Shepherd of Hermas*, which tries to renew the urgency of the eschatological expectation and even sees the unblemished community, not just the individuals, as the entity that Christ expects to find at his return, nevertheless defines this community as the sum total of morally unblemished individuals.[34] Where the eschatological expectation is absent, as in the letters of Ignatius of Antioch, it has been transformed into an ideology of martyrdom. In a grandiose vision, Ignatius' journey to his martyrdom in Rome is depicted by him as analogous to the triumphal procession of the victorious emperor.[35] But although Ignatius sees this victorious journey of the martyr as happening on behalf of the Church, he remains an individual human being, whose authority will be elevated to those of the apostles by his martyrdom. What is also accomplished by Ignatius' efforts, especially in his rejection of the docetists – who most likely had deep religious insights – is the emphasis upon the realities of physical and fleshly human existence, in which true spirituality is becoming a reality. This effort is also evident in the attempt to preserve normal marriage structures, directed against ascetic movements demanding sexual abstinence.

The Apostolic Fathers enabled the Christian movement to survive and to be built in the form of viable communities that were not just moral and pious but also concerned with principles of love and mutual care,

32. See also Poly. *Phil.* 3.2; 9.2.
33. *1 Clem.* 5.5–7 and Ign. *Rom.* 4.3, both times side by side with Peter.
34. *SH*, *Vis.* 3.3–7; *SH*, *Sim.* 9.3–8.
35. See A. Brent, 'Ignatius of Antioch and the Imperial Cult', *VC* 52 (1998), 30–58.

hospitality and concern for the poor, widows and orphans, and ritual that would bind the communities together in common celebration. They thus accomplished what the Gnosticizing followers of the Jesus tradition were unable to do. While those followers explored the depths of Jesus' sayings and also the profound theological insights of Paul's letters, they were unable to show the way for the building of viable communities in which the heritage of love, care and respect for each other could become a reality.

4. *The Transformation of Egalitarianism into Hierarchy*

The question remains of the price that had to be paid for this definition of Christian existence. One of the problems was the introduction of hierarchical structures. A central administration in major cities, especially of a central treasury for services to the needy, was certainly unavoidable. Christians would continue to meet in increasing numbers of small assemblies in house churches, while a meeting of all Christians in one place in a city would have been impossible. The supervision by one bishop in each city of these small assemblies and their charitable giving was therefore a necessity. The letters of Ignatius of Antioch give some good insights into this new episcopal organization of the churches. But the term 'monarchical episcopate' is misleading. Ignatius' letter to bishop Polycarp of Smyrna makes clear that the bishop is not the principal ruler of the Church but its primary servant and caretaker. It is also interesting to note that qualifications for the office of bishop were not spelled out in terms of spiritual achievements but in terms of the accepted general moral requirements for offices in the Graeco-Roman world.[36]

Another price that was paid was the disappearance of the egalitarian status of all members of the congregations. Paul's 'neither male nor female' (Gal. 3.28) no longer applies, as the duties and relationships of the different genders in their daily lives and in their status in the churches are spelled out in the tables of household duties. In the reproduction of Gal. 3.28 in Col. 3.11 the phrase 'neither male nor female' is omitted. 1 Tim. 2.11–12 even forbids women to speak and teach in the congregational assembly. While the Apostolic Fathers do not repeat this regulation explicitly, it seems that they shared the desire to keep women out of ecclesiastical offices. It is difficult to know what actually happened in the organization of communities. The mention in the letter of Pliny to Trajan of slave women he had apprehended who claimed to be deacons (= preachers?)[37] seems to prove that the recommendations of the

36. See especially the materials in the appendix of M. Dibelius and H. Conzelmann, *The Pastoral Epistles*, Hermeneia (Philadelphia: Fortress Press, 1972), 158–60.
37. Pliny, *Letters of Pliny the Younger to Trajan*, 10.96.

Pastoral Epistles regarding women were not generally in force. On the other hand, hierarchical structures were not only introduced into the organization of the churches, they were also maintained in the affairs of the household and family according to the moral and social orders of the day – to be sure, with the modification that love and mutual respect 'in the Lord' should accompany all family relationships.

One may lament and criticize the acceptance of Graeco-Roman morality and piety in the post-apostolic churches as evident in the Apostolic Fathers and other Christian writings from that period. The legacy of the price that was paid then is still a burden for many churches today. Yet in the absence of a definition of Christian existence and community under an eschatological perspective such accommodation to existing mores of society seems unavoidable. The task of the interpreter must be guided by an empathy that critically explores all of the issues related to the decisions made by these earliest fathers of the Church.

Chapter 2

THE *DIDACHE*

Jonathan A. Draper

Few of the writings of the Apostolic Fathers have occasioned such controversy and such a flood of literature as the *Didache* or 'Teaching of the Twelve Apostles'.[1] Published first in Athens by Archbishop Bryennios in 1883 from a twelfth-century manuscript containing a variety of texts, it was popularized by the learned text and commentary of the great German scholar Adolf von Harnack in 1884.[2] A work of this title had been known from its listing among the 'disputed' writings in Eusebius' canonical texts (*HE* 3.25) and the stichometry of Nicephorus, but had been lost. There remains some doubt as to whether Eusebius is referring to the full text of the *Didache* or to the shorter text of the Two Ways found in chapters 1—6, whose independent circulation is attested by the Latin text *Doctrina apostolorum*.[3] In any case, the entire work is taken up (and revised) in *Apostolic Constitutions* 7 and is treated as 'scripture' by a number of early Christian writers. Additional evidence for the text of the *Didache* has been found in a fragment from Oxyrhyncus, a Coptic translation of part of the text, and an Ethiopic translation of part of the text incorporated into the *Ethiopic Church Order*.

1. *Date and Origin of the Text*

Harnack found in this short text the key to the evolution of the early Christian church, since it portrays a community which still knows active

1. Many texts and commentaries on the *Didache* are available. The best critical text of the Greek, together with an excellent commentary, is provided by W. Rordorf and A. Tuilier, *La Doctrine des Douze Apôtres (Didaché)*, 2nd edn (Paris: Éditions du Cerf, 1998). A cautious historical-critical (redactional) approach is provided by K. Niederwimmer, *The Didache: A Commentary*, ET Hermeneia (Minneapolis: Fortress Press, 1998).

2. A. von Harnack, *Die Lehre der zwölf Apostel nebst Untersuchungen zur ältesten Geschichte der Kirchenverfassung und des Kirchenrechts* (Leipzig: Hinrichs, 1884).

3. The text of the *Doctrina apostolorum* is provided in Rordorf and Tuilier, *La Doctrine des Douze* Apôtres, 207–10.

apostles and prophets and which is beginning to elect bishops and deacons. He saw here a bridge in the process of 'early catholicization' of the Church from a charismatic to an institutional form, and this thesis formed the basis of his widely influential work translated into English in 1908 as *The Mission and Expansion of Christianity in the First Three Centuries.*[4]

This early enthusiasm for the text was overturned some thirty years later by the scepticism of a group of influential English scholars, who argued that the *Didache* was dependent on the *Epistle of Barnabas* and Matthew in particular, but in addition had borrowed from virtually every book of the New Testament to reconstruct a fraudulent and tendentious picture of life in the early Church.[5] As the eminent J. Armitage Robinson expresses it in his Donnellan Lectures in 1920: 'He disguises his borrowings indeed; but he also disguises the actual conditions of his own time. The result is that he contributes almost nothing, except doubtful exegesis, to advance our knowledge of the early Christian ministry.'[6] In the face of this uncertainty, few scholars referred any longer to the *Didache* in their historical reconstructions of Christian origins, except for those interested in the evolution of the Eucharist.[7] Even the late date in the third century given by Robinson still means that it provides the earliest extant Eucharistic prayer.

The discovery of the Dead Sea Scrolls in 1948 revolutionized the situation once again, since, as demonstrated by the French Canadian scholar Jean-Paul Audet, the Two Ways teaching, found in the first six chapters of the *Didache* and also in the *Epistle of Barnabas*, shows clearly that both Christian texts are dependent on an earlier, possibly Jewish,

---

4. A. von Harnack, *Die Mission und Ausbreitung des Christentums in den ersten drei Jahrhunderten* (1905), ET *The Mission and Expansion of Christianity in the First Three Centuries*, 2 vols (New York: G.P. Putnam, 1908).

5. J.A. Robinson, *Barnabas, Hermas and the Didache: Donnellan Lectures at the University of Dublin* (London: SPCK; New York: Macmillan, 1920); R.H. Connolly, 'The Didache in Relation to the Epistle of Barnabas', *JTS* 33 (1932), 237–53, and 'The Didache and Montanism', *Downside Review* n.s. 36 (1937), 339–47; J. Muilenburg, *The Literary Relations of the Epistle of Barnabas and the Teaching of the Twelve Apostles* (diss. Yale University; printed Marburg, 1929); F.E. Vokes, *The Riddle of the Didache: Fact, Fiction, Heresy or Catholicism?* (London: SCM Press, 1938). There were strong dissenting English voices, e.g. J.V. Bartlet, 'The Didache Reconsidered', *JTS* 22 (1921), 239–49; B.H. Streeter, 'The Much-Belaboured Didache', in B.H. Streeter, *The Primitive Church* (London: Macmillan, 1936), 369–74. But they were swept away in the tide of disillusionment.

6. Robinson, *Barnabas, Hermas and the Didache*, 102.

7. For example, G. Dix, *The Shape of the Liturgy* (Westminster: Dacre, 1945), and more recently, E. Mazza, *The Origins of the Eucharistic Prayer* (Collegeville, Minn.: Liturgical Press, 1995).

source best attested by the *Doctrina apostolorum*.[8] In addition, the watershed study of the New Testament in the Apostolic Fathers undertaken by Helmut Koester cast doubt on the dependence of the *Didache* on Matthew's Gospel.[9] While the debate over the relationship between the two writings has still not been settled,[10] and some, myself included, would argue contrariwise for a dependence of Matthew on the *Didache*,[11] few scholars now date the text later than the end of the first century CE or the first few decades of the second.[12] If dependence on Matthew is ruled out, then there is little to establish the date of the text except for internal evidence, so that a number of recent studies have even argued for a very early date in the mid-first century.[13] In any case, the recent shift in the dating of the *Didache* has led to a flurry of attention and a further flurry of books arguing for the importance of the work in understanding the evolution of the Church.

The place of origin has also been a matter of much dispute, but it is now widely accepted that the text originates from the general area of Syria, or more narrowly from Antioch. It seems to originate from a Jewish-Christian community trying to remain faithful to the Torah, even though it has opened itself to Gentile converts.[14] It also relates in some way to the Gospel of Matthew, with which it shares obvious parallels and to which it may well be subordinated in its final redactional phase (*Did.* 15.4).

8. J.-P. Audet, 'Affinités littéraires et doctrinales du "Manuel de Discipline"', *RB* 59 (1952), 219–38, ET 'Literary and Doctrinal Relationships of the "Manual of Discipline"', in J.A. Draper (ed.), *The Didache in Modern Research* (Leiden: Brill, 1996), 129–47. Audet went on to write a major commentary arguing for apostolic authorship in two redactional phases with interpolations: *La Didache: Instructions des apôtres* (Paris: Gabalda, 1958), which has carried rather less conviction.

9. H. Koester, *Synoptische Überlieferung bei den apostolischen Vätern*, Texte und Untersuchungen 65 (Berlin: Akademie-Verlag, 1957), 159–241.

10. See, for example, the dissenting voices in H. van de Sandt (ed.), *Matthew and the Didache: Two Documents from the Same Jewish-Christian Milieu?* (Assen: Royal Van Gorcum; Minneapolis: Fortress Press, 2005).

11. A.J.P. Garrow, *The Gospel of Matthew's Dependence on the Didache* (London and New York: T&T Clark, 2004); J.A. Draper, 'Do the Didache and Matthew Reflect an "Irrevocable Parting of the Ways" with Judaism?', in van de Sandt (ed.), *Matthew and the Didache*, 217–41.

12. A. Milavec, *The Didache: Faith, Hope, and Life of the Earliest Christian Communities, 50–70 CE* (New York and Mahwah, NJ: Newman Press, 2003); Garrow, *The Gospel of Matthew's Dependence on the Didache*.

13. See Milavec, *The Didache*, pp. xxvi–xxxiii, 693–739.

14. This has been most substantially argued by the recent work of H. van de Sandt and D. Flusser, *The Didache: Its Jewish Sources and its Place in Early Judaism and Christianity* (Assen: Royal van Gorcum; Philadelphia: Fortress Press, 2002). See most recently M. del Verme, *Didache and Judaism: The Jewish Roots of an Ancient Christian-Jewish Work* (New York and London: T&T Clark, 2004).

2. The Yoke of the Lord

One of the most intriguing issues raised by the *Didache*, if it is Jewish-Christian and Antiochene in origin, is the reference to the 'yoke of the Lord' at the conclusion to the Two Ways instruction (6.3), since it then appears to relate to the issue of Torah observance and table fellowship, which lay at the centre of a controversy in the earliest Christian communities that Acts describes as resolved amicably at the Council of Jerusalem (15.6–29). Gentiles joining the *Didache* community are not obligated to become 'perfect' Torah-observant Jews by 'taking the whole yoke of the Lord' upon themselves, but they are nevertheless instructed to keep as much of the Torah and the food laws as they can 'bear' and to keep strictly away from food offered to idols. Paul, on the other hand, forbids the Gentiles in Galatia to keep the Torah (to submit to the 'yoke of slavery', Gal. 5.1) or risk losing their salvation (Gal. 5.4), and also argues that eating food from the market which may have been offered to idols is no problem unless someone makes an issue of it (1 Cor. 10.25–30). The *Didache* may thus be a key text in understanding the nature of the issues between Paul and his opponents.[15] While the *Didache* is usually known by its shorter title, there is a second title, which has sometimes been taken as an interpolation but may indeed have been part of the original text: *Teaching of the Lord through the Twelve Apostles to the Gentiles/ Nations.*[16]

3. The Two Ways

The Two Ways instruction in *Didache* 1—6 is found in many forms in Jewish and early Christian writings,[17] where it passes into the monastic tradition in the *Rule of St Benedict*. Its function in the *Didache* is to provide catechesis for the preparation of new Gentile converts in extensive training at the hands of an instructor (4.1–2) prior to baptism ('Having said all these things beforehand, baptize . . .': 7.1). In the *Didache* the two ways are ethically conceived as ways of life and death (cf. Deut. 30.15), rather than drawing on the cosmic opposition of angels of light and darkness found in Qumran and the *Epistle of Barnabas*. Opening with the

15. See M. Slee, *The Church in Antioch in the First Century CE* (Sheffield: Sheffield Academic Press, 2003); J.A. Draper, 'A Continuing Enigma: The "Yoke of the Lord" in Didache 6.2–3 and Early Jewish-Christian Relations', in P.J. Tomson and D. Lambers-Petry, *The Image of the Judaeo-Christians in Ancient Jewish and Christian Literature* (Tübingen: Mohr-Siebeck, 2003), 106–23.

16. The provenance of this title has been the subject of much debate. See the extensive discussion in Audet, *La Didache*, 91–103.

17. See, for example, 1QS 3.14—4.26, *Testament of Asher, Derek Eretz, Epistle of Barnabas, Doctrina Apostolorum, Apostolic Church Order, Epitome, Life of Shenudi.*

double command to love God and neighbour as oneself, followed by the negative form of the Golden Rule, the Two Ways consists mostly of an elaboration of the ethical sections of the Ten Commandments. It targets particular Gentile practices regularly abhorred by Jewish writers: pederasty, abortion, exposure of infants, astrology, magic, idolatry and so on.

One of the interesting aspects of the Two Ways section is that a block of Jesus tradition is inserted at the beginning of the Way of Life as a first instruction (1.3–6), relegating the legal material to the status of a 'second commandment' (2.1). There is no indication in the *Didache* that this comes from Jesus, nor that it is part of the 'gospel'. The teaching comes mostly from Q material organized by Matthew in the Sermon on the Mount and by Luke in the Sermon on the Plain. It follows neither of these canonical Gospels in its structure and exact wording, though it is closer to Matthew than to Luke. This supports an interpretation of the origin of this Q material as a block of catechetical instruction, set on the lips of Jesus by the Evangelists to underpin its authority. In any case, the Two Ways material presents a rare glimpse of the kind of ordered programme of initiation undertaken by an early Christian community.[18]

4. *Baptism and Eucharist*

The *Didache* presents evidence of the utmost significance for the study of the origins of Christian liturgy and worship, since it offers the earliest picture of baptism (chs 7—8) and Eucharist (chs 9—10) in the early Church. It differs strikingly from traditional pictures and later practice, offering a markedly Jewish emphasis. Moreover, since liturgical practice was likely to have been long-established in the community before it was written down and collected in the *Didache*, it offers witness to a practice pre-dating the text by some time.

The emphasis in the baptismal instruction is not on repentance and forgiveness of sins, of which there is no mention, but on the ritual purity and therefore the purifying nature of the water (7.2–3). There is no mention of baptism into the death of Christ as this is set out in Paul (Rom. 6.1–11), and although baptism is 'in the name of the Father, Son and Holy Spirit' in chap. 7, there is a suspicion that this may have been a later redaction, since 9.5 speaks of baptism 'in the name of the Lord'. Fasting by the initiand and the officiator for one or two days is required before the baptism (7.4) and subsequent to baptism for two days a week, on Wednesdays and Fridays. Likewise, the *Didache* specifies that the newly

---

18.   For an extensive presentation of this position see Milavec, *The Didache*, esp. 70–168, and also J.A. Draper, 'The Role of Ritual in the Alternation of Social Universe: Jewish-Christian Initiation of Gentiles in the Didache', *Listening* 32 (1997), 48–67.

baptized person should pray the Lord's Prayer three times a day (8.2–3). In both instances, it appears that the instruction is intended to differentiate the new member from members of the community led by the 'hypocrites', probably the Pharisaic party.

Even more surprising is the Eucharistic liturgy provided in chaps 9—10, since it contains no mention of the 'Words of Institution' or of the sacrificial death of Christ. The blessing over the cup precedes the blessing over the broken bread, followed by a full meal and then by a further set of blessings (probably involving, though this is not mentioned, a further cup of wine in the Jewish fashion found also in Luke's description of the Last Supper, 22.17–20).[19] The *eucharistia* over the cup gives thanks to the Father for the 'holy vine of David' made known to the community in Jesus 'your son/servant' (παῖς, 9.2), reflecting a Davidic Christology found also in the final acclamation of the liturgy, 'Hosannah to the house of David' (10.6).[20] The Davidic emphasis matches the emphasis on the 'kingdom' into which members are gathered 'like broken bread which was scattered on the mountains' in the *eucharistia* over the bread (10.3–4) and in the *eucharistia* after the meal (10.5). As with baptism, the Eucharistic prayers reveal a concern with ritual purity: the unbaptized must be excluded from the meal because 'you shall not give what is holy to the dogs' (9.5), and only the holy may partake: 'If anyone is holy let that person come; if anyone is not let that person repent' (10.6; cf. 14.1–3).

While the usual officiant at the Eucharist is not mentioned, an unexpected concluding instruction, which prepares the hearer for what follows, allows a prophet to 'eucharistize as she or he wills' (10.7).

5. *Apostles, Prophets, Teachers, Bishops, Deacons and Visitors*

What first excited Harnack continues to fascinate and perplex interpreters of the *Didache*: itinerant apostles and prophets are envisaged as still active in the community, alongside bishops and deacons elected by the community itself. There seem to be tensions between 'charismatic' figures appointed by the Spirit, who wish to 'settle down' in the community, and this emerging local 'hierarchy' (15.1–2). Moreover, much in the description of the apostles and prophets in chap. 11 echoes themes running through the Gospel tradition: apostles are to move on after a stay of one or two days and should receive food but no money; prophets speak 'in the Spirit' and may not be contradicted for 'blasphemy against the Holy Spirit

19. For a summary of the discussion of the problems associated with the textual tradition of Luke at this point see B. Metzger, *A Textual Commentary on the Greek New Testament*, 3rd edn (London: United Bible Societies, 1971), 173–7.

20. Following the Coptic witness to the text, where the manuscript of Bryennios (H54) has 'God of David' and the *Apostolic Constitutions* has 'son of David'.

cannot be forgiven'. The renewed search for the 'historical Jesus' and his community has led to an increasing interest in this material, particularly in the light of Gerd Theissen's theory that Jesus 'the bearer of revelation' initiated a movement of wandering charismatic ascetics supported by a network of local communities, which has been taken up by J. Dominic Crossan, Burton Mack, Leif Vaage and many others.[21]

Another point of view would make the apostles emissaries of Jerusalem, carrying letters of authorization for their final destination but entitled to hospitality along the way. Any attempt by such people to stay for a longer period than a few days living off the community's goodwill would suggest that they were not genuine.[22] People who wish to settle must support themselves or else they are 'Christ traders' (13.5). Prophets, on the other hand, appear to be welcome settlers, whose charismatic work entitles them, like (full-time) teachers, to community support (14.1–2) from the 'first fruits' of their labour (14.3–7).

6. *The Return of the Lord*

The *Didache* concludes with eschatological teaching alluding back to the Two Ways instruction: 'Watch over your life' (16.1). It also echoes the Q material found in Matthew 24 and Luke 12.35–40, again in words and an order which indicate independent use of the same tradition. It envisages a time when members of its community will turn against that community, when lawlessness will increase and a 'world deceiver' will emerge to perform signs and wonders to lead the world astray and inaugurate a time of 'fiery testing' (16.4–5). Three 'true signs' indicate the coming end of all things: a sign 'spread out in the sky', the sound of the trumpet and the resurrection of the righteous departed. Finally the Lord comes on the clouds with his holy ones (16.6–7). Interestingly, Matthew seems to structure his use of the apocalypse in Mark 13 around these three signs, while the *Didache* shows no knowledge of the Markan material in Matthew at all, raising again the questions about redaction and priority with which this chapter began.[23] The text seems to break off suddenly in mid-sentence at the end of the apocalypse (16.8), where one would expect

---

21. G. Theissen, *The First Followers of Jesus: A Sociological Analysis of Earliest Christianity* (ET London: SCM Press, 1978); J.D. Crossan, *The Historical Jesus: The Life of a Mediterranean Jewish Peasant* (San Francisco: HarperSanFrancisco: 1991); B. Mack, *The Lost Gospel: The Book of Q and Christian Origins* (San Francisco: HarperSanFrancisco, 1993); For a contrary viewpoint, see (Valley Forge, Pa.: Trinity Press International, L. Vaage, *Galilean Upstarts: Jesus' First Followers According to Q*).

22. See J.A. Draper, 'Weber, Theissen, and "Wandering Charismatics" in the *Didache*', *JECS* 6 (1998), 541–76.

23. See J.S. Kloppenborg, 'Didache 16:6–8 and Special Matthean Tradition', *ZNW* 69–70 (1978–9), 54–67.

a description of the judgement of the wicked and the vindication of the righteous, and this has led to many attempts at reconstruction by scholars.[24]

7. Conclusions

The survival of the *Didache* as an independent text is, to some extent, accidental. It presents us with a moment frozen in time, a community which still lived within the Jewish worldview and practice, competing with the successors of the Pharisees for control of the same social space. It remains focused on the Torah and its fulfilment in practice, even though it admits Gentiles without requiring them to become Jews. It is concerned about ritual purity in baptism and Eucharist. Its Christology is Davidic and it envisages a return of the Lord on the clouds, accompanied by the righteous departed, to gather the Church from the four winds into the kingdom (10.5, perhaps echoing Ezek. 37.7–14), probably to establish it 'on earth as it is in heaven' (8.2). The Church's local elected leadership of bishops and deacons seems to be in contention with Spirit-inspired prophets and teachers, while apostles might present themselves at its door claiming their right to support on their journeys. This is a picture much at odds with the Church as it emerged in subsequent centuries. Jewish-Christian communities which tried to continue this kind of tradition were marginalized and even demonized as heretics, while few traces of their life and witness to Jesus have survived. The *Didache* is thus particularly valuable as evidence of, and a witness today to, the roots of the Christian movement in Torah-faithful Judaism.

24. See R.E. Aldridge, 'The Lost Ending of the Didache', *VC* 53 (1999), 1–15; Garrow, *Matthew's Dependence on the Didache*, 29–66.

Chapter 3

1 CLEMENT: AN INTRODUCTION

Andrew Gregory

Letters make up an important part of such early Christian literature as survives from the end of the first and the beginning of the second centuries.[1] By far the longest and perhaps the most significant of these letters is that of the church of Rome to the church of Corinth, commonly known as *1 Clement*. I shall follow scholarly convention in using this title, and referring to its author as Clement, even though this may be slightly misleading. Not only is there no internal evidence to associate the letter with an author named Clement, there is also no reason to identify this letter as the first of more than one by the same author; the text conventionally known as *2 Clement* is not a letter but a homily, and it is not clear why each text first came to be associated with the other. *1 Clement* may be the oldest Christian writing apart from those included in the New Testament, but the same claim might be made of either the *Didache* or the *Shepherd of Hermas*. Its importance for our knowledge of the development of Christianity can hardly be overestimated, even if assessments of its significance have varied considerably at different times,

---

1.   It is striking that 21 of the 27 books of the New Testament are written in the form of a letter. Two of the remaining six (Acts and the Apocalypse) each include letters within their texts (see Acts 15.22–35; Revelation 2—3, cf. 1.4). Only the Gospels are without any obvious influence from the form of the letter. The letter is also the most dominant genre in the texts referred to as the Apostolic Fathers. The other letters in that collection include the *Epistle of Barnabas* (described famously by Johannes Quasten as 'A theological tract and a letter only in appearance'), Polycarp's *Epistle to the Philippians*, the letters of Ignatius and the *Epistle to Diognetus* (an apology for Christianity composed in the form of a letter). The *Martyrdom of Polycarp* is also cast in the form of a letter and the opening of the *Didache* suggests the influence of the letter form. The only 'non-letters' in the collection are *2 Clement* (usually considered a homily), the *Shepherd of Hermas* (an apocalypse) and the fragments of Papias. Perhaps surprisingly, however, there are relatively few letters among the texts in the standard collections of New Testament apocrypha.

not least according to the particular theological commitments of its readers.[2]

1. *Text and Influence*

The text of *1 Clement* is preserved in two Greek manuscripts, the Codex Alexandrinus and the Codex Hierosolymitanus. Codex Alexandrinus, usually dated to the fifth century and now in the British Library, contains (with the exception of some missing leaves) a complete text of the Greek Bible (i.e. the Septuagint and the New Testament) and also *1* and *2 Clement*. These texts appear immediately after the Apocalypse; the last page of *1 Clement* (57.7—63.4) and part of *2 Clement* are missing, as are the Psalms of Solomon that followed them (as we know from an ancient table of contents prefixed to the manuscript). Codex Hierosolymitanus, dated to 1056, was discovered in Constantinople in 1873. It too contains both *1* and *2 Clement* as well as other writings. These include an introduction to the Old and New Testaments and (from among the Apostolic Fathers) the *Epistle of Barnabas*, the *Didache* and the longer recension of the letters of Ignatius. Two Coptic manuscripts of *1 Clement* are also partially extant, and there is a complete eleventh-century Latin manuscript that might go back to a translation made in the second or third century,[3] which appears to have been corrupted sometime in the early Middle Ages in order to promote the importance of the Pope.[4] The final manuscript is a twelfth-century Syriac manuscript of the New Testament, now in Cambridge, in which *1* and *2 Clement* appear after Acts and the Catholic Epistles but before the Epistles of Paul. *1 Clement* is headed 'The Catholic Epistle of Clement the disciple of Peter the apostle to the Church of the Corinthians', and both letters are divided into lessons in the same way as are Acts and the preceding Catholic Epistles.

1 Clement is quoted frequently in the early Church, particularly in the East by Greek-speaking authors. Significant parallels between *1 Clement* and Polycarp's *Epistle to the Philippians* suggest a literary relationship between these two texts; if *1 Clement* may be dated securely as the earlier of these two letters, Polycarp is the first secure witness to its reception,

---

2. See J. Fuellenbach, *Ecclesiastical Office and the Primacy of Rome: An Evaluation of Recent Theological Discussion of First Clement* (Washington, DC: Catholic University of America Press, 1980), for a survey of Protestant and Roman Catholic scholarship on aspects of the understanding of church office and ministry in the letter.

3. It was rediscovered only in 1894, i.e. after the important edition of Lightfoot had been published (J.B. Lightfoot, *The Apostolic Fathers*, part 1, *Clement* (London: Macmillan, 1889–90).

4. These alterations come at 60.4—61.1. By omitting the word 'our' the Latin translation suggests that it is to Clement and the Roman Church that God has given authority, not to temporal rulers and governors.

though some see an allusion to it in Ignatius. (See Ign. *Rom.* 3.1, where he writes that the Romans have taught others. If Ignatius is referring to written teaching, he might be thinking of 1 Peter, *1 Clement* or both – and/or other texts no longer extant.) Irenaeus makes use of the letter, but it is Clement of Alexandria who quotes it most frequently. On occasion he cites it as scripture. Didymus the Blind appears to have considered it part of his canon of scripture, and an approximately contemporary Syriac work, the *Apostolic Canons*, lists both *1* and *2 Clement* as part of the New Testament. In this list, which does not include the Apocalypse, *1* and *2 Clement* appear last, after the Catholic Epistles. It is difficult to know whether or not Didymus' canon is earlier or later than the thirty-ninth Festal Epistle of Athanasius (dated 367), which is our earliest evidence for the recognition of a New Testament canon identical to the twenty-seven books accepted as canonical today. However, the *Apostolic Canons* can be more confidently dated *c.* 380.

1 Clement appears not to have circulated widely in the Middle Ages. It seems to have been eclipsed by other writings associated with the figure of Clement – the *Pseudo-Clementine Recognitions* and the *Pseudo-Clementine Homilies*, two versions of an early Christian novel or romance that identifies Clement as the disciple and successor of Peter.

We do not know how *1 Clement* was received at first in Corinth. Eusebius, the fourth-century historian on whom we rely for so much of our knowledge of pre-Nicene Christianity, notes that it was known to Hegesippus *c.* 170(?), whose testimony is presented in such a way as to imply that the church in Corinth 'remained in the true doctrine' after receiving this letter (*HE* 4.22.1). Eusebius also quotes Dionysius, Bishop of Corinth, (*c.* 170) also writing to Rome *c.* 170 and saying that the Corinthians shall continue to read the letter to which he is now responding, just as they continue to read the letter sent to them through Clement (*HE* 4.23.11). This is in all probability a reference to *1 Clement*, and is the first surviving example of the letter being associated with a person named Clement. The reason why Dionysius made this association is unclear; the fact that the *Shepherd of Hermas* refers to a certain Clement as responsible for Rome's letters with other churches may be important (*SH, Vis.* 2.4.3). There the Clement to whom Hermas refers is clearly a functionary, not a leader, of the church at Rome.

2. *Authorship*

Irenaeus (*AH* 3.3.3) dates this letter to the time when an individual named Clement was said to be third in the line of bishops (after Linus and Anacletus). These bishops are portrayed as the successors of the apostles Peter and Paul, whom Irenaeus identifies as the founders of the church at

Rome. Irenaeus stops short of naming this Clement as its author, but other early (and uncontested) traditions make this leap. Clement's name appears in the titles of each manuscript in which the letter survives.

Various proposals have been made as to the identity of this Clement. According to Origen (*Commentary on John* 6.36), he was the Clement to whom Paul refers in Phil. 4.3. Eusebius also identifies him as the companion of Paul and as the third bishop of Rome (*HE* 3.4.8–9; 3.15.1; 3.34.1). According to Tertullian (*Prescription against Heresies* 32, followed by Epiphanius, *Panarion* 27.6) and the *Pseudo-Clementines*, Clement succeeded Peter directly. The *Pseudo-Clementines* also identify him as a Roman citizen of noble birth, and various modern scholars have identified him in one way or other with Flavius Clemens, consul in 95 and cousin of the emperor Domitian, or with a member of his household.

Such traditions notwithstanding, we simply do not know the name of the author of this letter, let alone whether he was a Gentile or a Jew. He was a Greek-speaker thoroughly at home in Rome, but it is unclear whether the rhetorical devices he uses and the topics that he discusses, apparently with great ease, require that he had enjoyed a pagan higher education, or whether such forms and motifs are no more than popular commonplaces with which many Hellenistic Jews of a certain standing would have been familiar.[5] The letter describes itself as being from 'The Church of God that dwells at Rome to the Church of God that dwells at Corinth' (prescript) and names three (or perhaps two) envoys who carry it, but no individual who is responsible for its composition. The letter is written in the plural (it refers to 'we' and to 'us', not to 'I' and to 'me') and may include some further evidence to suggest that there was no single leader in the church at Rome (see 44.1–2). Also, the fact that Ignatius fails to mention a monarchical bishop at Rome, though he refers to such bishops in other churches, has caused many scholars to question whether monarchical episcopacy was present in Rome by the early second century, the period to which Ignatius' letters are usually dated.[6]

3. *Occasion and Purpose*

The purpose of the letter and the occasion that gave rise to it are clearly stated, even if precise details are lacking. The church in Rome is aware of conflict in the church at Corinth, and writes to them in order that peace may be restored (1.1; 63.4; 65.1). Some younger men have deposed the elders (or presbyters) even though their conduct was honourable and blameless (3.3; 44.6), with the result that there is now factionalism and

---

5. For a comprehensive discussion, see P. Lampe, *From Paul to Valentinus: Christians at Rome in the First Two Centuries* (Minneapolis: Fortress Press, 2003), 206–17.
6. For an account of recent debates on this subject, see Chapter 9 below.

internal dissent (στάσις) in the church, albeit at the instigation of only a few (47.6; 1.1). Reports of this factionalism have reached Rome and appear to have come to the attention both of Christians and of others, leading to blasphemy against the Lord's name and danger (of damnation?) for those in Corinth (47.7).

To those who have tolerated the situation, the Romans appeal to them to restore the presbyters who have been deposed (44.3–6; 46.4; 47.6; 48.1) and seek forgiveness for what they have done (51.1).

To those who have caused it by deposing those very leaders, the Romans appeal to them to consider giving up their own position for the sake of the community as a whole, accepting voluntary exile (54.2). They should subject themselves to the elders whom they have deposed and repent for what they have done (57.1–2). This exile – if that is what the believers at Corinth collectively consider to be appropriate – is presented not so much as a punishment, but rather as an opportunity for the exiles to gain recognition and welcome among Christians wherever they may go. This rosy perspective may set it apart from the punishment more typically associated with exile in the Roman world. It is nevertheless noteworthy that the Roman Christians appeal to this way of dealing with a problem rather than to Paul's approach to dealing with troublesome offenders in 1 Corinthians 5, which itself appears to be modelled on the Jewish practice of putting people out of the synagogue. Clement appeals to a model that stands quite outside the Jewish tradition, but is familiar in Roman culture.

The letter from Rome appears to have been written at the initiative of its senders. They have heard news from Corinth (47.6), but there is no suggestion that they have received an official request for help or a letter of any kind. According to its authors, it is motivated by concern for the reputation of the Corinthians (1.1f.), by their fervent and prayerful hope that peace be quickly restored (63.2, 4; 65.1), and by the wish that their own consciences be clear (59.2). If they do not speak, perhaps they will appear to give assent to what has happened in Corinth, just as the majority of Christians there appear to have done already (46.1—48.6; 59.2). Thus the church at Rome shows concern for the situation in Corinth, but makes no claim of authority over the Christians there. For the Corinthians, they pray for submission not to Rome but to the will of God (56.1); for themselves, they pray that they may be innocent of such factionalism as the Corinthians face (59.2). They write not to condemn, but in full awareness that they are engaged in the same struggle as those whom they address (7.1). It is the problem of internal strife at Corinth that concerns them, not questions of church order as such.[7]

The observation that most of this information about the situation that the letter addresses is found in only a small part of the letter raises

---

7. See further below, sect. 4.

questions about how the main body of the letter relates to its apparent purpose.[8] The fact that the information given is not very detailed also raises questions about the extent to which the church in Rome was informed about the details of the situation in Corinth. However, as recent scholarship has demonstrated, both concerns may be easily addressed in terms of the genre of the letter and the conventions it therefore presupposes.

4. *Genre*

As Willem van Unnik has demonstrated,[9] *1 Clement* is best understood as belonging to the literary genre of the συμβουλευτικον. This is a form of address that is identified in rhetorical handbooks and found in other texts that are contemporary with *1 Clement*. It is used by those who wish to persuade others to reach for themselves a successful resolution to difficulties that they face, not to force them to submit to those who offer them this counsel.

The identification of *1 Clement* as a συμβουλευτικον, a form of deliberative rhetoric that is attempted to persuade rather than to compel, depends on a number of factors. First, the letter describes itself as an appeal or petition (εντευκσις) and refers to its content as counsel (συμβουλη), something rather stronger than disinterested advice. Each word is typical of the genre, and indicates that the author of the letter knows that he must appeal to the goodwill of his audience. He hopes to persuade because he cannot compel or command, and he knows that he cannot take it for granted that those whom he addresses will welcome and act on the counsel that he gives. He avoids the use of the imperative, and speaks instead in the second person plural. This is why – the second key indication of its genre – the type of rhetoric that Clement uses is classified as deliberative. His purpose is to give advice to those who deliberate on a certain matter (in this case, the deposition of leaders in Corinth), so his goal is to make clear what is detrimental and what is good, and to persuade his audience to reject the former and to embrace the latter.

Third, the letter emphasizes the need for peace and harmony,

---

8. *1 Clement* alludes to the difficulties in Corinth in chap. 1 and returns to them at the end, in chap. 65, but the majority of information about the nature of the problems in Corinth comes in chaps 42—44 and 47.

9. W.C. van Unnik, 'Studies on the So-called First Epistle of Clement', tr. L.L. Welborn, in C. Breytenbach and L.L. Welborn (eds), *Encounters with Hellenism: Studies on the First Letter of Clement*, AGAJU 53 (Leiden: Brill, 2004), 116–81. For a fuller historical-rhetorical analysis of the letter, see O.M. Bakke, *'Concord and Peace': A Rhetorical Analysis of the Language of the First Letter of Clement with an Emphasis on the Language of Unity and Sedition*, WUNT 2.143 (Tübingen: Mohr-Siebeck, 2001).

ubiquitous concerns in the early second century. His letter is an appeal/ petition for peace and harmony (εντευκσις περι ειρηνης και ὀμονοια), a concern instantly recognizable to contemporary Greeks and Romans, who would recognize it as the opposite of divisions and factionalism in public life (στάσις), which is how Clement identifies the situation in Corinth. Both peace and harmony (in Latin, *pax et concordia*) were dominant concerns in the Roman Empire, so Clement's use of this language is suggestive of the serious and political nature of the situation that he addresses. στάσις has been the downfall of many a city; will that be the case for the Corinthian church? Fourth, the letter offers numerous examples of the need for, and benefits of, harmony (ὀμονοια). This is the characteristic exemplified by the examples he chooses. The idea of 'harmony' indicates the dominant concern of the letter, which demonstrates why his long discussion of these examples is not a digression, but is in fact directly relevant to the situation he addresses. Such examples are part of his strategy of persuasion, for they are introduced in order to counter any resistance that his addressees might feel towards the counsel he offers. They not only function as illustrations and proofs of the opinions that Clement expresses, but also give form to the ideal of Christian life. Those in Corinth should respect these examples and imitiate them in their lives (63.1).

At least two important corollaries follow from this understanding of *1 Clement* as belonging to the genre of the συμβουλευτικον. The first is that there is no need to believe that the Romans lacked detailed knowledge of the situation in Corinth on the grounds that in their letter they speak of the situation in Corinth in only the most general terms. This is completely in accord with the conventions of the genre, for the letter aims to give advice that might bring a future resolution to a conflict, not a narrative account of what has already taken place. Modern readers may regret that we do not know more of what had happened in Corinth, but there is no reason to suppose that our ignorance was shared any more by those in Rome than it was by those in Corinth. As van Unnik observes, we should be grateful rather that in chaps 44ff. Clement has in fact told us *more* than was demanded by the conventions according to which he worked.[10]

The second corollary is confirmation that this letter offers no evidence for the primacy of Rome at the time of its composition. The church at Rome writes to the church at Corinth of its own free will, but the form in which it does so makes clear that it could not take for granted that its counsel would be either welcome or in any way binding at Corinth. Nowhere does the Roman church demand obedience to its own authority, but only to that of God, as revealed in the Greek Bible and in certain Christian texts and traditions. Rome does not claim to speak in the name

10.   van Unnik, 'Studies on the So-called First Epistle of Clement', 164.

of the Lord, but always refers to the scriptures, to which authority the writer knows that the church at Rome is also subject (9.1; 13.3; 14.1). The Christians in Corinth should be obedient to God's will, not to Rome, for he alone is able to change hearts (56.1).

5. *Date*

1 Clement is customarily dated to *c.* 96, but there have been important challenges to this consensus.[11] The case for such precise dating depends on the interpretation of 1.1, where the author appeals to external events to explain why Rome has been slow to address the situation in Corinth. Much hinges on the translation of two nouns, συμφοράς and περιπιώσεις. If translated as 'misfortunes' and 'calamities' – as Kirsopp Lake translated them in his influential Loeb edition, published in 1912[12] – then it is possible to see how they could be taken, if other supporting evidence were available, to refer to persecution. However, it is much more difficult to take them in this way if they are translated 'misfortunes' and 'setbacks', as is the case in Bart Ehrman's new Loeb edition.[13] This more accurate translation, together with the recognition that firm independent evidence for persecution under Domitian is lacking, makes it difficult to date *1 Clement* to the period around the end of the emperor's life, on the grounds that his alleged persecution of Christians would have come to a stop around the time of his death. This does not preclude a date around the end of the first century, but it does mean that such a date must be based on other evidence than the very questionable view that the letter refers to persecution under Domitian.

Other factors may also be taken into account. Internal evidence suggests that the deaths of Peter and Paul are some time in the past (5.1–7); and that there has been time for presbyters appointed by the apostles to have died (44.2), and perhaps also their successors (44.3). The church at Corinth is called ancient (47.6); and the emissaries sent by Rome are said to have lived blamelessly as Christians from youth to old age (63.3). Such statements are usually thought to demand a date no earlier than the 80s or 90s, although the evidence for this is not compelling. The deaths of Peter

---

11. See L.L. Welborn, 'On the Date of First Clement', *BR* 24 (1984), 34–54, repr. in Breytenbach and Welborn (eds), *Encounters with Hellenism*, 197–216, and T.J. Herron, 'The Most Probable Date of the First Epistle of Clement to the Corinthians', *StPatr* 21 (1989), 106–21. Their arguments are summarized in A. Gregory, 'Disturbing Trajectories: *1 Clement*, the *Shepherd of Hermas* and the Development of Early Roman Christianity', in P. Oakes (ed.), *Rome in the Bible and the Early Church* (Carlisle: Paternoster Press, 2002).

12. K. Lake (ed. and tr.), *The Apostolic Fathers* (Cambridge, Mass.: Harvard University Press, 1912).

13. B.D. Ehrman (ed. and tr.), *The Apostolic Fathers* (Cambridge, Mass.: Harvard University Press, 2003).

and Paul are described as having been in the very recent past (a superlative rather than comparative form is used). If presbyters (elders!) appointed by the apostles were already quite old, it is quite possible that their successors were appointed from the 60s. Corinth might be said to be ancient (αρχαιαν) not because it is very old but because it goes back to the founding of the church at the beginning (ἀρχῇ) of Paul's preaching. If Roman emissaries have lived blamelessly at Rome since their youth, not necessarily as Christians, we have no way of knowing their age. Thus it is possible that the *terminus a quo* for the writing of *1 Clement* may be brought forward from the 80s to the 70s.

One piece of internal evidence sometimes used to provide a *terminus ad quem* for the composition of the letter is the fact that it appears not to quote from the written Gospels,[14] but this is a dubious argument from silence. The author might have known written Gospels even if he chose not to quote from them, and there remains continuing debate as to when the written Gospels were widely available. External evidence suggests that Hegesippus may have seen the letter in the mid- to late-second century, and Dionysius of Corinth sometime after that. If it could be shown that literary parallels between Polycarp's *Epistle to the Philippians* and *1 Clement* were evidence that Polycarp drew on Clement, not vice versa, this would bring forward even earlier the *terminus ad quem* that external evidence can supply.

6. *Authorities and Sources*

Approximately one quarter of *1 Clement* is given over to quotations from the Jewish scriptures – about 75 in total[15] – and there appear to be many allusions as well. Some may depend on *testimonia* collections, but the fact that the author uses so much Septuagintal language and draws on it both extensively and coherently to support the point he wishes to make suggests that he knew the Greek Jewish scriptures very well. At the same time he is creative in his approach to these writings, and not afraid to present them in a novel way in order to support the argument that he advances. Thus he uses the Jewish scriptures to emphasize the importance of ὁμονοια, even when that concern is not present in the scriptural text or in earlier extant traditions. For example, there is no precedent to his claim that the animals enter the ark in *homonoia* (9.4), or that the sin of Lot's wife was her failure to remain in *homonoia* with her husband (11.2). Clement blends biblical examples with contemporary Graeco-Roman mores and it is difficult to point to one or the other as more important to

14. See further below, sect. 6.
15. D.A. Hagner, *The Use of the Old and New Testaments in Clement of Rome*, NovTSup 34 (Leiden: Brill, 1973), 22.

his thought, although the introductory formulae that he uses leave no doubt that he considered the Jewish scriptures to be divinely inspired. Thus he refers to the one who speaks through scripture as God (10.4; 18.1; 33.5; 53.2), as Lord (8.2; 36.4), and as the Holy Spirit (13.1; 16.2). It is to the holy and true scriptures given through the Holy Spirit that he appeals in addressing the Corinthians (45.2; 53.1).[16]

Clement appeals also to a number of Christian writings that were later included in the New Testament,[17] as well as to the words of Jesus. He tells the Corinthians to take up a letter from Paul, and refers to enough of its content to leave no doubt that he means 1 Corinthians (47.1–8). In so doing he assumes that it is self-evident that he should appeal to Paul, and that Paul's letter was still available in Corinth as well as in Rome. Clement appears to draw on 1 Corinthians at various points in his letter, and there is evidence to suggest that he very probably knew Romans and Hebrews as well. Clement refers to Peter as well as to Paul by name and as apostles (5.3–7), but there is no clear evidence that he used any letters associated with the former. Most scholars agree that there is no evidence to demonstrate that Clement used any of the Gospels later included in the New Testament, although he appeals to sayings of Jesus that were included in Matthew and in Luke (*1 Clem.* 13.2; 46.7–8). He also appears to allude to the parable of the sower (24.5), but in the context of a discussion of the resurrection of the body in which he draws on 1 Corinthians 15 and makes no reference to the teaching of Jesus. There is no evidence to demonstrate any knowledge of John or of Acts.

Clement also draws on other sources in addition to the Jewish scriptures and Christian writings and traditions. These include the legend of the phoenix (25.1–5), possibly Stoic images of harmony (20.1–12; 37.1–3, but cf. Paul and Jesus), and various examples drawn not only from Jewish but also from Gentile (i.e. Graeco-Roman) history (6.2, 4; 55.1). These appeals have sometimes been used as evidence of the extent to which he has been influenced by non-Jewish and Christian traditions, but it is probably more important to note how few, rather than how many, such examples he notes. By far the majority of his examples and appeals to other sources of authority are drawn from Jewish scripture or from Christian tradition.

16. Hagner, *The Use of the Old and New Testaments in Clement of Rome*, 110–11.
17. For a fuller discussion, see A. Gregory, '*1 Clement* and the Writings that Became the New Testament', in A. Gregory and C.M. Tuckett (eds), *The Reception of the New Testament in the Apostolic Fathers* (Oxford: Oxford University Press, 2005), 129–57.

7. *Conclusion: Between Jerusalem, Corinth and Rome*

Commentators have variously evaluated *1 Clement* as either an essentially Hellenistic (often with particular reference to Stoicism in its Roman form) or Jewish-Christian text. Such debates seem futile, however, for it is very difficult to understand categories such as Jewish-Christian (whatever this very problematic term is taken to mean), Hellenistic and Roman as necessarily mutually exclusive. The Jewish scriptures that Clement quotes are a product of the Hellenistic world, just as the Greek that he writes from the capital of the Roman Empire to a church in a Roman colony in the Roman province of Achaia is a product of the confluence of Greek and Roman culture in the period of the Second Sophistic, a major resurgence of interest in Greek culture at this point in the history of the Roman Empire. Nor is Clement innovative in this respect. He shows greater facility than Paul in his use of Graeco-Roman rhetorical conventions, but Paul before him was a Jew who drew on Roman imagery in letters written in Greek. Clement no more 'encounters' Hellenism than does Paul, for each is a product of the Hellenistic world. The fact that all surviving Christian texts from the early second century were written in Greek, as were those that may have pre-dated *1 Clement*, can hardly be exaggerated.

Chapter 4

2 *CLEMENT* AND THE MEANING OF THE CHRISTIAN HOMILY

Paul Parvis

Of the motley collection of documents that make up the Apostolic
Fathers, *2 Clement* is in many ways the most unprepossessing. Its great
nineteenth-century editor, J.B. Lightfoot, concluded rather sadly that it is
'confused in thought and slipshod in expression' and 'as a literary work is
almost worthless'.[1] More than a thousand years earlier, Photius, the
learned and discriminating Patriarch of Constantinople, had decided that
'the ideas [in *2 Clement*] are somewhat scattered and do not maintain a
coherent continuity'.[2]

And yet – paradoxically – much of the interest and importance of the
document lies precisely in that apparently unprepossessing character. In
order to see why that might be so, we have to look at what kind of text *2
Clement* is. And in order to understand the evidence for that, we have to
say something about the history of its transmission – something about the
process by which the text has come down to us – and something about its
integrity as a literary work (whether or not it is 'almost worthless').

---

1.   J.B. Lightfoot, *The Apostolic Fathers*, part 1, *Clement of Rome*, vol. 2 (London:
MacMillan, 1890), 206, 208. Lightfoot includes a translation (306–16) as well as a critical
edition of the Greek text with commentary (211–61). A handy recent edition of the Greek
text with facing English translation is in B.D. Ehrman (ed. and tr.), *The Apostolic Fathers*,
vol. 1, 24 (Cambridge, Mass: Harvard University Press, 2003), 153–99. There is a useful
commentary on an English text of the letter in R.M. Grant and H.H. Graham, *The Apostolic
Fathers: A New Translation and Commentary*, vol. 2, *First and Second Clement* (New York:
Thomas Nelson and Sons, 1965), 107–38, and an excellent German commentary in A.
Lindemann, *Die Apostolischen Väter*, vol. 1, *Die Clemensbriefe*, HNT 17 (Tübingen: Mohr-
Siebeck, 1992), 183–261.

2.   Photius, *Bibliotheca*, cod. 126. Photius is actually referring to *both* letters of Clement
('the ideas *in them*'), but in the context he has just been speaking about the second letter in
particular, and his remarks apply to it much more than they do to the first.

1. *How the Text Came to Us*

Eusebius of Caesarea, in his great *Ecclesiastical History*, the last edition of which was produced towards the end of the year 324, knows of the existence of two letters of Clement, the second of which – presumably identical with our text – 'we do not acknowledge as recognized, as we do the first, because we are not aware that it too was used by those of olden times' (*HE* 3.38.4).

The fact that Eusebius bothers to say that he does not 'recognize' the letter of course itself implies that there were others who did – others, that is, who regarded it as authoritative and, indeed (once the concept was formulated), as canonical. That view is represented by a collection of disciplinary regulations known as the *Apostolic Canons*, which probably comes from Antioch towards the end of the fourth century. The last canon in the collection (85) numbers among 'our books, that is the books of the New Covenant, . . . two epistles of Clement'.[3]

The text Eusebius and the *Apostolic Canons* are referring to was, however, completely unknown in the Latin West until 1627, when the magnificent manuscript of the whole Greek Bible known as Codex Alexandrinus arrived at the British court, a present from Cyril Lucar, the controversial, Protestantizing Patriarch of Constantinople, to James I of England and VI of Scotland. The manuscript probably dates from the fifth century and contains, at the end of our New Testament, *1* and *2 Clement*, undifferentiated in any way from the 'canonical' texts that have preceded them. But *2 Clement* is incomplete and breaks off in the middle of a sentence, since the last pages of the manuscript are missing. It was in this truncated and mutilated form that it was first edited, in 1633, by Patrick Young.

Recovery of the full text had to wait until the last quarter of the nineteenth century – and it was only then that the genre of the work could really be understood. In 1875 the Orthodox scholar Philotheos Bryennios published, for the first time, the document in its entirety, from an eleventh-century manuscript in Constantinople. And then, a few months later, a Syriac version of the complete text came to light, in a manuscript acquired by the Cambridge University Library. In Bryennios's manuscript, *2 Clement* appears with other works which we would class as belonging to the Apostolic Fathers,[4] but in the Cambridge Syriac

---

3. Text in M. Metzger (ed.), *Les Constitutions Apostoliques*, vol. 3, *Livres VII et VIII*, SC 336 (Paris: Éditions du Cerf, 1987), 308.

4. Indeed, it was in this same manuscript that the *Didache* – also first edited by Bryennios – was discovered.

manuscript, as in Codex Alexandrinus, it is found with the books that make up our New Testament. Here, though, *1* and *2 Clement* come not at the end, but sandwiched between the Catholic Epistles and the letters of Paul. These three manuscripts – two Greek and one Syriac – remain the only primary witnesses to the text of *2 Clement* (there are also a few quotations in later patristic writings).

2. *The Homily and Its Context*

What kind of document do these manuscripts attest? Though known as the Second Letter of Clement to the Corinthians,[5] the text is not a letter, does not claim to be by anyone named Clement, and has no clear connection with Corinth. It is in fact a homily, and it is apparent from the full text that it was valued enough in at least one church to be itself read out to the congregation after the reading of the scriptures. Indeed, if – as we will see is most likely – it belongs to the middle of the second century, it is in fact the earliest surviving Christian homily, apart from the polished and literary sermons which Luke includes in Acts. (The next candidate would be the paschal homily by Melito of Sardis, which was perhaps written some twenty years later.[6])

The literary unity of the text has been a matter of some debate. The theory that seems to me overwhelmingly likely is that there is a suture near the end of the work, at the beginning of the nineteenth of the 20 chapters into which the text is divided.[7] That is apparent partly on stylistic grounds and partly from content. Thus, the first 18 chapters repeatedly address the audience (in the second person plural) as 'brethren' (1.1; 4.3; 5.1; 7.1; 10.1; 11.5; 13.1; 14.1; 16.1), while chaps 19—20 speak of 'brothers and sisters' (19.1; 20.2). That is actually quite a suggestive change. 'Brothers' is ἀδελφοί; 'sisters' is the corresponding feminine form ἀδελφαί. Normal Greek usage, pagan as well as Christian, would have been to address a group of mixed gender as ἀδελφοί. The differentiation of ἀδελφοί from ἀδελφαί may suggest a setting in which men are seated or standing on one side of the assembly and women on the other – as became the norm in the ancient church and was perhaps already true of the synagogue; we can

5.   That is the title in both the Bryennios and Cambridge manuscripts. In Alexandrinus the title would have come at the end of the work, rather than at the beginning, and the ending is lost, but in the list of contents prefixed to the whole manuscript it is called Second Epistle of Clement (with no mention of the Corinthians).

6.   There is an excellent edition of this work in Melito of Sardis, *On Pascha and Fragments*, ed. and tr. S.G. Hall, Oxford Early Christian Texts (Oxford: Clarendon Press, 1979); for the date, see pp. xxi–xxii.

7.   See the very good discussion in Lindemann, *Die Clemensbriefe*, 190–1 and 255–6.

even imagine the speaker turning from one to the other as he proceeds.[8] In other words, in chaps 19—20 we may be hearing an echo of a more fully developed, more carefully articulated liturgical context.

In terms of content, these last two chapters look more like an introduction than a conclusion. The beginning of this section professes to explain what is going on:

> So, brothers and sisters, after the God of truth, I am reading you a supplication to pay heed to what has been written, that you might save both yourselves and the one who is reading in your midst. For I ask as my payment that you repent from your whole heart, giving yourselves salvation and life. (19.1)

The text that is here being referred to – the 'supplication' – seems, then, to have followed the reading of scripture ('the God of truth') and to be a set piece, read rather than delivered spontaneously. Moreover, this introduction to the last section picks up themes and phrases from the main body of the text. In 15.1 the preacher had said (as if concluding), 'And I think I have given no small counsel about chastity; anyone who has fulfilled it will not be sorry, but will rather save both himself and me, the counsellor. For it is no small reward to turn a wandering and perishing soul toward salvation.' And in chap. 17, in a sort of peroration, he had urged, 'Let us, then, repent from our whole heart . . . And let us not only seem to believe and to pay heed now while we are being admonished by the presbyters, but when we have gone off home too let us remember the commandments of the Lord' (17.1, 3).

Now, it seems distinctly odd for someone reading a text actually to say 'I am reading you' a text about what the audience has just heard. But it would make sense if chaps 19—20 were really a sort of trailer for chaps 1—18. We then get quite a vivid snapshot of a Christian service in the middle of the second century.

There were scripture readings: Justin Martyr, writing in Rome at almost the same time, says that 'the memoirs of the apostles or the writings of the prophets are read – as much as there is time for' (*1 Apology* 67.3). Then there were exhortations, applying the readings and driving them home, delivered by the various presbyters who were present. Our original homily – *2 Clement* 1—18 – was one of them, and, for whatever reason, a written copy of it was preserved. Perhaps the presbyter who delivered it had written it down to be used again; perhaps it was taken down by stenographers, as frequently happened to sermons later in the patristic period. In any event, on one occasion when it was reused – perhaps by a presbyter diffident about his own abilities as a speaker – it was preceded

---

8.   See E. Schürer, *The History of the Jewish People in the Age of Jesus Christ*, new English version, ed. G. Vermes *et al.*, vol. 2 (Edinburgh: T. & T. Clark, 1979), 447 with n. 98.

by a short explanation,[9] and the composite document, chaps 1—18 plus 19—20, became the fountainhead of our thin manuscript tradition.

We can say more about the situation of the preacher and his audience. The basic opposition between confessing and denying – so fundamental to the rhetoric and the reality of life in the second-century church – does occur, but the emphasis is almost entirely moral. The threat of persecution may be in the background, but it is a long way off, like the rumble of thunder on a warm summer evening. We are to confess

> the one through whom we were saved. And how do we confess him? In doing what he says and not disobeying his commandments . . . So then, brethren, let us confess him in works – in loving one another, in not committing adultery or slandering one another or being jealous, but rather chaste, merciful, good. And we ought to show compassion for one another and not love money. In these works let us confess him and not in their opposites. (3.3–4; 4.3)

And, conversely, the temptation to deny Christ has to be resisted in daily life at least as much as it does before the magistrate's tribunal:

> The righteous who have done well and endured torments and hated the disturbance of the soul by sweet pleasures will give glory to their God when they see how those who have gone awry and denied Jesus in their words or in their deeds are punished with terrible torments in unquenchable fire. (17.7)

It is, moreover, a community that seems open to its pagan neighbours and indeed basks in their approbation. The problem is living up to their expectations: 'Let us not wish to please ourselves alone, but also people outside, on the basis of our righteousness, that the name might not be blasphemed because of us' (13.1). And it is blasphemed when we fail to do what the Lord wants:

> For the Gentiles, when they hear the words of God from our mouth, are amazed at them as being beautiful and great. Then, when they realize that what we do is unworthy of what we say, they are turned to blasphemy, declaring that it is some myth and deceit. (13.3)

When and where would we find such a context? *2 Clement* belongs to the middle of the second century. That is the virtually unanimous view, and it

---

9. The assumption here, following Lindemann, *Die Clemensbriefe*, 152–3, is that when the papers were gathered up to be recopied, 1—18 and 19—20 were, in effect, put in the wrong order. But the essential point would not be affected if it were assumed that the explanation actually followed the reading of the written text of the original homily.

must, I think, be right.[10] There is no external evidence earlier than the
fourth century, so we have to rely largely on our evaluation of the feel of
the piece. The most compelling single piece of evidence is the way it cites
texts, and especially sayings of Jesus. On the one hand, the work appeals
to the authority of 'the books and the apostles' (14.2), but, on the other –
as we will soon see – appeals several times to strikingly non-canonical
sayings. In other words, it belongs to a time when the idea of a normative
collection of writings, including Christian, 'apostolic' ones, has emerged,
but there is as yet no notion of a closed canonical list, even of Gospels. We
are still a long way from Irenaeus' assertion (in the 180s) that there must
be four and only four Gospels just as there can be four and only four
winds (*AH* 3.11.8).

Geographical location is more uncertain. Rome, Alexandria and
Corinth have all been favoured candidates. The most attractive suggestion
is based on an athletic analogy in chap. 7, where the homilist appeals to
the example of the 'many' who 'sail down to perishable games' (7.3). Zahn
in 1876 and Lightfoot in 1890 both saw in that a topical reference to the
Isthmian Games, which were held every other year, about ten miles east of
Corinth, and which drew competitors and spectators from all over the
Graeco-Roman world. A Corinthian origin would also, of course, offer at
least a partial explanation of the way in which *2 Clement* became attached
to *1 Clement* in the manuscript tradition, if both documents were
preserved in the archives of the same church. This theory is speculative,
but remains the best bet.

The second century, for both pagans and Christians, darkened towards
the end. Our text comes from a time of openness and possibility. It lets us
see a church still at peace, reflecting on what it is and what it needs to do.

3. *The Preacher's Message*

And the message this mid-second-century preacher addresses to his
audience is that they have to pull up their moral socks. But though the
theme of repentance appears over and over again (8.1–3: 'let us repent
from our whole heart, that we might be saved by the Lord, while there is
still time for repentance'; 9.8; 13.1; 16.1; 17.1), it would be a mistake to
think of *2 Clement* as a clarion call to radical conversion – and that for
two reasons.

---

10.   See the discussion in Lindemann, *Die Clemensbriefe*, 195, who concludes that 'a more
precise affirmation than "middle of the second century" does not appear to be possible'.
Lightfoot preferred 120–40, but thought that a date either earlier or later could not be
excluded (*Clement of Rome*, 202). I would myself prefer a date rather nearer 150 on the
grounds of the covert polemic against Gnosticizing views, for which I will argue below.

First, repentance is only one of the virtuous responses toward which the congregation is admonished. The author can say, for example,

> Almsgiving is a good thing, as is repentance of sin. Fasting is better than prayer, but almsgiving is better than both. And love covers a multitude of sins, but prayer from a good conscience rescues from death. Blessed is everyone who has been found full of these things, for almsgiving lightens the burden of sins. (16.4)

When commentators on this passage try to sort out a logical sequence, they miss the point. Repentance is one of a whole package of attitudes and actions which together constitute the life to which the Christian is ever being called.

And the second reason why repentance from sin should not be uniquely privileged as the message of *2 Clement* is that it is only one of the models used to describe the renewal the Gospel brings. Our sight was dim and our vision fogged, but 'we regained our sight, laying aside the cloud that surrounded us' (1.6; see also 9.2). We should entrust ourselves to the God who brings health, 'while we have time to be healed' (9.7). 'Let us at last repent,' the preacher says, but he immediately adds, 'Let us sober up towards the good, for we are full of much folly and evil' (13.1). The prevalent language of sin and repentance is, then, nuanced and qualified by other images – blindness and sight, sickness and healing, moral drunkenness and sobriety. It is not – or at least not just – a sort of camp-meeting conversion experience to which the homilist is calling his audience; it is, rather, a process – a process of growth and conversion: 'Praying more frequently, let us attempt to make progress in the commandments of the Lord, that we might all, being of one mind, be brought together in life' (17.3); 'Let us pursue virtue all the more, and let us leave behind vice, as the forerunner of our sins' (10.1).

As the threat of persecution is but the rumble of distant thunder, so the theological and ecclesial climate seems to be largely tranquil as well. Here, though, appearances could be deliberately deceptive.

There are 'evil teachers of innocent souls' (10.5), but it is moral, not doctrinal, evil that they teach, 'preferring enjoyment here to the promise that is to come' (10.4), and the threat of heresy is never adverted to. But there is a stress on the value and importance of the flesh, so typical of second-century polemic against docetists and gnostics of various persuasions: 'Let none among you say that *this* flesh is not judged or does not rise' (9.1). And in varied and complex ways flesh is made the bearer of the divine.

There is a fundamental tension and contrast between flesh and Spirit. Thus (as often in second-century thought) 'Spirit' designates the divine aspect of Jesus, and 'flesh' the human aspect: 'Christ the Lord, who saved us, being first Spirit, became flesh' (9.5). But that tension and contrast is not a simple opposition, and the same duality is used to express the underlying reality of Christian life.

'The first Church . . . was created before sun and moon' (14.1).[11] In other words, it belonged to the realm of Spirit, but was realized and concretized in the realm of flesh in a movement that is at once parallel to and an expression of the appearance in flesh of the spiritual Christ: 'For it was spiritual, as was our Jesus too, but he was made manifest in the last days that he might save us. And the Church, being spiritual, was made manifest in the flesh of Christ' (14.2–3).

The complex relationship between Christ and his Church is expressed in terms of the Pauline idea that 'the living Church is the body of Christ', but also in terms of the sexual imagery of Gen. 1.27, 'God made the human being male and female', where 'the male is Christ, the female is the Church' (14.2). At first these pictures seem to sit ill together, and certainly the progression in the whole passage is kaleidoscopic rather than strictly logical. But in fact it is coherent because the payoff, as always for *2 Clement*, is moral.

The conclusion drawn from the fact that the Church, like Christ, was made manifest in flesh is that

> if any of us keeps it [that is, the Church] in his flesh and does not corrupt it, he will receive it in the Holy Spirit. For this flesh corresponds to and expresses[12] the Spirit . . . Keep the flesh that you might partake of the Spirit. And if we say that the flesh is the Church and the Spirit is Christ, then the one who has abused the flesh has abused the Church. Such a person will not, then, partake of the Spirit, which is Christ. (14.3–4)

This strongly theological stress on the significance of flesh is, I think, both significant and deliberate. It represents a covert polemic against those in the second-century Church who denied its reality or its worth. But instead of engaging in head-to-head polemic – as Ignatius of Antioch does, for example – *2 Clement* prefers to turn its back on overt debate and to imply instead that the important thing is not so much what you say about the flesh as what you do with it and in it.

The author makes the same move elsewhere. There are several texts in *2 Clement* which are presented as authoritative sayings of Jesus, but which

11. The idea of the pre-existence of the Church is also found in the *Shepherd of Hermas*: she 'was created first of all things' (*SH, Vis.* 2.4.1).

12. I have used the phrase 'corresponds to and expresses' to translate 'is an *antitype* of'. The idea is that a *type* is something that leaves an impress that represents it and replicates it in a different order of reality, like a seal leaving its imprint in wax or a die stamping a coin.

do not in fact come from our canonical Gospels.[13] Perhaps the most revealing is that cited in 12.2:

> For the Lord himself, when someone asked him when his kingdom will come, said, 'When the two will be one and the outside will be as the inside and the male with the female will be neither male nor female.'

Again, as in the discussion of the primeval Church, there is an appeal to sexual imagery. And, again, there is a lot going on behind the scenes. The text turns out to have a very close parallel in the riddling and enigmatic collection of sayings of Jesus that make up the *Gospel of Thomas*, preserved in the Coptic Gnostic library that was discovered at Nag Hammadi in the middle of the last century. There we read,

> Jesus said to them, 'When you make the two one and you make the inside like the outside and the outside like the inside and the top like the bottom and you make the male with the female a single one so that the male is not male and the female is not female . . . then you will go in to the kingdom.' (logion 22)

In *Thomas* sexual differentiation is an integral part of a deep mystery, a central part of the existential puzzle and religious problem of unity and diversity, the one and the many. It has an ultimate, mythical, cosmic significance.

   2 Clement's exegesis moves on an entirely different plane:

> The two are one when we speak the truth to one another, and there is one soul, without pretence, in two bodies. And this is what 'the outside like the inside' is saying: the inside means the soul and the outside means the body. Just as your body, then, appears to view, so let your soul too be manifest in good works. And this is what 'the male with the female neither male nor female' means, that when a brother sees a sister, he should think nothing about her sexually, nor should she think anything about him sexually. When you do these things, he says, the kingdom of my Father will come. (12.3–6)

The interpretation in *2 Clement* is, typically, moralizing. Does that mean that the homilist is trivializing something he fails to understand? Or does it rather mean that for him the mystery at the heart of things finds expression, not in cosmic myth, but in the practicalities of living together with honesty and integrity?

   If we take the latter view – as I think we must – we can see why it is precisely in the apparent banality of the text that its real significance lies. The flesh 'corresponds to and expresses' – is the 'antitype' of – the Spirit.

---

13.   See 4.5 ('the Lord said . . .') and 5.2–4 (a conversation between Jesus and Peter). In 11.2–4 a long non-canonical saying is introduced by the phrase, 'For the prophetic word too says . . .'

Ultimate meaning and value and truth find expression in and through our material world and our fleshly, bodily lives. To approach such a text with notions of works-righteousness derived from much, much later debates would be to miss the whole point of it. It would be to miss precisely what made it, in that world, Good News.

The homilist has a deep sense of what Christ has done for his people: 'Our whole life was nothing other than death'; 'In us' was 'much error and destruction'; but 'he gave us the light; he named us sons as a father does; he saved us when we were perishing'. In short, 'he called us when we were not and willed that we come into being from non-being' (1.4–8). And so 'we who are living do not sacrifice to dead gods and we do not worship them, but through him we have come to know the Father of truth' (3.1).

2 Clement is not a profound theological text, and, as critics from Photius on have not failed to observe, it is neither well written nor well organized. But what it is struggling to give expression to is the idea that it is precisely in the nitty-gritty of everyday life that we can see the Gospel at work. It spoke to the men and women of the second century of new possibilities for the transformation of human life, and that is what made it, for them, something worth reading and rereading, copying and recopying, and preserving for us.

Chapter 5

THE FRAGMENTS OF PAPIAS

Charles E. Hill

If there is one figure from the early Church who battles a persistent Jekyll
and Hyde image, it is Papias of Hierapolis. On the one hand, the primitive
nature, and therefore intrinsic importance, of his testimony cannot be
denied; and indeed, interest in his information about the Gospels of Mark
and Matthew has never waned. On the other hand, Eusebius of Caesarea,
one of his earliest, educated readers, who ought to have been in basic
sympathy with him, called him 'a man of exceedingly small intelligence' (*HE*
3.39.13). And some have concluded that Eusebius was being charitable!

The variety of interpretations to which Papias' statements seem open
may at least tell us he was not the clearest of writers, though perhaps
Eusebius bears some blame for short-changing us on context. Eusebius'
remark about Papias' intelligence pertained explicitly to the latter's
chiliastic traditions. Eusebius also might have had in mind the grotesque
and, at best, 'exaggerated' account, preserved only by Apollonius of
Laodicea, about Judas the Betrayer's final end (LHH, fr. 18).

Yet, his disparagement of Papias notwithstanding, the church historian
also valued many of the things Papias recorded as historically reliable.
One essential thing should be kept in mind: Papias was above all a
collector of traditions, and some traditions will necessarily be more
trustworthy than others.

1. *Life, Times and Sources*

Papias was probably born sometime around 70 CE. He wrote perhaps as
early as about 110 and probably no later than the early 130s, with several
recent scholars opting for the earlier end of the spectrum.[1] It is not known

---

1. For example, U.H.J. Körtner, *Papias von Hierapolis: Ein Beitrag zur Geschichte des
frühren Christentums*, FRLANT 133 (Göttingen: Vandenhoeck and Ruprecht, 1983); R.W.
Yarbrough, 'The Date of Papias: A Reassessment', *JETS* 26 (1983), 181–91; W.R. Schoedel,
'Papias', *ANRW* 2.27.1, 235–70.

when he died. His residence in Asia Minor at this early time makes it possible that he had contact with primitive, Palestinian Christian émigrés to his region. He personally heard stories from the 'daughters of Philip' (*HE* 3.3–9, though Eusebius is confusing here: is this the apostle or the evangelist?) who settled in Hierapolis in later life. According to Irenaeus, Papias was both an Asian companion of Polycarp and a hearer of John (*AH* 5.33.4) – Which John is not quite clear. Most (including Eusebius) have understood him to mean the apostle, but Eusebius searched Papias' five-volume *Expositions of the Dominical Logia* (see sect. 2 below) and determined that Papias had known none of the apostles, but had known an elder named John, whom he often quoted.

To prove his reading, Eusebius quotes from Papias' introduction:

> I will not hesitate to set down for you, along with my interpretations, everything I carefully learned then from the elders and carefully remembered, guaranteeing their truth. For unlike most people I did not enjoy those who have a great deal to say, but those who teach the truth. Nor did I enjoy those who recall someone else's commandments, but those who remember the commandments given by the Lord to the faith and proceeding from the truth itself. And if by chance someone who had been a follower of the elders should come my way, I enquired about the words of the elders – what Andrew or Peter said,[2] or Philip, or Thomas or James, or John or Matthew or any other of the Lord's disciples, and whatever Aristion and the elder John, the Lord's disciples, were saying. For I did not think that information from books would profit me as much as information from a living and abiding voice. (*HE* 3.39.3–4)[3]

In this excerpt Papias never uses the term 'apostle', but only 'disciples' and 'elders'. He uses 'the Lord's disciples' to describe both Jesus' apostles (Andrew, Peter, Philip, Thomas, James, John and Matthew) and another group, which included Aristion and the other John. Whether this means that the last two knew Jesus personally is unclear; Eusebius apparently concluded that Papias had no direct contact with any who had known the Lord. In fact, from this quotation alone we cannot even be sure that Papias ever heard Aristion or the elder John in person (though Eusebius assumes that he had). Papias speaks of his actual sources as 'elders', or as 'followers of the elders'. The elders could be (i) apostles of Jesus; (ii) disciples of apostles (as in Irenaeus, *AH* 5.36.2); or (iii) later elders. It is

---

2. This is probably not to be taken as appositional to 'the words of the elders', but as the content of their words. That is, Papias was interested in what the elders reported of the sayings of the men he goes on to name.

3. Michael Holmes's translation, LHH 565.

also possible that by 'elders' he means 'aged ones'[4] and not necessarily those who held church office. The only person definitely named as 'elder' is the famous second 'John'. While some identify this man as the apostle, and therefore understand 'elders' in the entire passage to mean apostles, he is evidently called 'elder' to distinguish him from the apostle John, who has just been mentioned.[5] Others, including recently Martin Hengel and Richard Bauckham, argue that this second John was the author of some or all of the Johannine literature.[6]

2. Expositions of the Dominical Logia

The essential (though not exclusive) contents of Papias' only known work, the five-volume *Expositions of the Dominical Logia*, as both the title and the surviving fragments suggest, had to do with interpretations and oral traditions relating to things Jesus had said in certain *written* Gospels. Even the 'unwritten' eschatological saying attributed to Jesus in *AH* 5.33.3 (LHH, fr. 14) appears to be an 'exposition' of a Gospel passage, Matt. 26.27–9. According to the earliest sources (Irenaeus and Eusebius), these 'expositions' contained a wide assortment of intriguing information, including: circumstances of the writing of (at least some of) the Gospels; a saying about the fecundity of the earth in the coming kingdom, attributed to Jesus himself; the tale about Judas already mentioned; a story about a woman accused of many sins before the Lord, which must have some relation to the *pericope adulterae*, which appears in some manuscripts of John (7.53—8.11); a story Papias heard from one of Philip's daughters about the raising of a corpse; and an account of Justus Barsabbas, mentioned in the book of Acts, drinking deadly poison and suffering no ill effects.

Much of the information alleged to be culled from Papias by post-Eusebian writers has been treated with greater suspicion by scholars. Late reports have Papias as none other than John's amanuensis, who wrote the Gospel at the Evangelist's dictation (LHH, frs 19, 20). Another attributes to him the statement that John, like his brother James, was killed by the Jews. Despite recurring speculation, this last item, even if not spurious, does not imply that John's death was early.

In addition, several of Irenaeus' appeals to tradition from unnamed

---

4. 'The old fathers', as von Campenhausen calls them: H. von Campenhausen, *The Formation of the Christian Bible*, tr. J.A. Baker (Philadelphia: Fortress Press, 1972), 131.

5. J. Munck, 'Presbyters and Disciples of the Lord in Papias', *HTR* 52 (1959), 223–43; Schoedel, 'Papias', 251.

6. M. Hengel, *Die johanneische Frage: Ein Lösungsversuch* (Tübingen: Mohr-Siebeck, 1993); R.J. Bauckham, 'Papias and Polycrates on the Origin of the Fourth Gospel', *JTS* n.s. 44 (1993), 24–69.

'elders' also appear to have come from Papias' book.[7] These include eschatological traditions about Paradise and about the final abodes of the saved, and the reading 666 (as opposed to 616, a reading which has lately turned up in an Oxyrhynchus papyrus) from Rev. 13.18.

The fragmentary state of our information about Papias and his teaching has resulted in major differences in the editions of his work. Lightfoot took an inclusive approach, accepting in his collection statements about Papias or his views in ancient authors, as well as actual quotations. Most questionably, he even printed the *pericope adulterae* from Codex Bezae as from Papias, based on his interpretation of Eusebius' words in *HE* 3.39.17. The latest Lightfoot–Harmer–Holmes edition (used here) contains 26 fragments, including three Armenian ones (whose authenticity has been questioned) only published in 1981,[8] plus five 'traditions of the elders' which Irenaeus very likely found in Papias' book. Bihlmeyer took a narrower approach, printing only 13 fragments which contain actual citations or summaries.[9] This approach is reflected in the recent Loeb edition by Bart Ehrman, which contains 16 fragments of direct quotations (and does not include the Armenian fragments).[10]

3. *Gospels Tradition*

Probably the most widely discussed aspect of Papias' witness is his testimony concerning written Gospels. It is from him that we first hear that Matthew's Gospel was originally written in Hebrew or Aramaic, and that Mark's is based on the preaching of the apostle Peter. The use of the word *logia*, sayings, in the title and fragments has prompted some to seek a connection with 'Q' or some other hypothetical source for Jesus' words. But the *logia* must be essentially, if not strictly, the sayings (or even narratives) Papias knew from the written Gospels, or a name for the Gospels themselves.[11] This is deduced from near-contemporary sources (Justin, *Dial.* 17; *2 Clem*ent 13), from the bulk of the remaining Papian fragments,

7. F. Loofs, *Theophilus von Antiochien Adversus Marcionem und die anderen theologischen Quellen bei Irenaeus*, Texte und Untersuchungen 46 (Leipzig: Hinrichs, 1930), 311–12.

8. F. Siegert, 'Unbeachtete Papiaszitate bei armenischen Schriftstellern', *NTS* 27 (1981), 605–14. One of the Armenian fragments is a translation of a portion of Andrew of Caesarea's commentary on Revelation; two are from Vardan Vardapet's thirteenth-century *Explanations of Holy Scripture*.

9. K. Bihlmeyer, *Die apostolischen Väter: Neubearbiteung der Funkschen Ausgabe* (Tübingen: Mohr-Siebeck, 1924).

10. B.D. Ehrman, *The Apostolic Fathers*, vol. 2, LCL 25 (Cambridge, Mass. and London: Harvard University Press, 2003), 92–119.

11. H.J. Lawlor, 'Eusebius on Papias', *Hermathena* 19 (1922), 167–222; A.D. Baum, 'Papias als Kommentator evangelischer Aussprüche Jesu: Erwägungen zur Art seines Werkes', *NovT* 38 (1996), 257–76.

and from *HE* 3.39.15–16, where the elder speaks of both Mark and Matthew as containing the *logia* of the Lord. These show that Papias was using at least these two written Gospels (or some early version of them); and his description of Mark as containing 'the things either said or done by Christ' shows that these books contained narrative accounts as well.

In *HE* 3.39.15–16 Eusebius quotes Papias, who quotes 'the elder' (probably John the elder), who used to say that Mark wrote down what he had memorized of Peter's teaching. The elder also gives a sort of apology for Mark, who did not produce an 'orderly arrangement' because his writing was based upon the preaching of Peter, who used to teach as need arose. Mark only made sure not to omit anything he had heard and not to falsify anything. Matthew by contrast, he says, did make an 'orderly arrangement' of the *logia* of Jesus, in Hebrew (or Aramaic), which each interpreted as best he could.

These tantalizing bits, precious as they are, have left scholars with a host of things to puzzle over. Already in the elder's day 'Mark' had come under some degree of criticism, but by whom, and for what exactly? And what are we to make of the assertion that Matthew wrote originally in a Semitic dialect,[12] when scholars today are all but unanimous that Matthew was originally written in Greek?

And what about Luke and John, not mentioned in *HE* 3.39.15–16? Did Papias say nothing about these or any other Gospels? This would be unlikely, as some of the fragments and traditions of the elders appear to reflect knowledge of John, in particular,[13] but also Luke (LHH, fr. 24). Furthermore, ancient authors who knew Papias' words about Mark and Matthew also speak in similar strains about Luke and John (but no other Gospels), which could suggest that they were indebted to Papias regarding these too. A satisfying resolution of this problem may be achieved if we recognize that Eusebius did not give Papias' tradition about John in 3.39.15–16 because he had already given it some chapters earlier, in 3.24.5–13, though without mentioning Papias' name. I have recently argued that this passage contains Eusebius' paraphrase of Papias' tradition about John (and to a lesser degree, Luke, in 3.24.14–16), preserving much of Papias' original vocabulary.[14] Both passages (3.24.5–16 on John and Luke and 3.39.15–16 on Mark and Matthew) discuss several common topics, including (i) that each Gospel had its origin in the preaching of one or more of the apostles of Jesus, (ii) that the Evangelists wrote at the request

---

12. J. Kürzinger, *Papias von Hierapolis und die Evangelien des Neuen Testaments* (Regensburg: Verlag Friedrich Pustet, 1983), interprets this as Semitic 'style'.

13. Cf. Hengel, *Die johanneische Frage*, 79–87.

14. C.E. Hill, 'What Papias Said About John (and Luke): A "New" Papian Fragment', *JTS* n.s. 49 (1998); C.E. Hill, *The Johannine Corpus in the Early Church* (Oxford: Oxford University Press, 2004), 385–94, 409–16.

of others, (iii) a form of the word 'remember' (cf. John 14.26) to describe these Gospels as firsthand reports of the Lord's disciples, (iv) a concern for the 'order' or 'arrangement' of their contents, and (v) the attempt to find an 'endorsement' for each Gospel from another accepted, apostolic source. Recognizing these passages as 'new' Papian material would also enable us to explain much of the tradition concerning the four Gospels in later writers who are known to have used Papias' work.

All of this would mean not only that these four Gospels were known to the elder at around the turn of the second century, but that they were already becoming or had become textual authorities, held to be the direct or indirect preaching of Jesus' eyewitness disciples. Fairly sophisticated efforts were already being made at that time to account for their origins, expound their meaning, and deal with some of the difficulties they posed.

4. *Papias and Other New Testament writings*

Papias, then, is an extremely early witness to the interested and in some sense authoritative use of certain new books in the Church. Most probably these included Matthew, Mark, Luke, John, 1 Peter, 1 John, Revelation and, though this is disputed, Acts. In none of the earliest fragments is there a mention of Paul or a clear allusion to anything he wrote, and this has led some to conclude that Papias held the apostle to the Gentiles in disrepute. Yet a recently published Armenian fragment from Andrew of Caesarea and two of the elders' traditions do contain Pauline allusions. Papias' book was concerned foremost with sayings (and acts) of the Lord, not with apostolic writings as such. Even his references to 1 Peter and 1 John (only reported, not excerpted, by Eusebius) evidently were only used to support the interpretation or the authenticity of the Gospels. Any Pauline references therefore would most likely have been illustrative or corroborative.

5. *Papias and Oral Tradition*

Perhaps the single most quoted line from Papias is his comment, 'for I did not think that information from books would profit me as much as information from a living and abiding voice' (*HE* 3.39.4; for the context see the quotation in sect. 1 above). This seems to reflect a common and proverbial preference for oral instruction from qualified teachers over what can be derived solely from books.[15] The contrast should not be seen

15. L. Alexander, 'The Living Voice: Scepticism towards the Written Word in Early Christian and in Graeco-Roman Texts', in D.J.A. Clines, S.E. Fowl and S.E. Porter (eds), *The Bible in Three Dimensions: Essays in Celebration of Forty Years of Biblical Studies in the University of Sheffield*, JSOTSup 87 (Sheffield: Sheffield Academic Press, 1990), 221-47.

as a blanket disparagement of books, or what would be the sense of adding five more to the world? Nor does it make sense to interpret them, as some have done, as a swipe at the written Gospels. Such Gospel books were, after all, the chief if not exclusive source of 'the Lord's *logia*' for him,[16] and a negative attitude towards them does not square with the interest expressed in the traditions he gives about them. The 'books' here being contrasted to the living and abiding voice are clearly an alternative to the tradition he recorded, both apparently intended in some way to expound the *logia*.[17]

In this light, it is even possible that Papias' words had something to do with the curiously similar reports about one of his contemporaries, the 'Gnostic' Basilides, active in Alexandria, according to Clement of Alexandria (*Strom.* 7.106.4), during the reign of Hadrian (117–38). Agrippa Castor reported that Basilides wrote 24 books 'on the Gospel' (Eusebius, *HE* 4.7.7). Papias wrote five books on 'the Lord's oracles'. The titles, too, are similar, the work of Papias being called *Exposition* [or *Exegesis*] *of the Dominical Logia* (λογίων κυριακῶν ἐξήγησις), that of Basilides going under the title *Exegetica* (*Strom.* 4.81.1), possibly *Exegetica concerning the Gospel* (ἐξηγητικὰ περὶ τοῦ εὐαγγελίου). Another one of Clement's sources tells us that Basilides claimed he got his Gospel tradition from a man named Glaucias, who is said to have been Peter's interpreter (ἑρμηνέα, *Strom.* 7.106.4). This sounds like a counter to the elder's tradition that Mark the author of the Gospel was the interpreter (ἑρμηνευτής) of Peter. These aspects of Basilides' work might well have been a response to that of Papias.[18] Yet we cannot be quite sure that the dependence was not the other way around. The claim about Glaucias may indeed have been developed in antithesis to the one which accompanied Mark,[19] but Basilides need not have learned of the Markan tradition from Papias. Since Papias learned it from the elder, this tradition about Mark goes back at least another generation, to about the end of the first century if not earlier. It is likely that already in the first century this tradition accompanied Mark's Gospel to Alexandria, where Basilides could have known it well before Papias wrote. It would then be possible to suppose that Papias, writing perhaps around 120–5, when contrasting the traditions he had collected on the words and deeds of Jesus to what could

16. As W.R. Schoedel notes, 'he clearly is also well disposed to his written sources': 'Papias', in *ABD*, vol. 5, 141.

17. J.B. Lightfoot, *Essays on the Work Entitled* Supernatural Religion (London and New York: Macmillan, 1893), 60; Hill, 'What Papias Said', 623–4.

18. See M. Hengel, *The Four Gospels and the One Gospel of Jesus Chris: An Investigation of the Collection and Origin of the Canonical Gospels*, tr. by J. Bowden (Harrisburg, Pa.: Trinity Press International, 2000), 58.

19. So also M. Hengel, *Studies in the Gospel of Mark*, tr. by J. Bowden (London: SCM Press, 1985), 153 n. 64, 167 n. 46.

be gained 'from books', criticizing at the same time those who 'have a great deal to say', and who 'recall the commandments of others', is alluding to the likes of Basilides' *24 books* on the Gospel, based partly on the alleged tradition from Glaucias. The coincidences are certainly suggestive, but so much remains unknown that this explanation too must remain a conjecture.

6. *Papias and Eschatology*

Some of the traditions attributed to Papias are of an eschatological nature. There are two quotations of Papias and one statement about him in Andrew of Caesarea's commentary on Revelation (LHH, frs 10, 11, 24, the last of these among the newly recovered Armenian fragments). These comments are a bit out of character with the rest of the fragments in two respects. First, they appear to be substantive comments of Papias himself, not traditions of others reported by him. Second, they appear to be comments based upon Rev. 12.7–9, the account of the war in heaven and the defeat of the Dragon and his hosts, not on Gospel-like acts or sayings of Jesus (though the citation of Luke 10.18 in the midst of the preserved comments may indicate a Gospel source).

Other eschatological traditions recorded by Papias show that at least some Christians of Asia Minor in his day maintained significant contact with Jewish apocalyptic ideas. The best known of these is a long saying passed down by Irenaeus about the marvellous fecundity of nature and peacefulness in the natural order during the coming earthly kingdom (LHH, fr. 14). The saying predicts a time when every vine will produce ten thousand shoots, every shoot ten thousand branches, every branch ten thousand twigs, etc., with each individual grape yielding 25 measures of wine. Irenaeus tells us he read the saying in Papias' book; Papias attributed it to certain 'elders' who allegedly heard it from 'John, the disciple of the Lord', who in turn attributed it to Jesus himself. Yet today, all seem to agree that this chain of tradition breaks down at some point,[20] for the quotation does not resemble anything attributed to Jesus in any of the Gospels. What it does resemble, and very closely, is a passage from the Jewish apocalypse *2 (Syriac) Baruch*, where the saying about nature's bounty in the kingdom appears as a prophecy given to Baruch, the scribe of the prophet Jeremiah (*2 Bar.* 29.5–6). Another point the Papian fragment has in common with Jewish apocalyptic eschatology is in the answer Jesus gives to Judas, who asks, incredulous, how such growth could be accomplished by the Lord. Jesus is said to have responded,

20. Most likely, with the unnamed 'elders', whose persons or stories were not properly vetted.

'Those who live until those times will see.' This sounds like the view of *4 Ezra* (7.28; 13.24), in which the Messiah's kingdom is 'seen' only by the last generation of humans, who 'live until those times'. By contrast, the 'millennial reign' of Christ with his saints in the Christian apocalypse written by John (Rev. 20.1–10) is explicitly for those who have already 'died' and 'come to life' as partakers in 'the first resurrection'.

Then there is a tradition about Paradise which Irenaeus attributes to certain elders, probably through the medium of Papias (LHH, tradn 2). According to them, Paradise during the present age is the dwelling place only of those few men who had been preserved from death and translated bodily thereto.[21] This view of Paradise, too, like the previous saying recorded by Papias, has much more in common with the views of *2 Baruch* and *4 Ezra* than with Revelation,[22] or with Paul (cf. 2 Cor. 12.3), or with anything said by Jesus in the Gospels (cf. Luke 23.43).

Thus Papias' millennial traditions in particular would seem to signify the presence in Asia Minor in his day of Jewish converts[23] who carried over eschatological ideas from nationalistic apocalypses and perhaps from the synagogues.[24] Possibly, however, these 'elders' were not Jewish in origin but were closely engaged in Jewish-Christian dialogue and debate. As we see more clearly in Justin, one approach of Christians involved in such dialogues (whether Jewish or Gentile) was to claim and adapt as much of Judaism as possible for Christianity, in this case including the expectation of a glorious messianic kingdom on earth. That such hopes were prominent among Diaspora Jews in Papias' day is evidenced not only in the apocalypses mentioned above, but also in the Jewish insurrections which broke out, first in Cyrene in 115 CE, then elsewhere in the immediately ensuing years and then, climactically, in the Bar-Cochba revolt in Palestine in 132. The stinger for those Christians who sought to adapt this eschatology was therefore not a denial of the coming kingdom but the claim that the people chosen to populate it, alongside the risen patriarchs and prophets, would not be Jews but Christians, the spiritual seed of Abraham (cf. Justin, *Dial.* 80.1; 135; Irenaeus, *AH*

21. See C.E. Hill, *Regnum Caelorum: Patterns of Millennial Thought in the Early Church* (Grand Rapids: Eerdmans, 2001), 22–3.

22. Hill, *Regnum Caelorum*, 227–35; cf. Körtner, *Papias von Hierapolis*, 104.

23. Some have suggested that Papias himself was a Jew. See e.g. A.C. Perumalil, 'Are Not Papias and Irenaeus Competent to Report on the Gospels?', *ExpT* 91 (1980), 335.

24. Cf. also the exegetical 'midrash' involving the 'many mansions' of John 14.2, the parable of the sower (Matt. 13.3–23), the parable of the marriage feast (Matt. 22.1–14), and 1 Cor. 15.25 preserved in one of Irenaeus' traditions of the elders (LHH, tradn 5), in which the hundred-, sixty-, and thirty-fold fruit of Matt. 13.8, 23 are said to represent heaven, Paradise, and the city as eschatological abodes of the saints. This eschatological 'midrash', however, while it shows the influence of Jewish exegetical techniques (see Hill, *The Johannine Corpus*, 407–9), is not necessarily chiliastic.

5.32.2). Whether ethnically Jewish themselves or not, the originators of these eschatological traditions repeated by Papias reflect a situation in which contemporary Jewish views continued to exercise an influence on the development of Christian eschatology.

7. *Conclusion*

Is Papias of Hierapolis then Dr Jekyll – a responsible guide, exuding qualities which inspire implicit trust, or is he a Mr Hyde – a gullible addict of rumour and legend, in whom 'everything is sinking back into the flood of chaotic tradition'?[25] The answer, of course, is that he is neither. Both his traditions and his commentary should be scrutinized with care. Close attention has to be paid to the historical and literary contexts, great parts of which we often lack, not only of the fragments themselves but also of the secondary authors who preserve them. But while the historical value of his traditions is uneven and their interpretation seldom straightforward, Papias of Hierapolis will remain a key figure in the study of early Christianity. For despite all the enigmas, this early Asian bishop still puts us in touch with a generation of Christians – actually two – about whom far too little is known. The information he passes on from 'the elder' about Gospel origins has a permanent place among the *instrumenta studiorum* of both Church and academy. And the few samples of New Testament exegetical traditions recoverable in his fragments are still among the earliest we have. Any new discoveries of fragments (or convincing new interpretations of old ones) would hold great potential for enhancing our understanding of Christianity in this critical time and place.

---

25. von Campenhausen, *The Formation of the Christian Bible*, 134; in full, 'In Papias everything is sinking back into the flood of chaotic tradition, whether written or oral, which despite his alleged sifting is at most only a little restricted by his own theological judgment, and is mostly in practice uncontrollable, bursting all banks and defences and spreading far and wide'.

Chapter 6

THE *APOLOGY OF QUADRATUS*

Paul Foster

Of all the writings discussed in this book, the *Apology of Quadratus* is the only one for which the complete extant text will be provided. The reason for this is simple. Only one small quotation of this apology is preserved, in the works of Eusebius of Caesarea. The place of *Quadratus* among the writings known as the Apostolic Fathers is somewhat contentious. Although the matter is not explicitly discussed, many editions of these texts simply omit the fragment. The original Loeb edition, produced by Kirsopp Lake, does not include *Quadratus*, although it also omits the fragments of Papias.[1] Similarly, the Lightfoot edition, most conveniently available in the revised form edited by Michael Holmes, omits this text as a separate entry[2] (while it includes the Papias fragments[3]). The text, however, is printed in the revised Bihlmeyer version,[4] and the new Loeb edition, edited by Bart Ehrman.[5] Yet, both in terms of the text's claims to antiquity and its generic similarities to the *Epistle to Diognetus*, it has at least equal claim to inclusion in comparison to some of the other writings in the admittedly artificial corpus that has become known as the Apostolic Fathers.

---

1. K. Lake, *The Apostolic Fathers*, 2 vols, LCL 24 and 25 (Cambridge, Mass. and London: Harvard University Press, 1912, 1913).

2. Holmes discusses *Quadratus* in relation to the question of the authorship of the *Epistle to Diognetus*: M.W. Holmes, *The Apostolic Fathers: Greek Texts and English Translations*, 2nd edn (Grand Rapids: Baker Book House, 1999), 529–30.

3. The discussion relating to the fragments of Papias is contained in Holmes, *The Apostolic Fathers*, 556–95.

4. A. Lindemann and H. Paulsen, *Die Apostolischen Vater: Griechisch–deutsche Parallelausgabe* (Tübingen: Mohr-Siebeck, 1992); see 302–3.

5. B.D. Ehrman, *The Apostolic Fathers*, vol. 2, LCL 25 (Cambridge, Mass. and London: Harvard University Press, 2003), 86–91, 118–19.

1. *The Text*

The fragment of the *Apology of Quadratus* has no independent extant manuscript tradition outside that represented by copies of Eusebius of Caesarea's *Historia Ecclesiastica*, where it is cited in 4.3. The textual history of the *Historia Ecclesiastica* is itself extremely complicated, with the primary manuscripts falling into two main groups.[6] Among the Greek manuscripts even the earliest, Codex Laurentianus (E), is dated to the tenth century. Fortunately, none of these textual problems, especially the divergences between the two major manuscript groupings, appears to impinge greatly on the *Quadratus* citation. In addition to quoting a short extract from the apology, Eusebius also provides some interesting background about *Quadratus*, such as the date of composition, the intended addressee, and the purpose of the writing. The brevity of the description and the citation mean that it can be given in full:

> When Trajan had reigned for nineteen and a half years Aelius Hadrian succeeded to the sovereignty. To him Quadratus addressed and delivered a writing in which he set forth a defence of our religion, since some wicked men were attempting to cause a disturbance in our affairs. It is still in circulation among most of our brothers; we have a copy ourselves, from which one can see clear signs of his intelligence and apostolic orthodoxy. He shows his early date by what he reveals in his own utterances:
>
>> But the works of our Saviour were always present, for they were true – those who were healed, those who were raised from the dead, who were not only seen when healed and raised, but were always present – and not just while the Saviour was here, but even when he had gone they remained for a long time, so that some of them survived even to our own time.
>
> Such a person was he. Also Aristides, a man of faith and committed to our religion, like Quadratus left an apology, on behalf of the faith, addressed to Hadrian. His writing, too, is still preserved among most people. (*HE* 4.3)

Although details are lacking, if the dating described by Eusebius is accurate, the text provides a glimpse into the intellectual thought-world of Christianity during the second or third decade of the second century. In the face of growing opposition to Christianity, which characterized the new religion as morally depraved, socially destabilizing and intellectually discredited, the response was robust, portraying the new movement as superior to other religions or philosophical schools of thought. *Quadratus*, like a number of other apologies, was unashamedly addressed to the

---

6. See K. Lake (ed.), *Eusebius, Ecclesiastical History: Books I–V*, LCL 153 (Cambridge, Mass. and London: Harvard University Press, 1926), pp. xxvii–xxx.

supreme political authority, the emperor himself, although it may be doubted whether the holder of the imperial office ever read the treatise.

2. *Date and Setting for the* Apology

Eusebius states that the apology composed by Quadratus was written during the reign of Hadrian. In fact the opening reference in the passage to Trajan may appear to be no more than an extraneous detail, until it is read in the wider context of Book 4 of the *Historia Ecclesiastica*. The previous two chapters describe events that took place during the reign of Trajan (98–117 CE). One event in particular is described in detail: the rebellion of Diaspora Jews. This sedition appears to have had its origins in Alexandria and Cyrene, but the ramifications were felt as far away as Mesopotamia. Eusebius describes this revolt as starting 'in the course of the eighteenth year' (*HE* 4.2.1) of the Trajanic reign, i.e. 115 CE. Griffin notes the geographical scope of the uprising when she comments, 'Failing in health, Trajan sent Lucius Quietus to Judaea to put down a Jewish revolt that had started under a messianic leader in Cyrene and spread to Cyprus, to Palestine and to the new province of Mesopotamia.'[7] The rebellion was protracted, especially since it had multiple epicentres, and was finally suppressed during the final year of Trajan's reign, 117 CE. Apart from the account of the revolt provided by Eusebius, another brief description is found in the epitome of Dio, although Goodman notes the somewhat divergent features in these accounts.[8] It is claimed by Dio that Jews killed up to 220,000 Greeks and Romans in Cyrene and a further 240,000 in Cyprus. Bennett's comments on these figures appear sensible: 'While the alleged atrocities are likely to be grossly exaggerated, as is usual in such cases, some measure of the seriousness that Trajan attached to the matter was his dispatch of Marcius Turbo to (probably) Alexandria to help subdue the disturbances.'[9] Thus, having mentioned the final significant religio-political event that occurred during the Trajanic period, Eusebius continues his history of the Church by describing events of relevance to Christianity that happened at the beginning of Hadrian's imperial office. The first of these is the production of the apology written by Quadratus, which was presented to the emperor (*HE* 4.3.1).

Immediately after relating this description concerning the *Apology of Quadratus*, Eusebius describes the death of Alexander the bishop of Rome

---

7. M. Griffin, 'Nerva to Hadrian', in A.K. Bowman, P. Garnsey and D. Rathbone (eds), *The Cambridge Ancient History*, 2nd edn, vol. 11, *The High Empire, A.D. 70–192* (Cambridge: Cambridge University Press, 2000), 125.

8. M.D. Goodman, 'Judaea', in Bowman, Garnsey and Rathbone (eds), *The High Empire, A.D. 70–192*, 669–71.

9. J. Bennett, *Trajan: Optimus Princeps* (London: Routledge, 1997), 201.

in the third year of Hadrian's reign, i.e. 120 CE (*HE* 4.4). Assuming the events are described in chronological order (which is indeed the general pattern of Eusebius' work), this would appear to imply a date for the composition of the apology after the accession of Hadrian in 117 CE, but prior to the death of Alexander in 120 CE. The issue of dating, however, is not this simple. In another work by Eusebius, his *Chronicon*, it is stated that Quadratus addressed a discourse to Hadrian containing an apology, during a visit which the emperor made to Athens in 124 or 125 CE. There appears to be no decisive way to arbitrate between these two competing dates, apart from an assessment of the relative chronological accuracy of the two works. The few scholars who refer to *Quadratus* opt for the later date, but there is no discussion of the alternative possibility of a date in the earlier range of 117–20 CE. Perhaps it is best to conclude that either set of dates is possible.

Furthermore, while the *Historia Ecclesiastica* gives no clue to the geographical locale in which the apology was composed, the *Chronicon* links the composition with Athens (*Chron.*, ad ann. Abrah. 2041). The tradition that associates Quadratus with Athens is taken up and expanded by Jerome, who makes reference to Quadratus on two occasions (*De Vir.* 3.19; *Ep.* 70, *ad Magnum*). The account in *De Viris Illustribus* is the fullest:

> Quadratus, disciple of the apostles, after Publius bishop of Athens had been crowned with martyrdom on account of his faith in Christ, was substituted in his place, and by his faith and industry gathered the church scattered by reason of its great fear. And when Hadrian passed the winter at Athens to witness the Eleusinian mysteries and was initiated into almost all the sacred mysteries of Greece, those who hated the Christians took opportunity without instructions from the Emperor to harass the believers. At this time he presented to Hadrian a work composed on behalf of our religion, indispensable, full of sound argument and faith and worthy of the apostolic teaching. In which, illustrating the antiquity of his period, he says that he has seen many who, oppressed by various ills, were healed by the Lord in Judea as well as some who had been raised from the dead.

The identification of Quadratus the apologist with Quadratus the Bishop of Athens, who held office around 180 CE, appears to be erroneous on chronological grounds.[10] Notwithstanding the opinion, expressed in *The*

---

10. Even this dating appears to be extremely generous. The official succession lists of the Greek Orthodox Church in Athens seem to acknowledge a lacuna in the list between Publius (161–80 CE) and Quadratus, whose date is listed simply as 'about 200': see 'The Bishops of Athens', available on the Archdiocese of Athens website (at <www.ecclesia.gr/English/EnArchdiocese/EnArchdiocese_bishops.html>). It presents Quadratus as the sixth named person on the list, although there are obvious gaps at a number of points. If the date of 200 CE correctly indicates that bishop Quadratus was in office at this point, his identification with the apologist would make him at least one hundred years old.

Oxford Dictionary of the Christian Church, that 'there is also perhaps no compelling reason for rejecting his identification with the Bp. of Athens',[11] precisely the opposite seems to be the case. It may appear to be possible to force the data to cohere by assuming that the apology was written around 125 CE, when Quadratus was young, perhaps in his twenties, and exhibiting a precocious talent. Then, approximately 55 years later, when Quadratus may have been an octogenarian, he ascended to the bishopric. However, this fails to take into consideration the fact that the most natural way to read Jerome's account is to assume that the apology was composed subsequent to Quadratus being installed in the episcopal office. Hence, it seems that Jerome has incorrectly conflated traditions about two separate figures named Quadratus, one an apologist, the other a bishop of Athens. Thus it is best to reject the tradition provided by Jerome that Quadratus, the writer of the treatise addressed to Hadrian, also held episcopal office in Athens towards the end of the second century.

More productive is consideration of the social and political climate in which Quadratus wrote, at some stage during the first decade of Hadrian's reign. The proconsul of Asia, Licinius Silvanus Granianus, consulted Hadrian concerning imperial policy in relation to those practising the Christian faith. The surviving version of the emperor's reply (by the time it was composed it was addressed to Granianus' successor, Minicus Fundanus) counsels that Christians could only be prosecuted for specific crimes and not for confession of being Christians alone. The problem in determining whether this is an accurate version of the imperial corres-pondence revolves around the fact that the text of the edict is preserved only through Eusebius' *Historia Ecclesiastica*. As Birley comments, 'It looks like Christians may have "adapted" his rescript: other evidence indicates that there was no change in the practice followed by Pliny and confirmed by Trajan.'[12] The general imperial policy that was in force during the first half of the second century appears to have held sway during Hadrian's reign: Christians were not to be actively sought out for persecution; if, however, they confessed their faith to the authorities, or were denounced as Christians, they were required to sacrifice to the emperor to gain immunity from punishment or persecution. Practice differed from province to province, with some officials adopting a particularly lax attitude, while others were more rigorous in the suppression of Christianity. During this partially tolerant era, Christians were able to begin developing intellectual arguments in order to support the validity of their faith. The work of the apologists had twin aims: to

---

11. 'Quadratus, St', in F.L. Cross and E.A. Livingstone (eds), *The Oxford Dictionary of the Christian Church*, 3rd rev. edn (Oxford: Oxford University Press, 2005), 1363.

12. A.R. Birley, *Hadrian: The Restless Emperor* (London: Routledge, 1997), 127.

demonstrate that the claims of Christianity were legitimate, and also that the religion was not a threat to the social fabric of the empire.

3. *The Argument given by Quadratus*

The single argument that is preserved in the *Quadratus* fragment revolves around establishing the veracity of the miracle tradition associated with the ministry of Jesus. The testimony that is invoked is the survival of those who had received healing from the period when Jesus was alive until what Quadratus describes as 'our own time'. The verbal aspect of the entire description implies that such survivors from the time of Jesus had died by the time of the composition of the apology. However, there were people among the current generation of Christians who could remember those who claimed to have received dominical healing. Such a conclusion is suggested by the phrasing which Quadratus uses. This states that those healed 'were always present', employing the imperfect tense to imply a continual state in the past. Thus, ultimately what Quadratus presents as confirming the truth of the claim that Jesus was a true miracle-worker is first-hand testimony presented over many years by the recipients of healing, although in Quadratus' own contemporary setting this has become second-hand testimony, mediated through those who knew the earlier generation.

Interestingly, this 'chain of tradition' argument also surfaces in the fragments of the writings of Papias, who wrote during the period roughly contemporaneous with *Quadratus*. In a fragment preserved in the writings of Eusebius, Papias comments on his practice of consulting visitors who had been companions of the elders, to learn what those travelling Christians remembered of the words of the foundational figures of the faith. Thus Papias states,

> But whenever someone arrived who had been a companion of one of the elders, I would carefully enquire after their words, what Andrew or Peter had said, or what Philip or Thomas had said, or James or John or Matthew, or any of the other disciples of the Lord, and what things Aristion and the elder John, disciples of the Lord, were saying. For I did not suppose that things that came out of books would benefit me as much as that which came from a living and abiding voice. (*HE* 3.39.4)

In addition to general similarities with *Quadratus* in advocating 'a chain of tradition', Papias, also in common with *Quadratus*, places much weight on the value of the testimony of living witnesses.[13]

Another possible purpose of the argument contained in the *Quadratus*

13. For a fuller treatment of the issues surrounding this fragment of *Papias*, see Chapter 5 above.

fragment, suggested by Otto,[14] is that it was an attempt to respond to claims of performing healings and miracles made by groups labelled heretical by their opponents. As an example of a similar argument, Otto cites Irenaeus' response to the miracles performed by the Carpocratians and the followers of Simon Magus (who became the eponymous arch-heretic in much early Christian literature).[15] The contrast is drawn between the enduring quality of true and abiding miracles performed by genuine followers of Jesus, and the false and fleeting tricks that opponents attempted to pass off as miracles:

> And if they [i.e. Carpocratians and the followers of Simon] have in truth accomplished anything by means of magic, they strive deceitfully to lead foolish people astray, since they confer no real benefit or blessing on those over whom they declare that they exert power; but, bringing forward mere boys, and deceiving their sight, while they exhibit phantasms that instantly cease, and do not endure even a moment of time, they are proved to be like, not Jesus our Lord, but Simon the magician. It is certain, too, from the fact that the Lord rose from the dead on the third day, and manifested Himself to His disciples, and was in their sight received up into heaven, that, inasmuch as these men die, and do not rise again, nor manifest themselves to any, they are proved as possessing souls in no respect similar to that of Jesus. (*AH* 2.32.3)

Thus for Otto, the rhetoric in *Quadratus*, which both describes 'some wicked men who were attempting to cause a disturbance in our affairs' and affirms that 'the works of our Saviour were always present, for they were true', is responding to the same problem that Irenaeus tackles more explicitly. That is, it refutes the opponents' miracles as ephemeral and illusory, while the works of Jesus have a permanence which is unmatched.

There are a number of problems with this argument. First, if, as Eusebius informs his readers, the work was an apology addressed to Hadrian, it is a little strange that Quadratus describes an internal dispute. Secondly, the identity of the 'wicked men' can just as easily be understood as being either Jewish or pagan opponents of Christianity. Thirdly, unlike Irenaeus, Quadratus does not use labels such as 'Carpocratian' or 'Simon Magus'. This may be because the tormentors were in fact Roman officials, and in addressing the emperor Quadratus preferred some indefinite description rather than directly accusing Roman administrators of being 'wicked' in their persecution of Christians.

Grant speculates that the argument presented by Quadratus was not deemed persuasive, for it is not employed by later apologists or other Christian writers. He states, 'It is unlikely that Quadratus' apology enjoyed any success, for its theme is not repeated by later apologists of the

---

14. J.C.T. Otto, *Corpus Apologetarum Christianorum*, vol. 9 (Jena: Mauke, 1872), 333–41.
15. See Otto, *Corpus Apologetarum Christianorum*, vol. 9, 339–40.

2nd century.'[16] This reasoning may not be entirely cogent. First, the vagaries of manuscript survival, especially extra-canonical Christian texts that may have circulated in the first half of the second century, means that such arguments from silence are dubious. Secondly, the argument presented in *Quadratus* is predicated on a short chain of tradition, and with the passing of time the reasoning cannot be presented as successfully. Thirdly, Irenaeus describes the ongoing practice of healings in some sections of the Christian church as evidence of the power of the faith (*AH* 2.31.2, 2.32.4), which demonstrates the ongoing use of the miracle tradition for apologetic purposes. Moreover, while this single argument may not have resurfaced in extant works in a particularly visible manner, it is impossible to judge whether the presumably more extensive non-extant portions of Quadratus' apology shaped the subsequent thinking of later apologists. Hence, it appears that nothing can be concluded concerning the success, or otherwise, of the writing of this Christian apologist.

4. *Quadratus Among the Apologists*

Quadratus is often described as the 'earliest known Christian apologist'[17] or 'the first of the Christian apologists'.[18] Such a description may not be entirely accurate, and it may be better to describe Quadratus as a representative of the first stage in the apologist tradition. After providing the citation from the *Apology of Quadratus* Eusebius continues by mentioning Aristides, who, like Quadratus, also presented an apology to Hadrian. While Eusebius mentions Aristides after Quadratus, their close proximity in the account means they cannot be separated chronologically. In addition Jerome, though perhaps dependent upon Eusebius, provides further evidence for seeing the two men as contemporaries. He writes,

> Aristides, a most eloquent Athenian philosopher, and a disciple of Christ while yet retaining his philosopher's garb, presented a work to Hadrian at the same time that Quadratus presented his. The work contained a systematic statement of our doctrine, that is, an Apology for the Christians, which is still extant and is regarded by philologians as a monument to his genius. (*De Vir.* 3.20)

Unlike the work of Quadratus, which has been lost apart from the single short quotation preserved in the *Historia Ecclesiastica*, there are a number of manuscripts or fragments of the *Apology of Aristides*. These

---

16. R.M. Grant, 'Quadratus', in *ABD*, vol. 5, 583.
17. Grant, 'Quadratus', 582.
18. P.J. Healy, 'Quadratus', in *The Catholic Encyclopedia*, vol. 12 (New York: Robert Appleton, 1911), available at <www.newadvent.org/cathen/12589b.htm>.

consist of two fourth-century Greek papyrus fragments discovered at Oxyrhynchus (P. Oxy. 1778);[19] an Armenian fragment published in 1878 by the Mechitarists of Venice; and a complete copy of a seventh-century Syriac version of the apology discovered in the monastery of St Catherine on Mount Sinai in 1889 by Rendell Harris.[20] Once the Syriac text had been discovered, J.A. Robinson realized that most of the *Apology of Aristides* had been preserved as part of the Greek novel *Barlaam and Josaphat*, attributed to John of Damascus.[21] It is impossible to fathom any legitimate criterion that includes *Quadratus* in the corpus of the Apostolic Fathers (although admittedly it is on the periphery of that collection), but excludes *Aristides*.

As an aside, it should be stated that the dating of both *Quadratus* and *Aristides* has been questioned by Birley. He notes the tendency of Eusebius to confuse the names of the Antonines, because of the overlap in nomenclature. He comments, 'Quadratus and Aristides are assigned to Hadrian's reign by Eusebius who states they addressed that emperor (*HE* 4.3.3); but he may have confused Hadrian with Pius (who included Hadrian's names in his full style).'[22] In support of Birley's thesis, it can be observed that the Syriac version of *Aristides* is addressed to Antoninus (Pius), but it remains speculation to suggest that *Quadratus* was likewise addressed to Pius. For, unlike the *Apology of Aristides*, Eusebius actually claims to have seen and read the work produced by Quadratus. Another speculative proposal is that Quadratus was the author of the *Epistle to Diognetus*.[23] Three factors tell against accepting this identification. First, there is no overlap between the fragment preserved in *HE* 4.3 and *Diognetus*; secondly, whereas the former was addressed to Hadrian (according to Eusebius), the latter is directed to Diognetus; and thirdly, there is no significant similarity in stylistic features to suggest that the same author is at work in both documents.

While *Quadratus* and *Aristides* may be viewed as the first flowering of the apologist movement, the pattern developed in their works continued throughout the second century. This consisted of presenting a reasoned

---

19. A.S. Hunt (ed.), *Oxyrhynchus Papyrus*, pt 15 (London: Egypt Exploration Society, 1924). For photographs of the fragments see: <www.papyrology.ox.ac.uk/POxy>.

20. For further discussion of the discovery of the Greek fragments and their bearing on the Syriac tradition, see J.R. Harris and J.A. Robinson, *The Apology of Aristides*, Texts and Studies 1/1 (Cambridge: Cambridge University Press, 1893); recently republ. as J.R. Harris and J.A. Robinson, *The Apology of Aristides on Behalf of the Christians*, Text and Studies, First Series, vol. 1, no. 1 (Piscataway, NJ: Gorgias Press, 2004).

21. Again, see Harris and Robinson, 'Preface' to *The Apology of Aristides*, n.p.

22. A.R. Birley, *Marcus Aurelius: A Biography*, 2nd edn (London: Batsford, 1987; repr. London: Routledge, 2000), 258.

23. See 'Quadratus', in Cross and Livingstone (eds), *The Oxford Dictionary of the Christian Church*, 2nd rev. edn (Oxford: Oxford University Press, 1983), 1149.

defence of the Christian faith addressed to those in authority, often the emperor. The best-known representative among the apologists, Justin Martyr, principally addressed his *First Apology* to Hadrian's successor, Antoninus Pius, although other members of the imperial household, the Senate, and the whole people of Rome are included in the super-scription.[24] By contrast Tatian, Justin's pupil, addressed his apology, *Oratio ad Graecos*, as the name implies, to the Greeks. The *Epistle to Diognetus*, included among the Apostolic Fathers, is addressed to an otherwise unknown 'most excellent Diognetus' (*Diog.* 1.1). If this appellation represents a real person, and not just a literary cipher, then this may be a Roman citizen of equestrian rank.[25] Other second-century examples of apologetic writing are to be found in the works of Athenagoras, *Supplication for the Christians*, addressed to the emperors Marcus Aurelius and Commodus; Theophilus of Antioch, *Ad Autolycum*; and Hermias, *The Mockery of Heathen Philosophers*. It is, however, incorrect to confine the work of the apologists strictly to the second century. The arguments they developed and their form of writing continued into the third century as an ongoing attempt to rebut the charges brought against Christianity by its opponents. Two of the most significant third-century apologies were the *Octavius* of Minucius Felix, and Origen's classic defence, *Contra Celsum*.[26]

5. *Conclusion: The Contribution of Quadratus*

It would be a mistake to overplay the significance of the single fragment of text of the *Apology of Quadratus* preserved in the *Historia Ecclesiastica* of Eusebius. Like the work of Aristides, it attests the activity of Christian apologists as early as the beginning of the reign of Hadrian. The author, Quadratus, is adjudged to be 'orthodox' by Eusebius.[27] The precise basis

24. The Greek text of Justin's works has recently been re-edited by Miroslav Marcovich, *Iustini Martyris: Apologiae pro Christianis Dialogus cum Tryphone*, PTS 38 (Berlin: de Gruyter, combined edn of the *Apologies* and *Dialogue with Trypho*, 2005; the *Apologies* volume was originally printed separately in 1994).

25. See H.G. Meecham, *The Epistle to Diognetus* (Manchester: Manchester University Press, 1949), 92–3, and Chapter 12 below.

26. See H. Chadwick, *Origen: Contra Celsum* (repr. Cambridge: Cambridge University Press, 1965).

27. It is anachronistic to apply the term 'orthodox' to the time of Quadratus: see W. Bauer, *Orthodoxy and Heresy in Earliest Christianity* (London: SCM Press, 1972). The term 'proto-orthodox', as coined by Ehrman, is to be preferred as a description of those who held beliefs during this period which were later viewed as aligning with the emergent orthodox position of the fourth and fifth centuries. See the discussion in B. Ehrman, *The Orthodox Corruption of Scripture: The Effect of Early Christological Controversies on the Text of the New Testament* (Oxford: Oxford University Press, 1993), esp. 3–46.

for this assessment is not clear, although such 'orthodoxy' is described as being apostolic in nature. Eusebius' judgement may therefore be due to the chain of tradition on which Quadratus himself places so much weight, which is the measure that Eusebius employs to deem him orthodox in the sense that his beliefs aligned with those of the apostles – at least as those beliefs were understood by Eusebius in the fourth century. Alternatively, Eusebius also praises the intelligence of Quadratus along with his orthodoxy, so perhaps the very arguments employed by Quadratus were seen as establishing his orthodox credentials. Of course these options are not mutually exclusive, and Eusebius may have viewed them as acting in concert to establish the soundness of both the person and teaching of Quadratus.

The citation that Eusebius preserves from the apology is also of much interest. It represents a form of argument that is not explicitly taken up by the later Christian apologists, namely that the veracity of the claim that Jesus was a true worker of miracles was established by the continuing and abiding testimony of those who were healed, and that although they were no longer living, their confession of the miraculous cures of which they were recipients was remembered by those still alive in Quadratus' day. It is understandable that the impact of such 'eyewitness' testimony diminished with the passage of time. However, it is significant that the single extant fragment of the apology shows how early generations of Christians may have revered the words of those who had had first-hand contact with Jesus.

Chapter 7

The SHEPHERD OF HERMAS

Joseph Verheyden

In many respects the *Shepherd of Hermas* (*SH*) is a quite peculiar work among the writings of the post-apostolic age and much about it remains debated and puzzling.[1] The work is commonly listed among the so-called Apostolic Fathers, though one sometimes also finds it mentioned among the New Testament apocrypha. Its title as given above is a modern construct. The manuscripts offer various other titles, shorter (ΠΟΙΜΗΝ, i.e. 'Shepherd') and longer ones.

1. *The Textual Witnesses and Style of Writing*

SH was regarded very highly in the ancient Church. It was first mentioned by Irenaeus in the West and by Clement of Alexandria in the East, and it was known to several other ancient authors. At one time it was even very much in the running for acceptance in the canon. Originally written in Greek, it was translated into Latin (twice) early on, and, somewhat later, also into Coptic. The Greek text had long been thought to be lost. In 1855, however, a fifteenth-century manuscript was discovered on Mt Athos with an almost complete version of the work, except for the last chapters (*Sim.* 9.31.3ff. [108—14]). In addition we now also possess a good number of other witnesses of the Greek text, all partial or even just fragmentary, and some offering rather variant versions. Most important among these are the biblical Codex Sinaiticus, which contains a significant portion of *SH* (up to *Mand.* 4.3.6 [31.6]), Papyrus Michigan 129 (*Sim.* 2.8—9.5.1 [51.8— 82.1]), Papyrus Bodmer 38 (the first three *Visions*), and also ms. Paris. gr. 1143, Papyrus Amherst 190, fr. 7, and Papyrus Oxyrynchus 404, all three

---

1. In the literature, passages from *SH* are referred to in two ways, an older one that distinguishes between the three parts that together constitute the work, and a more recent one that divides the whole of *SH* into 114 chapters. I use both, with the latter in square brackets: thus, for example, *Vis.* 1.3.11 [19].

of which contain fragments of the missing chapters that otherwise have to be complemented with the Latin.[2]

SH is imbued with symbolism and allegorization. On this there is broad agreement. But too often *SH*'s interest in symbols and allegories has played tricks on commentators discussing the usual introductory questions regarding this work, as well as its content and purpose. For one, *SH* does not offer any reliable and straightforward information on when it was composed. The Muratorian Canon dates the work towards the middle of the second century. This information has been much debated, but so far no convincing arguments have been brought against it and plausible alternative proposals are lacking. Some elements in the text, such as the references to persecutions and to the way the community is structured, would point to an earlier date. However, there is no reason to do away with these elements by 'allegorizing' them. The picture of a threatened community can equally well be explained as echoing a recent past, or even, given the scarcity of our information, the real-life situation of mid-second-century communities, or again, the way these Christians perceived certain tensions with the outside world ('persecutions'). Moreover, what *SH* has to say about hierarchical structures in the communities was most probably not meant as a blueprint of Church hierarchy.

2. Setting in the Early Church

The situation is somewhat better with regard to the question of where the work was composed. *SH* situates the opening scene in Rome and refers to places in or near Rome, but once also speaks of 'Arcadia'. The poetic and symbolic use of the latter is massively documented in ancient literature, and *SH* is most probably not different in this respect, but it does not have to mean that the 'Roman' geography is totally imaginary.

The author identifies himself as one Hermas, a freedman. There is no reason to suspect that the information he provides about himself, his troublesome family (his wife's 'immoral' behaviour and his unreliable children), and his ill-fated professional career (he seems to have been preoccupied too much by his 'business' and yet also to have gone bankrupt) is wholly untrustworthy, even though he has clearly picked out only such elements as can help to illustrate one or another point of his

2. For a more detailed discussion of the manuscript evidence, and the standard introductory issues of dating and provenance, see the following: N. Brox, *Der Hirt des Hermas*, KAV 7 (Göttingen: Vandenhoeck and Ruprecht, 1991); R. Joly, *Hermas le Pasteur*, SC 53 (Paris: Éditions Cerf, 1958, 2nd edn 1968); C. Osiek, *Shepherd of Hermas*, Hermeneia (Minneapolis: Fortress Press, 1999); M. Whittaker, *Der Hirt des Hermas*, Griechischen Christlichen Schriftsteller 48 (Berlin: Akademie-Verlag, 1956, 2nd edn 1967).

argument. Hermas is a Christian, but he does not appear to have any formal function in the community. As the privileged subject of visionary experiences, he acts like a kind of prophet, but while he clearly has great sympathy for persons who have been granted this charisma, which was rapidly becoming more and more disputed, he does not refer to himself by that title and he takes care to distinguish in detail between 'true' and 'false' prophets, the latter speaking under false pretences and without the support of the Spirit, something Hermas always avoids by painstakingly describing both the setting in which he receives his visions and the dialogues he has with the divine messenger.

3. *The Genre and Structure of the Work*

The genre and structure of the work are most difficult to establish. *SH* contains features of an apocalypse, with Hermas in the role of the visionary mediating a series of divine messages. On the other hand, however, *SH* is not interested in revealing hidden schemes of world history or in speculating about the sequence of the events announcing the end-time. Its message rather is about what should be done in the here and now to prepare oneself for the end. At best this could be described as apocalyptic procedure in action, but with a clear-cut focus on the present and serving catechetical and pastoral purposes.

As for its structure, the work seems to be a composite. *SH* consists of three parts of different natures and different extents – five Visions (*Vis.*; chs 1—25), ten Commandments or 'Mandates' (*Mand.*; chs 26—49), and twelve Parables or 'Similitudes' (*Sim.*; chs 50—114) – that are only loosely connected to each other (*Visions* 5 serves as a sort of introduction to *Mandates*) and partly repetitious and overlapping (see e.g. *Visions* 3 and *Similitudes* 9). This strange combination of subgenres has made some scholars suspicious about the unity of the work and has given rise to various quite speculative and contrasting hypotheses of multiple author- ship, none of which have met with much success. There is no straight- forward logic or development in the treatment of the subject-matter. The author rather likes to take up a restricted set of topics time and again, looking at them from different angles and perspectives and introducing slight variations, as a way of imprinting the message on the audience. Perhaps the best we can come up with as an explanation for now is that *SH* was composed by one author pondering the same questions over and over again over a rather long time-span, with clearly pastoral concerns. This would account for both the repetitious and at times somewhat contradictory treatment of the same material, in part using the same symbols and allegories.

4. *Key Themes and Topics*

SH deals with a number of topics, among them the Spirit, community-building, church structures, virtues and vices and the foundations of ethical behaviour in general, salvation, God and the Son of God, but also persecution, relations and social tensions between the faithful, and conversion and/or penance. Most of these are dealt with in relation to others. In any case it would certainly be wrong to argue that *SH* is a systematic treatise on one or more of these topics. Hermas did not receive any formal theological training and has only a very limited acquaintance with theological reasoning and argumentation. It is above all the practical dimension that dominates his teaching. Clearly not all of these topics are equally important to him, to judge from the space he gives to each, but it has proven a most difficult question to find out what are the major points of interest to Hermas and for what purpose he is tackling these.

Three topics in particular seem to have attracted a great deal of *SH*'s attention and they have all been mentioned in the literature as representing the core message of the work.

(i) *Repentance*

Many have said that *SH* is above all, if perhaps not exclusively, about repentance – more specifically, about the possibility of repenting as a Christian. *SH* speaks repeatedly and at length about how to be and how to remain a member of the Church, and especially how to regain membership of the Church. The Greek word *metanoia* is a key notion of its paraenesis[3] and much energy is devoted to describing in full detail the criteria one has to meet to be judged a worthy member of the community, be it in the form of ethical instruction in *Mandates*, or in the more poetic forms of the stone imagery in *Visions* 3 and *Similitudes* 9 or of other similes from nature that are used throughout *Similitudes*. There can be no doubt that *metanoia* is a central concept of *SH*.

However, there is a two-fold problem. First, the word has often been mistakenly understood to refer to a 'discipline of penance'. Nothing of this sort can be found in *SH*. It has therefore been argued to the contrary that *metanoia* should be taken as referring to an experience one has to go through as an individual and not some kind of rite of 'public amendment', and consequently that it should perhaps best be translated as 'conversion' rather than as 'repentance' or 'penance'. But perhaps this view draws too sharp a distinction between the (psychological) process of conversion and the formal-procedural ('canonical') one of returning into the community after performing an act of repentance. Clearly, *SH* is not interested in

3.   The rhetorical tone adopted by an author or orator when giving exhortation, advice or counsel to the audience.

spelling out formal procedures for confessing sins and being accepted again by the community leaders and members, but it is equally obvious that *metanoia* is not just a matter of personal experience but of meeting 'objective' criteria. Second, it has been much debated what precisely *SH* is arguing for and what this meant for the community. On at least two occasions it clearly seems to promote the view that it is possible for one to be forgiven even those sins committed after baptism into the Church (see *Vis.* 2.2.4–5 [6]; *Mand.* 4.3 [31]). The fact that this is 'revealed' to Hermas by the angel/Shepherd, and that he himself at first seems to object to it, would indicate that this represents a fairly new view on the question of how to deal with post-baptismal sin. But in what sense is this 'a new teaching'? It has been taken as a way of propagating lax attitudes, and *SH* has understandably been blamed for that by partisans of more rigorous-minded movements, as witnessed by Tertullian's 'Montanist' critique. Modern scholars have shown more subtlety, and it has also been argued that *SH* actually was intent upon defending a more rigorist position than the one commonly held in Christian communities, admitting only one such 'conversion' as acceptable. The latter view has little to recommend itself, in as much as it faces serious problems trying to explain Tertullian's criticism, which may well have been correct in pointing out what was really innovative in Hermas' teaching.

(ii) *The Church*

A second theme that receives a lot of attention in *SH* is that of the Church and what it represents. To capture its essence *SH* erects a whole battery of images and allegories. The Church is called the first of God's creation (*Vis.* 2.4.1 [8]), and it is further likened variously to a woman and a building. The first image serves above all a didactic and parenetic, rather than a dogmatic, function in summoning repentant sinners and making them aware of their true identity as members of the Church. The symbolism of the woman is developed in *Visions* in different ways which single out different aspects. As 'Lady' (Κυρία, *Vis.* 1.1.5 [1]), the Church is characterized as authoritative, but the image also incorporates aspects of the biblical Wisdom tradition. When depicted as 'an old woman' (πρεσβύτερα), the emphasis instead is on its decline as a result of the misbehaviour of some of its members (*Vis.* 2.1 [5]; 3.10–13 [18—20]). When described as a virgin (παρθένος, *Vis.* 4.2.1 [23]) it is the ethical dimension and the purity of the community that are stressed. Finally, the Church is also indirectly presented as a mother addressing her children (*Vis.* 3.9.1 [17]), which puts its pedagogical tasks in the foreground. The symbolism of the mighty tower, developed in full detail in *Similitudes* 9, opens up yet another perspective. The key for correctly understanding this symbolism within the context of the interest in conversion and remission of sins is to be found in *Sim.* 9.13.5 [90] and the image of the 'monolithic' tower. The whole symbolism revolves around the tension between the real and the ideal. The Church is a project still under construction. It is a dynamic process of ongoing inspection and improvement. For now the Church may be a *corpus mixtum*, but the goal is and should be ultimately to reach perfection. This should not be acquired, however, simply by throwing away all of the building material that is judged to be imperfect, but rather by trying to 'save' and 'recuperate' as much as possible in the firm conviction that perhaps not all of it can be made useful again, but also that under no condition will 'damaged goods' be allowed to remain in use. Behind the imagery one clearly sees a sincere concern for maintaining and furthering the moral qualities of the community and of its members, as well as a strong sentiment of realism which takes seriously the facts as they are.

(iii) *Sin and Weakness*

A third topic that occupies the author's attention is that of the sins and weaknesses that threaten the members of the Church. The long catalogues of advice and warnings that make up *Mandates* give a fairly complete overview. This may not be the most inventive section of the work, though at times the author shows a certain empathy with the psychology of the 'sinner' and also succeeds in introducing a personal touch (he is fond of the notion of 'double-mindedness' – *dipsychia* – which in the New Testament occurs only in James). But the list of opposing qualities of character is not limited to those mentioned in the *Mandates*. Two other issues in particular are worth mentioning because they may give us some insight into the composition, real-life situation and social network of Roman communities.

5. *Persecution and the Christian Community in Rome*

In *Vis.* 2.2.7 [6] and again in *Vis.* 2.3.4 [7], 4.1.1 [22], 4.2.4–5 [23] and 4.3.6 [24], *SH* speaks of 'the great affliction (θλίψεις)' that is to come. But besides this clearly eschatological perspective Hermas also knows of community members who have suffered and endured all kinds of persecutions in the (recent) past. As a result, these members are granted a privileged status in the community gatherings (*Vis.* 3.1.9 [9]) and in the Church (*Vis.* 3.5.2 [13]), and their suffering is described in more detail in *Vis.* 3.2.1 [10]. It has been argued that this does not actually represent the current situation of the Church at the time of Hermas, because there is no strong and reliable evidence that Roman Christians were persecuted in the first decades of the second century. *SH* alludes instead to the 'collective memory' of the community, recalling the horrible events under Nero which had nearly brought about the end of the newly founded community in Rome. But perhaps it is not a question of either/or. There are those who have suffered in the past, but the Church as Κυρία instructs Hermas about their fate so that he too will be given an opportunity to 'sit at her right hand', which he is still forbidden to do at present (*Vis.* 3.1.9 [9]). This suggests the observation that *SH* is reckoning with the possibility that Christians will continue to be threatened while at the same time explaining how they can make sense of it for the good of the community and the benefit of their own salvation. What little can be gained in this respect from Roman literary sources should not lead us astray. One should distinguish between 'facts' and the perception and assessment of Christians constantly trying to cope with feelings of insecurity.

My second observation has to do with the social mix of Roman Christianity according to *SH*. Hermas is much concerned with urging the well-to-do members of the community to take up their responsibilities. A long list of passages could be quoted that deal with 'business' and how to use its gains for the relief of the poorer members. Among the recurrent themes are that of the rich person who is in danger of losing out on the more important share because of his wealth (*Vis.* 1.1.8 [1]; 3.9.2–10 [17]) and that of the rich person needing the poor for his own salvation, a theme that is developed at length in *Similitudes* 2 [51–2] through the image of the vine (the rich one) leaning on the elm tree (the poor). As a matter of fact this appeal to care for the poor and the destitute is present throughout the work until the very last chapter, where it is once more expressed in most dramatic language:

> Tell everyone who is able to do what is right not to stop practicing good works; for doing them is useful. But I say that everyone should be helped out of his misfortunes. For the one who is destitute and suffers misfortunes in his daily life is in great torment and misery. And so, whoever helps such a person out of his misery obtains great joy for himself. . . . For many who experience this kind of calamity, when they can no longer bear it, take their own lives. And so, whoever knows that someone like this is suffering calamity and does not help him out of it has committed a great sin and bears the guilt for his blood. Therefore, you who have received something from the Lord should do good works; otherwise the building of the tower may be completed while you delay. (*Sim.* 10.4.2–4 [114])[4]

But there is still another way in which Roman Christianity seems to have been a composite entity. Hermas has no need to reveal or identify his sources. Only once does he say he is quoting another (*Vis.* 2.3.4 [7]: from the otherwise lost apocryphal *Book of Eldad and Modad*). But he must

---

4. Translation from B.D. Ehrman (ed. and tr.), *The Apostolic Fathers*, vol. 2, LCL 25 (Cambridge Mass.: Harvard University Press, 2003), 473.

have read at least some of Judaism's sacred literature, as he was most probably also familiar with some of the earliest Christian writings. Among these may have been one of the Gospels (Matthew) or possibly more, some letters of Paul, and also the Epistle of James. But it is very difficult to point to convincing evidence that he actually also used these writings in composing *SH*, though in the recent past scholars may have been all too sceptical. Hermas addresses an audience that is clearly acquainted with certain doctrines which were widespread in Jewish milieus, be they matters of anthropology (the word 'flesh' (*sarx*) designating the whole person in *Similitudes* 5), or more esoteric ones, such as angelology. But *SH* also contains a fair number of ideas and notions that have their closest parallels in various Graeco-Roman philosophical traditions, both literary (note the almost exact similarity between the descriptions of vices and virtues in *Vis.* 3.8 [16] and in the so-called 'Tables of Cebes', a document that combines Stoic with Cynic wisdom) and more popular (e.g. the guardian angel of *Vis.* 5.3.4 [25]). It would appear rather improbable that Christianity in cosmopolitan Rome was still uniformly or even predominantly of Jewish stock in at the time of Hermas, if it ever was. But it would certainly also be too simple an explanation to assign all of the 'pagan' material to the impact of Gentile converts, with Hermas accommodating both sides. *SH* cannot be split up into a 'Jewish' and a 'Gentile' part. Elements from various traditions could find expression in one and the same document and apparently both could be understood and appreciated by the audience.

Hermas does not link this two-fold form of social diversity of the communities he addresses in any specific way to the leadership. Nowhere is it said that wealth is a condition for becoming an 'elder'. The original background of the leaders – Jewish or Gentile – must have had some influence on the way they taught and preached, but the Christian community functioned as a bridge to cross cultural differences. Hermas can first quote from an obscure Jewish book (*Vis.* 2.3.4 [7]) and then in the following lines (2.4.1 [8]) once more identify the elderly woman of his visions with the Sibyl, a character that may have called forth rather different associations among his Gentile-Christian and Jewish-Christian readers.

6. Conclusions

SH may often be rather too repetitive and verbose for our taste, but this did not prevent it from becoming quite popular in subsequent generations of the early Church. One may assume that the rich imagery and parabolic teaching must also have appealed to its very first audience. Hermas does not present himself as a leader of any sort, yet he speaks with divinely inspired authority. His teaching is rooted in Jewish and Christian tradition alike, both of which are handled with the freedom that characterizes the homilist and the prophet. The subjects Hermas deals with are more diverse than some modern commentators have been willing to grant. By associating social praxis and salvation he is fundamentally in line with basic Christian teaching. In calling for conversion and for endurance, he displays a sense of urgency that he may have felt was slipping away from the communities he was addressing. These topics offer us an insight into the life of the community. As such they also demonstrate that Hermas may perhaps behave as a prophet, but his aims and intentions are primarily pastoral.

Chapter 8

The *Epistle of Barnabas*

James Carleton Paget

The *Epistle of Barnabas* was probably a popular text in the early Church –
its place at the end of the Codex Sinaiticus, between Revelation and the
Shepherd of Hermas, and its incidental and confident citation by Clement
of Alexandria,[1] Origen,[2] Didymus the Blind[3] and Jerome,[4] together with
its place on the fringes of the canon,[5] would suggest as much. And yet in
spite of this evidence of its popularity, to many modern scholars it appears
a strange and peculiar document.[6] In part this judgement arises from its
somewhat lumbering argumentative style, which makes it very difficult at
times to follow the author's train of thought.[7] But more particularly
strangeness is associated with the author's singular mode of interpreting
the Old Testament, especially as this relates to the Jewish law. In a number
of passages, and in what some, but not all, scholars have perceived as a
strongly anti-Jewish manner, the author claims not only that people
should desist from observing the law in a literal way but that the law
should never have been observed in such a way. A related peculiarity is the
author's unscriptural claim that the Jews lost their covenant as a result of
worshipping the golden calf. The questions of where such ideas came from

---

1. *Strom.* 2.6.31; 2.7.35; 2.15.67; 2.18.84; 2.20.116; 5.8.51–2; 5.10.63.

2. *De Princ.* 3.2.4; *Cels.* 1.63.

3. Did. *Zech.* 259.21–4; Did. *Ps.* 300.12–13.

4. *Comm. Ezek.* 43.19.

5. See Eusebius, *HE* 3.25.1f., where *Barnabas* is placed in group 3 amongst the spurious
books (*notha*). But the same author states that Clement of Alexandria placed *Barnabas* in
group 2 amongst the disputed books (*antilegomena*). For a discussion of these two categories
and the implication of *Barnabas*' place in the Sinaitic Codex see J.C. Paget, *The Epistle of
Barnabas: Outlook and Background*, WUNT 2.64 (Tübingen: Mohr-Siebeck, 1994), 251–3.

6. See P. Vielhauer *Geschichte der urchristlichen Literatur* (New York and Berlin: W. de
Gruyter, 1975), who describes *Barnabas* as 'early Christian literature's strangest document'
(612).

7. Precisely this lumbering style has suggested to some that *Barnabas* contains
interpolations. This seems unlikely: see Paget, *The Epistle of Barnabas*, 73–8.

and for what purpose the author has used them has elicited much discussion.

1. *The Text*[8]

A complete version of *Barnabas* in Greek exists in Codex Sinaiticus (אַ) and Codex Hierosolymitanus (H), the latter of which also contains the *Didache*, *1* and *2 Clement* and the longer form of the letters of Ignatius. A family of manuscripts whose archetype is *Codex Vaticanus graecus* 859 (G) contains a version of the epistle running from 5.7 and immediately following Polycarp's *Epistle to the Philippians*. Additional to these are a papyrus (PSI 757b) containing *Barn.* 9.1–6, dated between the third and the fifth century; a possibly third-century Latin translation (Codex Petropolitanus, normally referred to as L), where the epistle appears between Pseudo-Tertullian's *De Cibis* and the Epistle of James, and which often witnesses to shorter readings; and Syriac fragments of verses from chaps 1, 19 and 20. The major Greek witnesses do not differ greatly between themselves,[9] although there are some significant variants, to which we shall have reason to refer below. Indirect witnesses to the text are found most importantly in Clement of Alexandria and also Origen, Didymus and Jerome. The first version of the text (in Latin) was produced by James Ussher but it was destroyed by a fire in Oxford in 1644, and the *editio princeps* appeared a year later in 1645. A Greek version of the text only appeared more than 200 years later when Tischendorf published the Codex Sinaiticus (1862) and then, 13 years later, when Bryennios published the Codex Hierosolymitanus (1875).

2. *Authorship, Date and Provenance*

Clement of Alexandria, the earliest author to cite *Barnabas*, attributes the epistle to Paul's companion, the apostle Barnabas.[10] This attribution is explicitly found in some manuscripts[11] and later authors.[12] Most would

---

8.   For the fullest discussions of the question of the text of *Barnabas* see P. Prigent and R.A. Kraft, *L'Épître de Barnabé*, SC 172 (Paris: Éditions de Cerf, 1971), 49–66, and F.R. Prostmeier, *Der Barnabasbrief*, KAV 8 (Göttingen: Vandenhoeck and Ruprecht, 1999), 11–62.

9.   אַ and H usually agree with each other against G, which sometimes has readings in common with L.

10. See *Strom.* 2.6.31; 2.7.35; 2.20.116; 5.10.63.

11. See G and L.

12. See the references in nn. 2–4 above.

now argue that such an attribution is wrong.[13] Not only does the date of the epistle – certainly after 70 CE, and probably much later than that – make it unlikely, but most scholars agree that the content of *Barnabas* would not appear to be compatible with what we know of Paul's companion.[14] Some even doubt that *Barnabas* is a genuine pseudepigraph, not least because there seems to be no attempt in the actual body of the text to exploit the attribution to the apostle.[15] If this is so, and the ascription is secondary, then this raises the interesting question as to why the text was ever attributed to Barnabas. A variety of answers have been offered, none of which is entirely satisfactory.[16]

Whether or not the author was originally a Jew is unclear. In favour of a Jewish origin are the presence in the epistle of what look like rabbinic traditions,[17] the use and knowledge of Jewish exegetical methods,[18] and an outlook shared with some Jewish apocalypses[19] and the Two Ways material (chaps 19—20). But none of these points need indicate a Jewish provenance, and the fact that at one point the author refers to a time before 'we believed in God' (16.7) might make a Gentile origin more likely.

Scholars have identified two cruces in their attempts to date *Barnabas*, 4.3–5 and 16.3–4. The first passage appears to cite, somewhat loosely, two passages from Daniel 7 in which an excrescent horn (the word παραφυάδιον, the word translated 'excrescent', is an addition to the Danielic text) appears to destroy three big horns at one stroke or at the same time. Scholars have suggested a variety of candidates for the excrescent horn, including Vespasian, who succeeded the three emperors Galba, Otho and Vitellius, and Nerva, whose reign brought to an end the dynasty of three Flavian emperors. But some have deemed the passage irrelevant to the question of date, arguing that it comes from an earlier source calling its audience in a general way to attend to the signs of the time. The same scholars have usually attributed more significance, at least with respect to date, to 16.3–4. Here, in a passage in which *Barnabas* attacks the Jewish decision to build a temple, he cites Isa. 49.17 ('See, those who destroyed this temple will themselves build it up'), and then

---

13. For an exception see S. Tugwell, *The Apostolic Fathers* (London: Geoffrey Chapman, 1989), 44.

14. Would the Levite Barnabas, who had shown himself somewhat conservative on occasions in relation to the Jewish law (Gal. 2.11f.), have subscribed to *Barnabas*' radically hostile attitude to literal implementation of the Jewish law?

15. See H. Windisch, *Die apostolischen Väter*, vol. 3, *Der Barnabasbrief*, HNT Ergänzungsband (Tübingen: Mohr, 1920), 413.

16. See Paget, *The Epistle of Barnabas*, 5–7.

17. See chaps 7 and 8.

18. See esp. chap. 10.

19. See, for instance, the strongly anti-Roman tone of 4.3–5 and compare this with *4 Ezra* 11—12, 13 and *Sib. Or.* 5.403–33.

goes on to note: 'It is happening. For because of their war, it was destroyed by their enemies. And now the servants of the enemies will themselves rebuild it.' Aside from the fact that there exist some potentially important textual variants here,[20] it is not straightforwardly clear what in fact is being referred to. Most scholars opt for the view that the passage refers either to a mooted rebuilding of the Jewish temple at the time of Hadrian, although the evidence for this is quite slim,[21] or the same emperor's decision to build a temple to Jupiter Capitolinus on the site of the destroyed temple, either before or after the Bar-Cochba revolt.[22] Either way the developing consensus would seem to be for a Hadrianic date sometime in the 130s.[23]

The question of provenance is an equally contested one. Egypt is favoured by a large number of scholars, mainly on the grounds that the epistle seems to have some traditions in common with known Alexandrian sources, in particular Philo, and because of its earliest attested use by Egyptian Christians.[24] Neither argument is, of course, infallible and the unconvinced have been led to suggest alternative provenances such as Syria or Asia Minor.[25] But these proposals seem to have less in their favour than those associated with Egypt.

3. *Genre and Content*

Barnabas is described as an ἐπιστολή or letter in the manuscripts in which it is found and by the ancient authors who refer to it. Some have suspected, however, that such a description is misleading and overlooks what they take to be the extent to which *Barnabas* does not display typically epistolary features. In particular they note the absence of a *superscriptio* in which the sender's name is mentioned and of any reference to the name of the addressee, and what they take to be the rather general tone of the text. On the basis of these observations Windisch was led to describe *Barnabas* as a 'Traktat',[26] and others have preferred such designations as 'homily' or 'word of exhortation'. But some more recent

20. ℵ and H omit the words 'It is happening'; and ℵ reads 'And now *they and* the servants of the enemies will rebuild it.'

21. See Paget, *The Epistle of Barnabas*, 22.

22. Cassius Dio, *Roman History* 69.12, records that Hadrian did this before the revolt, whereas Eusebius, *HE* 4.6.4, states that Hadrian rebuilt the temple after the revolt.

23. See R. Hvalvik, *The Struggle for Scripture and Covenant*, WUNT 2.82 (Tübingen: Mohr, 1996), 23. He prefers a date before the outbreak of the revolt, not least because he sees no indication in *Barnabas* that the revolt has started.

24. See Paget, *The Epistle of Barnabas*, 30–42.

25. See Hvalvik, *The Struggle for Scripture and Covenant*, 44, for general scepticism on the subject.

26. Windisch, *Der Barnabasbrief*, 411, followed by Prostmeier, *Der Barnabasbrief*, 87–8.

research has tended in the main to support the epistolary designation, arguing in particular that the perceived deviations from the letter form are not as telling as some have thought,[27] that there are other features of *Barnabas* which would point more strongly to an epistolary genre,[28] and that the personal character of many of *Barnabas'* interjections (1.8; 4.6, 9; 6.5; 6.7, 9; 7.4; 9.9; 15.4; 16.8) as well as the apparent evidence of the existence of opponents points away from seeing the text as too general to support an epistolary classification. Others have gone further and sought to give *Barnabas* a more specific genre definition, with Hvalvik most recently suggesting the designation 'protreptic epistle'.[29]

In the end, arriving at a conclusion on this matter is very difficult. We are probably right to accept some sort of epistolary classification even if attempts to explain away *Barnabas'* deviation from this form are not always convincing. Certainly it is true that attempts at arguing for other classifications have proved unconvincing. But to what extent a clear genre definition for the work is a necessary prerequisite for its interpretation is unclear.

Barnabas divides itself up into broadly two sections. After the introductory chapter, in which the author greets his readers and in somewhat vague terms states that his purpose in writing to them is 'that you may have perfect knowledge to accompany your faith' (1.5), he proceeds with an extended section which runs from chap. 2 to chap. 16. Here he presents his readers with various teachings, almost all of which have as their central concern the interpretation of scripture, that is, the Christian Old Testament.[30] Some of this teaching concerns the right interpretation of the Jewish law. So chap. 2 concerns sacrifice, chap. 3 fasts, chap. 9 circumcision, chap. 10 the food laws, chap. 15 the Sabbath, and chap. 16 the temple. In all of these chapters the clear implication is that these commandments should never have been observed literally, or put another way, as commandments they have an ongoing legitimacy as long as they are interpreted in a non-literal way.[31] Other chapters are taken up with the subject of Christ's death and its meaning (see chaps 5—7). Here, amongst other things, it is made clear that this event was foreseen in the scriptures. Finally there are chapters devoted to the

27.   See Hvalvik, *The Struggle for Scripture and Covenant*, 72–4. Amongst other things he notes that it might have been quite common at the time of *Barnabas* to put the writer's and the addresee's name on the outside of a letter.

28.   See Hvalvik, *The Struggle for Scripture and Covenant*, 76–8.

29.   This is an essentially persuasive text in which one way of life is attacked and another way of life exhorted. See Hvalvik, *The Struggle for Scripture and Covenant*, 159.

30.   *Barnabas'* knowledge of the New Testament is much disputed. Some think that he quotes Matt. 22.14 at 4.14 but this is uncertain.

31.   For a clear endorsement of the Mosaic law seen through the prism of *Barnabas'* own interpretation, see 10.11 and the words, 'Do you see how well Moses has legislated?'

covenant (chaps 4 and 13—14), in which Jewish loss and Christian ownership of that covenant are emphasized, and baptism (chaps 11—12). Chapter 16 is then followed by a transitional chapter (17) and then an exposition of the Two Ways, 'the path of light and the path of darkness', described by *Barnabas* as 'another area of knowledge'. The epistle ends with a hortatory chapter in which *Barnabas*' readers are called to righteous behaviour and to 'fulfil every commandment' (21.8).

Broadly speaking we might then categorize the distinctions between the two identified sections as exegetical and ethical, although this would be to overlook the strongly ethical thrust of much that is written in chaps 2—16.[32] Certainly it would be somewhat glib to follow Muilenberg and describe the two sections as haggadic and halakhic respectively.[33] What is clear is that any interpretation of the epistle must make sense of the presence of these two sections in determining its purpose.

4. *Major Concerns*

As noted above, a central concern of *Barnabas* lies in the interpretation of scripture. The author asserts that he is writing to a privileged community, 'For through the prophets the Master has made known to us what has happened and what now is; and he has given us the first fruits of the taste of what is yet to be' (1.7; see also 5.3; 7.1; 21.1, 5). As such a privileged community Christians are uniquely placed to understand the meaning of scripture and interpret it correctly. Central to this is a correct understanding of Torah, and at strategically important places in the epistle (chaps 2—3 at the beginning, 9—10 in the middle, and 15—16 at the end), we find extended attempts to interpret these Jewish laws. Some of these interpretations are allegorical,[34] some literal,[35] and some typological,[36] but all aim at presenting a non-literal understanding of these laws. Radically, and in contrast to Paul and other New Testament and early Christian writers, *Barnabas* asserts that this non-literal interpretation, which he appears quite consciously to contrast with Jewish interpretation – although neither of the terms 'Jew' and 'Jewish' ever appear in the epistle[37] – comports with the original meaning of the scriptural text. Such

32.   See *inter alia* 4.1f. and chap. 10.
33.   J. Muilenberg, 'The Literary Relations of the Epistle of Barnabas and the Teaching of the Twelve Apostles', diss., Yale University (Printed Marbury, 1929).
34.   See esp. chap.10.
35.   See 2.6–7.
36.   See 9.7f.
37.   Note the frequent occurrence in the epistle of the words 'to them' and 'to us': see esp. 2.7, 9, 10; 3.1, 3, 6; 7.5; 9.5; 11.1. In the Latin translation 'them' is sometimes replaced with *judaei*.

a view might be said to reach its most extraordinary expression in the assertion that the commandment literally to circumcise oneself was given by an evil angel (9.4). When we also note the possibility that some of *Barnabas'* community appear intent upon Judaizing (3.6; 4.6b; 9.6; 12.10), the fact that the author is noticeably concerned to assert that the Christians are now the rightful heirs of the covenant – a covenant which the Jews in fact lost after they worshipped the golden calf (4.8f.; chaps 13 and 14) – and the author's appropriation for the Christians of central Jewish symbols such as the land (chap. 6) and the temple (16.7f.), then a view of the epistle as implying the presence of a perceived Jewish threat can come to seem inevitable. *Barnabas'* radical position, in which scripture is viewed almost monolithically as only ever having had one reference and that a Christian one, and only ever referring to one covenant, the Christian covenant, emerges out of a straightforwardly polemical situation.

But for many years such a view of *Barnabas* has been challenged. Windisch, for instance, argued that *Barnabas* perceived the Jews in abstract terms and as no actual danger.[38] The absence of any reference to a perceived Jewish threat in the opening and closing chapter of the epistle seemed to support such a view. More recently scholars have argued that *Barnabas* is nothing more than a medley of sources and from this observation have gone on to assert that his anti-Judaism was simply part of his heritage and should not, therefore, be interpreted as implying anything specific about the circumstances he is addressing.[39] In most of these views of the epistle, *paranaesis*, or general building-up, of the community emerges as the author's central concern.[40]

None of these points is straightforwardly convincing. A purely abstract interpretation of the Jews in *Barnabas* underestimates the frequency with which the terms 'to them' and 'to us' appear. The absence of reference to the Jews or Judaizing in the opening and closing parts of the epistle is potentially more problematic but can be explained in a way that is compatible with a polemical interpretation of the epistle.[41] While we need not doubt that *Barnabas* has used sources, and the evidence for this is good,[42] it does not follow that his selection of material should be seen as

38. Windisch, *Der Barnabasbrief*, 323.

39. See e.g. R.A. Kraft, *The Apostolic Fathers: A New Translation and Commentary*, vol. 3, *Barnabas and the Didache* (New York and London: Thomas Nelson, 1965), 2–16, 19–22, 59–65.

40. Prostmeier, *Der Barnabasbrief*, 86–9.

41. See Paget, *The Epistle of Barnabas*, 64–5.

42. The use of sources is suggested by 1.5a, where *Barnabas* refers to handing over a portion of what he has received; by the presence of what Klaus Wengst (*Tradition und Theologie der Barnabasbriefes* (New York and Berlin: W. de Gruyter, 1971), 14–15), referred to as 'ad hoc Bildungen', or seams composed by the author, which seem to act as connections

irrelevant to his purpose. Moreover, it can be convincingly argued that *Barnabas* does not hail from a unitary tradition to whose views he gives uncritical expression, but rather that he is responsible for some of the more radical opinions expressed in his epistle.[43]

In the end the difficulty in arriving at a clear view of *Barnabas'* purpose lies in making sense of the strongly paranaetic and ethical element of chaps 1 and 21, together with the Two Ways section (chaps 19—20), and the more polemical/anti-Jewish character of chaps. 2—16. There have been serious attempts to do this, in particular in the work of Hvalvik,[44] and more recently, Rhodes,[45] but no one solution appears entirely satisfactory.

However we perceive *Barnabas'* major concern, it is clear that he is keen to point to the urgent character of the present time (cf. esp. 4.1f.) and to make plain that even though Christians may be the rightful inheritors of the covenant and may in fact be those who are reborn, embodiments of a revitalized temple (16.11f.; see also 11.11), they are still waiting for their final redemption (6.19). That final redemption appears to involve a return of Christ (7.9f.) and possibly a millennial kingdom (chap. 15). Christ's return follows on naturally from his suffering, death and resurrection. *Barnabas* pays particular attentionto Christ's passion and death, showing how, in a variety of ways, they fulfil the scriptures (see esp. chaps 5 and 7; see also chap. 12, with its interest in finding types for the cross). Christ, the central point of scriptural reference (12.5, 9), through his death brings about the creation of a new covenant in which Christians' hearts are

---

between different types of material (see 4.9a; 5.3; 6.5; 7.1); and by some evidence of the use of testimonies or collections of Old Testament citations (see esp. 2.5–10 and the discussion of this passage in Paget, *The Epistle of Barnabas*, 103–5).

43. This can be illustrated in at least two ways. First, we can demonstrate how in various chapters *Barnabas* has arrived at his final position by drawing together arguments from different quarters. See in this respect esp. chap. 9. Second, we can show how at certain points in his epistle there are shards of opinions not compatible with *Barnabas'* final opinion. See esp. 2.6, with its reference to a 'new law of Christ', apparently in contradiction of his own view that there is one law, the Mosaic law interpreted correctly.

44. Hvalvik argues that the way of light and the way of darkness, referred to in 18.1, are to be associated with Christianity and Judaism respectively: *The Struggle for Scripture and Covenant*, 200–1. The positive ethical dimension of the letter is linked to *Barnabas'* desire to show what the right interpretation of scripture actually is.

45. J.N. Rhodes, *The Epistle of Barnabas and the Deuteronomic Tradition*, WUNT 2.188 (Tübingen: Mohr-Siebeck, 2004) argues that *Barnabas'* principal concern is to warn Christians, by reference to Jewish failure – manifest in their worship of the golden calf, their killing of Jesus and the subsequent fall of the temple – of the consequences to them of their sins. In this interpretation, Rhodes emphasizes in particular the fact that chap. 4 can be read to support such a view (see in particular his own reading of 4.6b in terms of those who pile up sins by saying the covenant remains ours). In this reading he also lays particular stress upon what he sees as the nomistic character of *Barnabas'* language, and the covenantal/ Deuteronomic character of his language.

redeemed from darkness, and which, by extension, enables the Christian to understand the meaning of the covenantal commands (see 4.8f. and 14.5f.). In much of this *Barnabas* seems to embody an eschatological viewpoint continuous with that of Paul, in which there is a tension between what we already are and what we will become (see 4.10f.).

5. Some Concluding Observations

Whether or not we perceive *Barnabas* to be enigmatic, in at least two ways it reflects important themes in early, and specifically second-century, Christian history. The first of these relates to the place of the Old Testament. Almost more than any of the other Apostolic Fathers, with the possible exception of *1 Clement*, *Barnabas* attributes ultimate importance to this body of texts. Even if his interpretative take on these texts is singular, his dependence upon them is very typical of early Christian writers of the second century. The second of these relates to the question of Jewish–Christian interaction. The extent to which *Barnabas* reflects viva voce contact with non-Christian Jews itself feeds into a broader debate about Jewish–Christian interaction in this period and the extent to which texts allow us a clear view of this matter. On one reading *Barnabas* might be said to reflect an absolute division between the two communities. On another reading the letter could be seen to reflect a complex form of interaction.[46]

So *Barnabas* may in various ways be strange, and may lack a clear trajectory backwards or forwards, but it is a text reflecting some of the major concerns of the early part of the second century and this may in part account for its popularity in some parts of the Roman Empire.

---

46. It is possible to see *Barbabas* as an inter-Jewish text, one which need not imply separation between something called Judaism and something called Christianity. In arguing this case, one would highlight the many points in the epistle which betray Jewish influence; the failure of the author to refer to the Jews explicitly; and the continuity of his radical position on the law with opinions attributed to other Jews by Philo (*De Migratione Abrahami* 89–94). Appropriation of the covenant and other Jewish symbols has its analogue in the writings of the sect at Qumran. For something approximating to this opinion see W. Horbury, 'Jewish–Christian Relations in Barnabas and Justin Martyr', in W. Horbury (ed.), *Jews and Christians in Contact and Controversy* (Edinburgh: T&T Clark, 1998), 127–61, and for general scepticism about a separation between Judaism and Christainity before the fourth century see in particular A.Y. Reed, 'Jewish Christianity after the Parting of the Ways: Approaches to Historiography and Self-Definition in the Pseudo-Clementines', in A.Y. Reed and A.H. Becker, *The Ways that Never Parted* (Tübingen: Mohr-Siebeck, 2003), esp. 231. The whole discussion of this book is related to the use of the categories 'Judaism', 'Christianity', and 'Jewish Christianity', and the relationships between these groups in the aftermath of the destruction of the temple in 70 CE.

Chapter 9

The Epistles of Ignatius of Antioch

Paul Foster

With two exceptions, the authors of the texts known as the Apostolic Fathers remain shadowy or even totally invisible figures. One of the exceptions is Polycarp, the Bishop of Smyrna, for whom we have a graphic description of the events surrounding his martyrdom, an epistle written by him to the Philippians, and an epistle addressed to him.[1] The writer of that last document, the epistle addressed to Polycarp, is the other exception to the general phenomenon of anonymous or shadowy authors of the texts in the corpus of the Apostolic Fathers: Polycarp's earlier contemporary, Ignatius, Bishop of Antioch. Like Polycarp, we have a martyrdom account for Ignatius (although because of its late date this is not included among the Apostolic Fathers) and epistles written by Ignatius. Yet while Ignatius emerges from the shadows of anonymity, the epistles he composed come from a very brief period of his life, all being penned while he journeyed to Rome to face martyrdom. Although the epistles may have been written in as little as a few weeks, they provide a remarkable insight into the nature of the person facing martyrdom, as well as conveying much about the beliefs and theological positions he held.

1. *How Many Epistles?*

Open any modern version of the writings of Ignatius and it will contain seven epistles. Five of these are addressed to communities with which Ignatius had had contact during his journey to Rome, namely the epistles to the Ephesians, Magnesians, Trallians, Philadelphians and Smyrneans. Another is addressed to the Roman church prior to the arrival of Ignatius

---

1. Ehrman makes a similar assessment concerning Polycarp: 'In some ways we are better informed about Polycarp of Smyrna than any other Christian of the early second century. Among the writings of the Apostolic Fathers, there is one text written to him (by Ignatius), another written about him (the *Martyrdom of Polycarp*), and yet another written by him, a letter sent to the Christians of Philippi': B.D. Ehrman, *The Apostolic Fathers*, vol. 1, LCL 24 (Cambridge, Mass. and London: Harvard University Press, 2003), 324.

in the imperial capital. In that letter he counsels them not to intervene on his behalf by trying to prevent his martyrdom (Ign. *Rom.* 4.1). The remaining letter is directed to Polycarp, urging him to be steadfast and dignified in his episcopal office (Ign.*Poly.* 1.2; 3.1; 6.1).

Yet this consensus surrounding a sevenfold corpus of Ignatian epistles took a long time to establish itself. In the late Middle Ages at least 13 letters written in Greek circulated in various collections under the name of Ignatius. Such collections contained letters written to the Bishop of Antioch. These additional epistles included a letter from a certain Mary of Cassobola and the reply from Ignatius, letters to the Tarsian, Philippian and Antiochean communities, as well as an epistle addressed to Hero, deacon in Ignatius' see of Antioch. To this corpus was often added the prayer written by Hero to Ignatius. These letters, in conjunction with expanded versions of the seven letters printed in modern critical editions, form what is termed the Long Recension of the epistles.[2] Furthermore, although not usually referred to in the discussion of the Ignatian writings, additional texts are ascribed to the Bishop of Antioch in the Latin tradition. These consist of correspondence with St John the elder and the Virgin Mary. As no Greek manuscript evidence exists for these documents and their textual history cannot be traced back earlier than the Middle Ages, scholars regard these letters as spurious.[3]

When one reads the theological orientation of the Ignatian epistles it becomes fully apparent why they were not congenial to Puritan writers, who espoused and even intensified many of the anti-ecclesiastical notions of certain Reformation thinkers. Thus, the entire corpus was deemed by Puritan writers to be a forgery, while Roman Catholic writers affirmed the authenticity of the entire collection.

This impasse was overcome by the careful and scholarly work of James Ussher, Archbishop of Armagh. Ussher noted the divergence between the form of text that Faber Stapulensis had published in 1498 and the quotations given by medieval English writers – Robert (Grosseteste) of Lincoln (*c.* 1250), John Tyssington (*c.* 1381), and William Wodeford (*c.* 1396) – which agreed with those of the Church Fathers.[4] Conjecturing that the printed text represented an interpolated recension, and observing that English authors appeared to know a shorter form, Ussher went manuscript hunting around the libraries of England. His labours did not go unrewarded. Ussher discovered two Latin manuscripts, Caiensis 395,

2. For what is still the most readily accessible cataloguing of the manuscripts of the Long Recension see the work of J.B. Lightfoot, *The Apostolic Fathers*, part 2, *Ignatius and Polycarp*, 3 vols (London: Macmillan, 1889–90), vol. 1, 109–34.

3. The Latin text of the correspondence with St John and the Virgin Mary is given in Lightfoot, *The Apostolic Fathers*, part 2, *Ignatius and Polycarp*, vol. 3, 69–72.

4. 'Ignatius, St.', in *The Oxford Dictionary of the Christian Church*, 3rd edn, ed. F.L. Cross and E.A. Livingstone (Oxford: Oxford University Press, 2005), 822.

held at Gonville and Caius College, Cambridge, and Monticutianus, now lost, but part of the library of Richard Montague, Bishop of Norwich 1638–41.[5] These manuscripts contained the short form of the seven epistles, the same text that appears in modern printed editions, now known as the Middle Recension, along with the other epistles in the same form as they appear in the Long Recension. Ussher was able to conclude that the additional epistles were spurious, and that the genuine Ignatian letters had originally circulated in a shorter form. His one mistake was to judge the letter to Polycarp to be spurious.[6] This Middle Recension was first published in its Latin form by Ussher in 1644.[7] Two years later Isaac Voss published the first printed edition of the Greek version of the Middle Recension,[8] based upon the manuscript Mediceo-Laurentianus 57.7, housed in Florence. This manuscript was lacking the *Epistle to the Romans*, which has had a transmission history different to that of the rest of the corpus.[9] This letter was published in its Middle Recension form in 1689 by Ruinart, from the manuscript Parisinus Graec. 1451, housed in the Bibliotheque Nationale, Paris. Since these initial publications three further manuscripts of the Middle Recension of *Romans* have been discovered, but of the other six epistles of the Middle Recension only a single fragment of *Smyrneans* 3.3—12.1 (Berlin Papyrus, Codex 10581) has come to light. The significance of this fifth-century manuscript is that it pre-dates other Greek texts of the Middle Recension by at least five centuries.

The textual problems surrounding the form of the epistles appeared to have been finally settled by the meticulous investigations of Ussher and his fellow seventeenth-century scholars. However, this consensus, which held sway for almost exactly two hundred years, was challenged when, in 1845, William Cureton published three Syriac manuscripts of the epistles of Ignatius.[10] The earliest of these manuscripts, British Museum Add. 12175, dated to the first half of the sixth century, contained only the *Epistle to Polycarp*. The other two manuscripts, British Museum Add. 14618, dated to the seventh or eighth century, and British Museum Add. 17192, dated by Cureton to the sixth or seventh century, but by Wright to the tenth century,[11] both contain the *Epistle to Polycarp*, *Ephesians* and *Romans* in

---

5. Lightfoot, *The Apostolic Fathers*, part 2, *Ignatius and Polycarp*, vol. 1, 76–86.

6. 'Ignatius, St.', *Oxford Dictionary of the Christian Church*, 822.

7. J. Ussher, *Polycarpi et Ignatii Epistolae* (Oxon., 1644).

8. As stated in the article on Ignatius in *The Oxford Dictionary of the Christian Church*, Voss was directed to this manuscript by Ussher: 'Voss edited the corresponding Greek text which Ussher had traced to a Florentine MS (Laur. Plut. l.vii.7)' (822).

9. Ehrman, *The Apostolic Fathers*, vol. 1, 214.

10. W. Cureton, *The Ancient Syriac Version of Saint Ignatius* (London: Rivington, 1845).

11. W. Wright, *Catalogue of Syriac MSS in the British Museum* (London: British Museum, 1870–2), 778.

that order. From this evidence Cureton postulated that this three-letter Syriac collection represented the whole of the authentic Ignatian correspondence. This became known as the Short Recension. Without rehearsing the arguments of Zahn[12] and Lightfoot[13] in favour of the opinion that the Short Recension is an epitome or abbreviation of the Middle Recension, we can add one important piece of evidence to the discussion: the discovery of the fragment of *Smyrneans* 3.3—12.1 dated to the fifth century. This undermines the claim that whereas the Short Recension is attested in the manuscript tradition as early as the first half of the sixth century, the additional four epistles of the Middle Recension cannot be dated prior to the tenth century. Thus the consensus which has emerged in modern scholarship and is reflected in printed editions is that the seven epistles of the Middle Recension represent the genuine form of the epistles of Ignatius, though perhaps it would be better from a text-critical perspective to say that they represent the earliest recoverable stage of the textual transmission of the Ignatian letters.

The differences between the various recensions are summarized in Table 1.

MIDDLE RECENSION	Seven epistles written in Greek: *Ephesians, Magnesians, Trallians, Romans, Philadelphians, Smyrnaeans, Epistle to Polycarp*
LONG RECENSION	Expanded forms of the seven epistles of the Middle Recension, with six or seven further works in Greek – letter from Mary of Cassobola, letter to Mary of Cassobola, letters to the Tarsian, Philippian and Antiochean communities, a letter to Hero, and the Prayer of Hero – and sometimes four additional works in Latin – two letters to John the Elder, one epistle to Mary the Christ-bearer and a letter from Mary
SHORT RECENSION	Three epistles in a Syriac collection: *Ephesians, Romans, Polycarp*

2. *Ignatius and the Date of the Epistles*

Information about the life of Ignatius is derived primarily from the seven epistles of the Middle Recension, early Christian writers, especially the writings of Eusebius of Caesarea, and an account of the martyrdom of Ignatius, which may date to the fourth or fifth century. From his own

12.   T. von Zahn, *Ignatius von Antiochien* (Gotha: Perthas, 1893).
13.   Lightfoot, *The Apostolic Fathers,* part 2, *Ignatius and Polycarp,* vol. 1, 280–327.

hand we learn that Ignatius was also known by the name Θεοφόρος ('Theophoros' = 'God-bearer'), that the occasion of writing these letters was during his transportation to Rome to face martyrdom (Ign.*Eph.* 21.1–2; *Romans* 4—5), and that he was the Bishop of Antioch (Ign.*Rom.* 2.2). The place of Ignatius in the episcopal succession lists of Antioch has been seen as confused, because of supposedly conflicting information provided by the Church Fathers (in particular the two references contained in Eusebius). Without stating the name of his predecessor, Origen describes Ignatius as the second bishop of Antioch (*Hom. vi in Luc.* 1). Eusebius both confirms and expands upon this tradition. First, he states, 'Ignatius was famous as the second bishop at Antioch where Euodius had been the first' (*HE* 3.22.1). Later, however, in book 3 Eusebius still maintains that Ignatius was the second to hold episcopal office in Antioch, but provides a more famous predecessor, although not labelling him as 'bishop'. Describing distinguished church leaders in Asia Minor Eusebius writes, 'Ignatius, still a name of note to most men, the second bishop of Antioch, received the succession from Peter' (*HE* 3.36.1). This tradition, which does not mention Euodius, appears to imply that Ignatius was second in a chain instigated by Peter, although Peter himself is not counted part of that episcopal succession.[14] The *Apostolic Constitutions* likewise refer to Ignatius as bishop of Antioch, but it may in fact envisage a joint episcopacy shared by Euodius and Ignatius, although it is still possible to read the tradition as describing Ignatius as the second bishop of Antioch. Providing succession lists for prominent cities it comments, 'Of Antioch, Euodius, ordained by me, Peter; and Ignatius by Paul' (7.46). The historical value of this tradition is questionable, and it may be more concerned to demonstrate apostolic succession than to represent accurate history. Ehrman comments that 'early tradition holds that he [Ignatius] was second bishop there [Antioch], after Peter (Origen, *Hom. 6 in Luke*) or third, following Peter and Euodius (Eusebius, *Eccl. Hist.* 3.22.36 [*sic*])'.[15] This is only partially true. The consistent testimony of early Christian writing is to describe Ignatius as the second bishop of Antioch, although there is some confusion surrounding his predecessor. This role is most commonly ascribed to Euodius, but an alternative tradition lists Peter as the predecessor. Modern scholarship has at times tried to harmonize this data by suggesting that in some traditions Ignatius is presented as the

14. Later succession lists for Antioch from the fifth century onwards mention Peter as the first bishop, but Eusebius does not designate Peter as Bishop of Antioch.

15. Ehrman, *The Apostolic Fathers*, vol. 1, 203–4; the correct reference is presumably *HE* 3.22, 36.

third bishop of Antioch after Peter and then Euodius. This formulation, however, does not occur in ancient sources.[16]

The date of the seven epistles is related to the period during which Ignatius lived. This remains the case even if the letters are a forgery circulated in his name, since they must be written after the period when the martyrdom of Ignatius appeared imminent. Fixing the date of even Ignatius' death is not, however, as straightforward as is often assumed. Eusebius places the description of the martyrdom of Ignatius in the context of events during Trajan's reign in the third book of his *Ecclesiastical History*. However, unlike the notice about Clement of Rome's death – 'In the third year of the aforementioned emperor [i.e. Trajan], Clement . . . departed this life' (*HE* 3.34.1) – there is no temporal indication of when the martyrdom of Ignatius took place. For this reason it may be the case that Eusebius has decided to locate the tradition he had concerning Ignatius during the Trajanic period, without any external indication of the date. In his *Chronicon* Eusebius provides further information about the date of martyrdom. In that work, under the entry for the tenth year of Trajan's reign (i.e. 107–8 CE), Eusebius lists three undated events: the martyrdom of Simon the son of Cleopas, the martyrdom of Ignatius and the persecution in Bithynia.[17] Having referred to Trajan at the beginning of the undated paragraph inserted after the data for the tenth year of the reign, Eusebius specifically states, 'Itidem Antiochensium episcopus [Ignatius] martyrium passus est' (*Chron., seg. Ann. Abr.* 2123). Thus, this undated entry appears to be the basis on which subsequent writers have affirmed that the martyrdom of Ignatius took place in the tenth (or ninth[18]) year of Trajan's reign. The accuracy of the *Chronicon* in relation to dates surrounding the life of Ignatius is called into further question by the fact that it places his elevation to episcopal office in Antioch in the year 69 CE. This seems improbably early. Lightfoot himself, while maintaining that the martyrdom occurred during Trajan's reign, preferred the slightly later date of 'within a few years of A.D. 110, before or after'.[19] This left open the possibility that the Eusebian date was still correct.

The problem with a date in the first or second decade of the second

16. Lake baldly states, 'He was the third bishop in Antioch in Syria' and in a footnote asserts, 'According to tradition Peter was first and Euodius the second (*Hist.Eccl.* 3.22)': K. Lake, *The Apostolic Fathers*, vol. 1, LCL 24 (Cambridge, Mass. and London: Harvard University Press, 1912), 166. Similarly the *Oxford Dictionary of the Christian Church* comments that 'Acc. to Origen he [Ignatius] was the second Bp. of Antioch, the successor of St Peter, acc. to Eusebius he was the third, following St Peter's successor Euodius, *c.* 69' ('Ignatius, St.', 822).
17. Lightfoot, *The Apostolic Fathers,* part 2, *Ignatius and Polycarp*, vol. 2, 449.
18. See the *Chronicon Paschale* and Brit. Mus. Add. 14642.
19. Lightfoot, *The Apostolic Fathers,* part 2, *Ignatius and Polycarp*, vol. 1, 30.

century is not based on uncertainty about the occurrence of martyrdoms during this period: they undoubtedly took place and are well documented. Rather, it is the theological character of the very writings of Ignatius, which seems somewhat discordant with what is known of early second-century Christian writers. If the year 110 were indeed the correct date, it needs to be remembered that some of the New Testament writings would be roughly contemporaneous. The Gospel of Luke may have been written only twenty years earlier,[20] the Pastorals towards the end of the first century, the Johannine epistles around the beginning of the second century, and 2 Peter maybe as late as 130. The problem is that the ecclesial concepts so prominent in the seven epistles of Ignatius are noticeable by their absence from these supposedly contemporary Christian writings. The later New Testament writings and the Epistles of Ignatius appear to inhabit different thought-worlds and very different stages in the development of church order in Christian congregations. The same problem was highlighted by Lightfoot (although he did not explore the implications) in relation to the corpus of the Apostolic Fathers. Commenting specifically on *1 Clement* he wrote,

> The transition from the first to the second Apostolic father – from Clement to Ignatius – is rapid; but, when it is made, we are conscious what a wide chasm has been passed. The interval of time indeed is not great. Twenty years at the outside separate the Epistle of Clement to the Corinthians from the letters of Ignatius. But these two decades were a period of exceptionally rapid progress in the career of the Church – in the outward extension of the Christian society, in its internal organization and government, in the progress and ramifications of theological opinion.[21]

Yet the writings of the New Testament that may well date from the reign of Trajan show that the developments evidenced in the epistles of Ignatius had not touched upon all strands of Christianity in the first quarter of the second century. How is this to be accounted for?

Two basic explanations are possible. Either Ignatius represented a localized ecclesial development in the Antiochene church, being himself the harbinger of monarchical episcopacy and a host of other theological

---

20. In fact Raymond Brown uses what he takes to be the secure date of the Ignatian corpus to date Luke's Gospel. He states, '*a date no later than 100 is indicated*. The Gospel's symbolic interest in Jerusalem as a Christian center does not match the outlook of 2d-century Christian literature. For Asia Minor in particular and specifically for Ephesus the writer of Acts seems to know only a church structure of presbyters (Acts 14:23; 20:17). There is no sign of the developed pattern of having one bishop in each church so clearly attested by Ignatius for that area in the decade before 110': R.E. Brown, *An Introduction to the New Testament* (New York: Doubleday, 1997), 273–4, italics in original.

21. Lightfoot, *The Apostolic Fathers,* part 2, *Ignatius and Polycarp,* vol. 1, 1.

innovations, or his epistles have been misdated. Both of these alternatives have had proponents, although the first option is more often than not supported *de facto* rather than overtly stated. Disquiet over the suitability of placing the theological ideas of Ignatius in the context of the early second century has led to a number of alternative proposals. It has been argued that although the historical Ignatius may have lived at the beginning of the second century, the letters associated with his name were forged at a later period in that century. Rius-Camps maintains that only four of the letters are genuine,[22] while Joly suggests that the whole collection of seven epistles is a fabrication.[23] Alternatively, Hübner argues that the epistles show knowledge of texts that were not composed before the mid-second century and, moreover, that they suppose a more developed form of Gnosticism which is not consistent with a date in the first few decades of the second century.[24] The arguments put forward by Hübner have been expanded and developed by his student Thomas Lechner.[25] Basically Lechner's study falls into two major parts. In the first he demonstrates the extremely weak foundation upon which the traditional dating of Ignatius' letters is based. The second part seeks to demonstrate that the 'Hymn of the Star' (*Eph.* 19) is a parody of Valentinian myth. Hence he argues that some of the polemic contained in the epistles is an intentional attack on Valentinian gnosis. Consequently he dates the epistle to the period between 165 and 175 CE.[26]

So far the scholarly consensus has not shifted to any marked extent because of the arguments mounted by Lechner and Hübner. In part this is because the points of literary contact between the epistles of Ignatius and Valentinian writings appear weak. The majority of scholars retain the traditional dating proposed by Lightfoot of around 110 CE, without showing awareness of its flimsy basis. It remains possible to maintain Ignatian authorship of the seven genuine epistles, but to recognize that the date of their composition could be significantly later than usually assumed. A *terminus ad quem* can be established if the epistles are from Ignatius' own hand, for the letters would pre-date the martyrdom of Polycarp (a problematic date in itself, with opinion encompassing the range of dates from 155–77 CE, most scholars favouring the earlier period) and Polycarp's *Epistle to the Philippians*, which refers to the death of

22. J. Rius-Camps, *The Four Authentic Letters of Ignatius* (Rome: Pontificium Institutum Orientalium Studiorum, 1980).

23. R. Joly, *Le dossier d'Ignace d'Antioche*, Université libre Bruxelles, Faculté de philosophie et lettres 69 (Brussels: Éditions de l'Université de Bruxelles, 1979).

24. R.M. Hübner, 'Thesen zur Echtheit und Datierung der sieben Briefe des Ignatius Antiochen', *ZAC* 1 (1997), 44–72.

25. T. Lechner, *Ignatius adversus Valentinianos? Chronologische und theologiegeschichtliche Studien zu Briefen des Ignatius von Antiochen*, VCSupp 47 (Leiden: Brill, 1999).

26. Lechner, *Ignatius adversus Valentinianos?*, 306-7.

Ignatius (Poly. *Phil.* 9.1) as well as the letters written by Ignatius (Poly. *Phil.* 13.2). In fact, as Holmes suggests, 'Chapter 13 [of Polycarp's epistle] was probably written within a month or two following 24 August (cf. Ign. *Rom.* 10.1–3) in the year in which Ignatius was apparently martyred.'[27] Although many date Polycarp's epistle around 135 CE,[28] various partition theories make this a less than straightforward datum.[29] Therefore, taking a cue from Eusebius' uncertainty in his *Chronicon* about the dating of information concerning Ignatius, one may conclude that the letters could have been composed at some stage during the second quarter of the second century, i.e. 125–50 CE, roughly corresponding to Hadrian's reign or the earlier part of Antoninus Pius' period in office.

3. *Ignatius' Opponents*

In Ignatius' discussion of the role of the bishop, one issue was the need for Ignatius to defend the development of episcopal leadership in the face of opposition. The identity of such opponents can be traced through the information Ignatius provides in his epistles. One of the fundamental issues that has arisen in scholarly debate is the number of groups of opponents to which Ignatius refers.[30] The problem revolves around the different ways in which Ignatius describes his detractors in the individual letters. In the *Epistle to the Ephesians* there is a generalized description of the heresy he is attacking, although the addressees are commended for 'speaking truthfully about Jesus Christ' (*Eph.* 6.3) and Ignatius describes Christ as 'both fleshly and spiritual, born and unborn, God come in the flesh, true life in death, from both Mary and God, first subject to suffering and then beyond suffering' (*Eph.* 7.2). When writing to the Trallians and describing similar tendencies, he is more explicit concerning the description of the opponents: 'But if, as some who are atheists – that is, unbelievers – say, that he only appeared [δοκεῖν] to suffer, it is they who are the appearance [δοκεῖν]' (*Trall.* 10.1). The same critique of heretics emerges in addressing the Smyrneans. This attacks the notion that Jesus Christ accomplished his redemptive work in appearance or semblance alone (*Smyr.* 4.2), and Ignatius continues by declaring,

> For how does anyone benefit me if he praises me but blasphemes my Lord, not confessing that he bore flesh? The one who refuses to say this

27. See futher Chapter 10, sect. 6(ii) below.

28. W.R. Schoedel, 'Polycarp, Epistle of', in *ABD*, vol. 5, 390.

29. For the original statement of the partition theory, see P.N. Harrison, *Polycarp's Two Epistles to the Philippians* (Cambridge: Cambridge University Press, 1936). For a fuller discussion of partition theories, see Chapter 10, sect. 6(i) below.

30. For a brief summary see C.N. Jefford, *The Apostolic Fathers: An Introduction* (Peabody, Mass.: Hendrickson, 1996), 61–2.

> denies him completely, as one who bears a corpse. But I see no point in recording their disbelieving names. I do not even want to recall them, until they repent concerning the Passion, which is our resurrection. (*Smyr.* 5.2–3)

Employing language reminiscent of that used against the secessionists by the author of 1 John, Ignatius levels against his opponents the charge that they likewise deny the reality of Christ appearing and suffering in the flesh. Trebilco, specifically discussing the situation Ignatius addressed in Ephesus, suggests that 'what Ignatius says about the *current* threat of docetists as he writes shows that the Johannine secessionists are still in town, have developed their teaching further in the docetic direction, and that Ignatius is concerned that they might continue to gain a hearing'.[31] Furthermore, the suggestion that the docetists were actively engaged in missionizing is supported by the presence of similar teachings among the Smyrneans and Trallians, as well as by the observation that those described in 1 John with such Christological views had gone into the world and 'the world listens to them' (1 John 4.5).[32] For Ignatius, those who hold such beliefs are blasphemers and have no hope of partaking in the resurrection, since by denying the physical suffering of Christ they deny the efficacy of the redemptive act.[33]

When one looks at the description in the other Ignatian epistles of opposition or false beliefs a noticeably different characterization emerges. The tendency towards maintaining Jewish practices is contested in vitriolic terms, most fully in the *Epistle to the Magnesians* (8.1—10.3). Thus, Ignatius declares in tones of obvious exasperation,

> It is outlandish to proclaim Jesus Christ and practise Judaism. For Christianity did not believe in Judaism, but Judaism in Christianity – in which every tongue that believes in God has been gathered together. (*Mag.* 10.3)

In specific terms the practices Ignatius criticizes include living by 'false opinions and old fables' (*Mag.* 8.1) and observing the Sabbath rather than 'living according to the Lord's day' (*Mag.* 9.1). The critique resembles that contained in the Pastoral Epistles, where Timothy is charged to instruct the congregation to 'have nothing to do with godless and foolish myths' (1 Tim. 4.7) and Titus is instructed to rebuke those who 'give heed to Jewish myths' (Titus 1.14).[34] The correspondence between the Pastorals and

---

31. P. Trebilco, *The Early Christians in Ephesus from Paul to Ignatius* (Tübingen: Mohr-Siebeck, 2004), 695, italics in original.

32. For a fuller explanation of this suggestion see Trebilco, *The Early Christians in Ephesus*, 695.

33. See Ign. *Smyr.* 5.2–3.

34. For an extended discussion see Lightfoot, *Ignatius and Polycarp*, vol. 2, 124.

Ignatius' description of his opponents here is much less explicit than that between Ignatius' docetic adversaries and the Johannine secessionists. For this reason we do well to heed Schoedel's warning that 'we cannot assume that the situation in the Pastorals and in Ignatius was the same simply because they share a common polemical vocabulary'.[35] The critique of Judaism presented by Ignatius also occurs in the *Epistle to the Philadelphians*, although the reference is far more fleeting (*Phil.* 6.1–2). It includes the rather enigmatic advice that 'if anybody should interpret Judaism to you, do not listen to him. For it is better to hear Christianity from a man who is circumcised than Judaism from one who is uncircumcised' (*Phil.* 6.1). The possibility of hearing Judaism from an uncircumcised person suggests that those whom Ignatius describes are not ethnic Jews or even proselytes to the Jewish faith, but rather certain Gentiles who held to a form of Christian faith that promoted Jewish observance without the necessity of circumcision. Here Grant is surely incorrect when he states that 'Ignatius seems to have Gentile converts to Jewish Christianity in mind, not unlike those whom Paul describes as not keeping the law but advocating circumcision (Gal 6.13)'.[36] Rather, Schoedel's explanation is far more plausible: 'no one was actually recommending circumcision, and the issue had probably been injected into the debate under the influence of Pauline models'.[37]

Ignatius' confrontation with both Jewish and docetic tendencies has led to a protracted debate concerning the number of groups of opponents that Ignatius confronted. Lightfoot argued for a close connection between these two tendencies and saw the Judaizing aspect that Ignatius rejects as closely aligned to the false teaching under discussion in Colossians. Hence, he suggested that the 'old fables' to which Ignatius refers were 'probably myths relating to cosmology and angelology',[38] as may be the case in Col. 2.18. This in turn is characterized as a Gnosticizing form of Judaism which embraces docetic tendencies. Lightfoot then announces that 'the foe in question therefore was Doceto-judaism'.[39] Others have not been as convinced by the connections that Lightfoot draws, nor even persuaded that 'Doceto-judaism' really existed. Bauer argued that part of the confusion was due to the tendency of Ignatius to collapse differentiated categories into a closer association for the sake of polemic.[40] Similarly,

---

35. W.R. Schoedel, *Ignatius of Antioch*, Hermeneia (Philadelphia: Fortress Press, 1985), 119.

36. R.M. Grant, *The Apostolic Fathers*, vol. 4, *Ignatius of Antioch* (Camden, NJ: Thomas Nelson and Sons, 1966), 103.

37. Schoedel, *Ignatius of Antioch*, 203.

38. Lightfoot, *The Apostolic Fathers*, part 2, *Ignatius and Polycarp*, vol. 2, 124.

39. Lightfoot, *The Apostolic Fathers*, part 2, *Ignatius and Polycarp*, vol. 2, 125.

40. W. Bauer, *Orthodoxy and Heresy in the Early Church*, tr. R. Kraft and G. Krodel (London: SCM Press, 1972), 61–94.

Schoedel argues for the existence of two discrete groups, but sees Ignatius as intentionally confusing categories. He states, 'It is my view that in *Mag.* 8—10 Ignatius is speaking about the observance of Jewish customs (based on what he regards as a mistaken approach to Scripture); that such Judaizing was not characterized by docetic thinking; and that the link between Judaizing and docetism was invented by Ignatius.'[41]

Recently, the alternative views of either a single group or two separate opposing parties have again been articulated. Marshall draws on Jewish speculation concerning angels attested by the Qumran scrolls to argue that an angelomorphic Christology was part of the belief system of Ignatius' opponents. He concludes that 'the people against whom Ignatius warns his readers may be understood as a single group of Jewish Christians who understand Jesus to be an angel'.[42] It is then suggested that the stress Ignatius places on the corporeal reality of the sufferings of Christ was intended as a counter to such 'angel christologies', which by their very nature stood in opposition to the affirmation of Christ suffering in the flesh.[43] By contrast, Myllykoski distinguishes two groups of opponents. The first, evidenced in correspondence to the Philadelphian and Magnesian communities, is a Jewish Christian group which, according to Myllykoski, views 'Jesus as the true and last high priest and prophet in a long chain of these anointed ones in the history of Israel'.[44] However, according to Myllykoski, such a view reflected an ongoing adherence to the Jewish priesthood and an appeal to the Old Testament scriptures in such a way that the Christian gospel was placed in a position of subservience to these authorities (cf. *Philad.* 8.2, where Ignatius declares, 'For I heard some saying: "If I do not find it in the ancient records, I do not believe in the Gospel" '). What is new in Myllykoski's treatment is the way he characterizes the other group of opponents. The term 'docetic' is rejected as an inadequate description of this group, not only because 'the idea of Docetism is obscure',[45] but more significantly because this group of opponents 'did not carry the idea so far as to assume that the Roman soldiers crucified a ghost or a phantasma'.[46] It may be fairly asked if any precision is available in determining what this group of opponents believed. Moreover, just because the term is obscure from a modern perspective, it does not follow that it was not clear to ancient audiences,

---

41. Schoedel, *Ignatius of Antioch*, 118.
42. J.W. Marshall, 'The Objects of Ignatius' Wrath and Jewish Angelic Mediators', *Journal of Ecclesiastical History* 56 (2005), 17–18.
43. Marshall, 'The Objects of Ignatius' Wrath', 20–1.
44. M. Myllykoski, 'Wild Beasts and Rabid Dogs: The Riddle of the Heretics in the Letters of Ignatius', in J. Ådna (ed.), *The Formation of the Early Church*, WUNT 183 (Tübingen: Mohr-Siebeck, 2005), 358.
45. Myllykoski, 'Wild Beasts and Rabid Dogs', 367.
46. Myllykoski, 'Wild Beasts and Rabid Dogs', 367.

though admittedly in the heresiological controversies terms are cast at opponents more for impact than accurately. Instead Myllykoski states that 'The heresy opposed in *Ephesians, Trallians,* and *Smyrneans*, in turn, denied the incarnation, virgin birth, true bodily suffering and resurrection of Jesus (particularly in *Trallians* 9—10 and *Smyrneans* 1—4).'[47] This list seems to present key aspects of what many scholars would understand the term 'docetic' to represent, even if this does not encompass the full-blown development of a system of docetic and Gnostic ideas that separated the highest form of divinity from the taint of the material realm. Notwithstanding reservations about the way in which Myllykoski describes the second group,[48] his arguments for maintaining a distinction between two groups appear to be the more compelling way to read the texts. This is primarily because on the whole Ignatius treats these heresies in distinct letters, even if he occasionally uses similar language to lambaste those whom he labels as heretics.

4. *Theological Concepts and Ideas*

What made the letters of Ignatius so controversial in the seventeenth century were the ideas they contained. To employ an overused term, they can be viewed as promoting 'early catholicism'. Such a designation can too easily be misunderstood, so it is important to look in detail at the actual ideas that Ignatius puts forward about church order – his core theological beliefs on this issue and his attitude to his opponents.

(i) *Ecclesiology, Episcopacy and Eucharist*

In his letters Ignatius espouses the threefold pattern of ministry, consisting of deacons, presbyters and bishops. The vigorous manner in which Ignatius advocates this system may well suggest that this pattern was something of an innovation, at least in terms of the hierarchical structure being described, or that it had come under attack. But it is important to bear in mind Grant's note of caution: 'Before we draw too sharp a line between the various orders, however, we should note that all the ministers are viewed as apostolic.'[49] The model that Ignatius deems as normative is leadership in the form of a single ἐπίσκοπος (bishop) supported by a

---

47. Myllykoski, 'Wild Beasts and Rabid Dogs', 373.

48. The main reservation is Myllykoski's reticence to apply the label 'docetic' to this group when so much of Ignatius' description would align with what is reported about this group's beliefs. Admittedly, docetism was not a monolithic entity, and this makes Myllykoski's demand for an explicit statement concerning the separation 'between the earthly Jesus and the heavenly Christ' an unreasonable datum. See Myllykoski, 'Wild Beasts and Rabid Dogs', 373.

49. Grant, *Ignatius of Antioch*, 21.

πρεοβῦτ έριον (presbytery, eldership) along with those filling the role of διάκονος (deacon). This pattern recurs in a number of his letters. All three titles are seen in the *Epistle to the Ephesians*. Onesimus is described as the one 'whose love passes utterance and who is moreover your bishop in the flesh'. Following on from this the congregation are exhorted to 'pray that you may love him according to Jesus Christ and that you all may be like him; for blessed is He that granted unto you according to your deserving to have such a bishop' (*Eph.* 1.3). A little later in the same epistle the office of deacon and the presbytery are also mentioned. A certain Burrhus is described as 'your godly deacon who is blessed in all things' (*Eph.* 2.1). Then the eldership is mentioned in conjunction with the bishop when Ignatius exhorts Ephesian believers to lead a sanctified life: 'be holy in all respects, being made complete through a single subjection, being subject to the bishop and presbytery' (*Eph.* 2.2). Similarly, the pattern is repeated in *Magnesians*, where the bishop Damas is named (*Mag.* 2.1). In *Trallians* the three offices are discussed in even closer connection, being viewed as a focal point for establishing Church unity:[50]

> And so – as is already the case – you should do nothing without the bishop; but be subject also to the presbytery, as to the Apostles of Jesus Christ our hope; for if we live in Him, we shall also be found in Him. And those likewise who are deacons of the mysteries of Jesus Christ must also be pleasing in every way to all people. For they are not deacons of foods and drinks, but servants of the Church of God. And so they must guard themselves against accusations as against fire. (*Trall.* 2.2–3)

Furthermore Ignatius makes a spiritual comparison between these figures and divine and heavenly beings:

> In like manner let all men respect the deacons as Jesus Christ, even as they should respect the bishop as being a type of the Father and the presbyters as the council of God and as the college of Apostles. Apart from these there is not even the name of a church. (*Trall.* 3.1)

Ignatius focuses on the office of bishop more than on the roles of deacon or the presbytery. The relationship of believers to the bishop reflects the union between the Church and Jesus, and that of Jesus to the Father (*Eph.* 5.1). Moreover, according to Ignatius, opposition to the bishop is a sign that one is not subservient to God (*Eph.* 5.3; *Trall.* 2.1). It is necessary to defer to a bishop as a possessor of the wisdom of God (*Mag.* 3.1), and nothing should be done by members of the congregation without the consent of the bishop (*Mag.* 4.1; 7.1). In relation to *Mag.* 4.1 Schoedel comments that 'obedience to the bishop is of such decisive

---

50. On the relationship between the offices and unity, see Schoedel, *Ignatius of Antioch*, 140.

importance to Ignatius that he goes on virtually to define being Christian in terms of it'.[51] Ignatius declares that he has received the embodiment of the love that exists among the Trallian community in the person of Polybius their bishop (*Trall.* 3.2). Only those who remain in fellowship with their bishop belong to God and Jesus Christ (*Phil.* 3.2), and the only valid Eucharist is that presided over, or sanctioned by, the local bishop (*Phil.* 4.1; *Smyr.* 8.1). In fact the passage contained in *Smyrneans* 8—9 is Ignatius' most fulsome description of the authority and status of bishops. Nothing involving the Church can be done without episcopal permission, both baptism and Eucharist are invalid without the bishop's presence or oversight,[52] and whatever he approves is acceptable to God. Furthermore, by honouring the bishop one honours God. Finally, in the piece of correspondence addressed to Polycarp, but intended to be heard by the whole congregation, Ignatius makes it clear that he views his death as vicarious, but not as an efficacious offering for those who renounce episcopal authority. He writes, 'I am giving my life in exchange for those who are subject to the bishop, the presbyters and the deacons' (*Poly.* 6.1).

What is to be made of the repeated, highly laudatory and theologically significant comments about bishops? First, the fact that Ignatius has to insist on the primacy of the episcopacy and its authority suggests that this was not a universally held view even in the cities where the various named bishops held office. In fact the epistles bear witness to opposition to the authority of the bishop. Grant notes that the clear implication of *Smyr.* 8.1–2 is 'that the heterodox had their own Eucharist'.[53] The response Ignatius presents to those who refuse the authority of Polycarp in Smyrna is to reject the validity of the opponents' cultic rituals. As Schoedel states, 'Ignatius wishes to make it doubly clear that only the bishop can give approval to such meals.'[54] Thus, Ignatius seeks to impose a standardization of structure upon the various churches he comes across during his journey. Sociologically, the epistles may be reflecting the transition of early Christian communities from a pattern of charismatic leadership to a more structured and clearly defined system of authority, and the tension resulting from this. Such routinization of the charisma is a common phenomenon in later generations of new religious movements.[55] In fact, Maier argues that 'Ignatius' authority is best understood as

---

51. Schoedel, *Ignatius of Antioch*, 109.

52. Sullivan observes that 'the new note introduced here is that the bishop can also delegate someone else to preside': F.A. Sullivan, *From Apostles to Bishops: The Development of Episcopacy in the Early Church* (New York and Mahwah, NJ: Newman Press, 2001), 119.

53. Grant, *Ignatius of Antioch*, 120.

54. Schoedel, *Ignatius of Antioch*, 243.

55. W.S. Bainbridge, *The Sociology of New Religious Movements* (New York and London: Routledge, 1997), 220–2.

charismatic',[56] although he uses his authority to promulgate a more regulated pattern of leadership that led to the emergence of a single episcopal figure in each geographical centre.[57] Prior to the arrest and deportation of Ignatius, his own church in Antioch appears to have been suffering considerable upheaval and he writes about the return of peace that has been communicated to him while he is travelling to Rome (*Phil.* 10.1; *Smyr.* 11.2–3; *Poly.* 7.1–2; 8.1). It is likely that Ignatius himself was the major source of such discord and this could have been due to his attempt to impose a more hierarchical leadership model on the church in Antioch. This may perhaps have created internal divisions within the community, especially among members who wished to retain a more traditional charismatic leadership structure. It is not impossible, however, that Ignatius' attempts to suppress alternative forms of church structure and leadership resulted in his opponents betraying him to Roman authorities in Antioch.

Second, it is interesting to note that the only church where Ignatius does not name the bishop is the church in Rome. Although he had not arrived in the imperial capital at the time of writing to that community, his silence on this matter may suggest that the office of bishop had not yet assumed significance in Rome, or even that there was not a single figure at this stage who was the leader of the Christians in Rome.[58] The latter alternative is supported by Lampe, who puts forward the thesis that

> the fractionation in Rome favoured a collegial presbyterial system of governance and prevented for a long time, until the second half of the second century, the development of a monarchical episcopacy in the city . . . Before the second half of the second century there was in Rome no monarchical episcopacy for circles mutually bound by friendship.[59]

56. H.O. Maier, *The Social Setting of the Ministry as Reflected in the Writings of Hermas, Clement and Ignatius*, ESCJ 11 (Waterloo, Ont.: Wilfred Laurier, 2002), 170.

57. Trebilco's study of early Christianity in Ephesus draws attention to competing strands within that city. In relation to Ignatius' description of those who 'resist the bishop' (*Eph.* 5.1—6.1) Trebilco attempts to identify those who are opposing the model of authority resting with a single episcopal figure: 'Those who oppose these developments may well have included some who favoured a greater emphasis on the forms of authority which John the Seer made use of in Revelation and others who were from the Johannine community and so favoured a much more collegial church structure': *The Early Christians in Ephesus*, 647.

58. In order to try to counter this implication Sullivan notes that Ignatius does not mention presbyters in his *Epistle to the Romans*, yet most scholars would still argue for the existence of a presbytery. While this is true, it does not account for the overwhelming attention that Ignatius devotes to the office of bishop in his letters and its remarkable absence from the *Epistle to the Romans*.

59. P. Lampe, *From Paul to Valentinus: Christians at Rome in the First Two Centuries* (London: T&T Clark, 2003), 397.

By 'fractionation' Lampe is referring to the scattered and largely discrete house congregations that operated in Rome. This lack of centralization may reflect both the geography of the imperial capital and also the desire of believers to remain inconspicuous.

Third, there is debate surrounding the correct use of terminology: whether it is appropriate to label the system being advocated by Ignatius as 'monarchical episcopacy', or if 'monepiscopacy' should be used as a more neutral term. Obviously the system proposed by Ignatius is not the full-blown monarchical episcopacy of the late antique or early medieval periods. For this reason, scholars such as Sullivan prefer the term 'monepiscopal' for the single-bishop leadership structure that is being advocated in the seven genuine epistles.[60] While this may be a helpful neutral term, it perhaps fails to acknowledge adequately the immense privileges and theological significance that Ignatius attributes to this office, and perhaps his thinking is best understood as proto-monarchical episcopacy, because of its obvious resonances with the system that emerged over the course of the ensuing centuries. Schoedel notes that 'Ignatius' high view of the authority of the bishop is probably still the single most important reason for doubting the authenticity of the middle recension'.[61] In fact, this is one of Joly's fundamental reasons for rejecting the genuineness of the seven letters.[62] However, if, as has been suggested above, the letters were written in the second quarter of the second century by Ignatius, they can still be affirmed as authentic and the developed episcopal doctrine becomes less problematic. Notwithstanding all the complexities surrounding Ignatius' view of the office of bishop, it must be acknowledged that considerable development has occurred in terms of the leadership structure envisaged, especially in comparison to that suggested in the Pauline letters and other early Christian documents. Perhaps one may justifiably feel that the ideas put forward by Ignatius would have a little more integrity if he himself were not a holder of episcopal office, with his own authority being threatened by dissenting voices. His high view of bishops appears somewhat self-aggrandizing, and perhaps was even an attempt to silence those voices in Antioch who wished to retain a more spontaneous or charismatic form of leadership.

The understanding of the Eucharist is another highly significant and controversial theological development in the thinking of Ignatius. Yet again care is required in relation to the terminology employed. It would be anachronistic to discuss his ideas in the light of later debates about transubstantiation. Perhaps a more appropriate way to discuss his understanding is in light of the place of cultic meals in the wider milieu

---

60. Sullivan, *From Apostles to Bishops*, 104.
61. Schoedel, *Ignatius of Antioch*, 22.
62. Joly, *Le dossier d'Ignace d'Antioch*, 75–85.

of Graeco-Roman religions. Just as Paul can describe the eating of idol meat as partaking in idols (1 Cor. 10.20), Ignatius sees the consumption of the Eucharistic elements as a participatory event. Thus Schoedel summarizes the perspective of the epistles in the following manner: 'The eucharist is the center of worship for Ignatius (cf. *Eph.* 5.2; 13.1; *Phd.* 4; *Smyr.* 7.1; 8.1) and serves as the focus for a sense of the presence of saving power in the Christian community (cf. *Eph.* 20.2).'[63] A close association between the elements of bread and wine and the physical body of Christ does emerge in *Smyr.* 7.1, where Ignatius attacks his opponents' absence from the cultic meal performed under the authority of the bishop: 'They abstain from the eucharist and prayer, since they do not confess the eucharist is the flesh of our saviour Jesus Christ, which suffered on behalf of our sins and which the Father raised in his kindness' (*Smyr.* 7.1). Yet even here the formulation is so tied up with combatting the opponents' denial of the reality of the sufferings of Christ that it is perhaps best to exercise caution rather than to overload this single reference with too much theological freight. Rather, Ignatius is happier to describe the Eucharist as the 'medicine of immortality' (*Eph.* 20.2), which in some sense denotes the real salvific presence of Christ in the elements, and affirms the significance of the Eucharist as a participatory event for the community, as a demonstration of both their fellowship with Christ and their fealty to the bishop.[64]

(ii) *Christology*

Traditionally an analysis of an author's beliefs concerning the nature of Jesus has been undertaken by investigating the titles that are employed as descriptions of status. One of the classical exponents of this approach is Oscar Cullmann. Describing his desire to be analytical in his methodology for deriving the Christological concepts of the New Testament, Cullmann provided the following explanation:

> This does not mean that we shall investigate in turn each New Testament writing with all the different titles that appear in it, but rather that we shall examine in its precise meaning each Christological title for itself as it appears throughout all the New Testament books.[65]

Although privileging this titular approach, Cullmann acknowledges that in some ways it creates a false dichotomy between the person and the work of Christ. He states, 'The New Testament hardly ever speaks of the

63. Schoedel, *Ignatius of Antioch*, 21.
64. Further on these points see Schoedel, *Ignatius of Antioch*, 21.
65. O. Cullmann, *The Christology of the New Testament*, tr. S.C. Guthrie and C.A.M. Hall (London: SCM Press, 1959), 6.

person of Christ without at the same time speaking of his work.'[66] Thus in discussing the Christology that Ignatius implicitly presents, it is necessary to consider both the titles used and the significance he attributes to the work of Christ. Tuckett notes the protest made by a number of scholars against the overuse of titles, but cautions against throwing the proverbial baby out with the bath-water. Thus he comments that 'we cannot ignore key christological terms or "titles" completely. In any case, many of these key terms or titles became important in subsequent Christian history when they were adapted and used as key descriptions of who Jesus was.'[67]

Discussing the names Ignatius uses to refer to Jesus, Grant observes that the favoured term employed 'is the double name "Jesus Christ" (112 times)'.[68] This compares with 'Christ Jesus' (13 times), 'Jesus' (3 times), and 'Christ' (4 times). Often the name 'Jesus Christ' is conjoined to other Christological titles.[69] Ignatius is not shy about calling Jesus 'God'. In the inscriptions of *Ephesians* and *Romans* he speaks confidently of 'Jesus Christ our God'. In one of his creedal affirmations he declares that Jesus is 'God come in the flesh' (*Eph.* 7.2), and in addressing the Romans, he speaks of 'the passion of my God' (*Rom.* 6.3). Further examples could be given where Ignatius freely identifies Jesus as God, in a manner that assumes this is a natural and uncontested designation, at least among the recipients of his letters.[70] From these data Grant concludes that 'Ignatius is insisting upon the divine function, and also upon the divine nature, of the incarnate Lord'.[71] Yet, in the face of docetic opposition, Ignatius is equally strong in his affirmations of the humanity of Jesus,[72] and in a number of the creedal statements he utilizes carefully balanced pairings that support the divine/human duality of Christ.[73] Perhaps one of the most striking examples of this occurs in *Eph.* 7.2, where Ignatius describes Jesus as the 'one physician' who is 'both fleshly and spiritual, begotton and unbegotten, God come in the flesh'. While both sides of Jesus' nature

66. Cullmann, *The Christology of the New Testament*, 3.

67. C.M. Tuckett, *Christology and the New Testament: Jesus and his Earliest Followers* (Edinburgh: Edinburgh University Press, 2001), 11.

68. Grant, *Ignatius of Antioch*, 7.

69. Grant, *Ignatius of Antioch*, 7.

70. Cf. 'the blood of God' (*Eph.* 1.1); 'our God in us' (*Eph.* 15.3); 'our God, Jesus Christ, was conceived by the virgin Mary' (*Eph.* 18.2); 'God became manifest in human form' (Ign. *Eph.* 19.3); 'our God, Jesus Christ' (*Rom.* 3.3); 'Jesus Christ, the God who made you so wise' (*Smyr.* 1.1); 'farewell in our God, Jesus Christ' (*Poly.* 8.3).

71. Grant, *Ignatius of Antioch*, 8.

72. This point is noted by Hurtado. He states, 'For his part, Ignatius, too, certainly affirms Jesus' divinity. Indeed, he is as noticeable for the way he does this as he is for his emphasis on Jesus' humanity': L.W. Hurtado, *Lord Jesus Christ: Devotion to Jesus in Earliest Christianity* (Grand Rapids: Eerdmans, 2003), 637.

73. See *Eph.* 7.2; *Smyr.* 1.1–2; *Poly.* 3.1.

are confessed, no attempt is made to explain how these twin aspects are held together in union.

Hurtado comments on the purpose of these formulae, which function as both doxological and doctrinal declarations. That is, while they may reflect the language of praise employed by Ignatius they also represent intellectually formulated beliefs about the nature of Jesus. Hurtado states,

> Of course, these all directly reflect Ignatius's deeply felt piety, but they are not simply emotionally tinged rhetoric. In the context of all that Ignatius attributes to Jesus, his application of the epithet *theos* to him surely signals that Jesus is genuinely divine.[74]

There was much distance yet to be travelled between the primitive Christological statements articulated by Ignatius and the more detailed and reflective creeds and discussions of the fourth and fifth centuries, which were formulated as responses to the Christological controversies of their own times. Notwithstanding this caveat, Ignatius can be seen as one who, at least in embryonic form, resonates with key features of those later 'orthodox' statements. He relentlessly declares the humanity and divinity of Christ, and his views of divinity incarnated in human form reveal that he does not hold to adoptionistic interpretations of Christ being clothed with divinity at either his baptism or resurrection. The resurrection, however, does represent a stative change as Jesus is transformed from a passible to an impassible being (*Eph.* 7.2).

(iii) *The Virgin Mary*

Another area in which Ignatius appears to show some noticeable development in thinking is the way in which he depicts Mary, the mother of Jesus. It should be noted, however, that the epistles evidence none of the Marian devotion that became so prominent later, especially in the Middle Ages. Instead, references to Mary serve the related purposes of affirming the real humanity of Jesus and undermining those who deny that he came and suffered in the flesh. It is interesting to observe that Mary is only referred to in three epistles, those three which have been seen as refuting docetic adversaries, namely *Ephesians*, *Trallians* and *Smyrneans*. In the former, Mary is mentioned on three separate occasions. First, in what may be an early creedal or hymnic formulation that celebrates the duality of Jesus' nature as 'both fleshly and spiritual, begotten and unbegotten' (*Eph.* 7.2) Ignatius continues by affirming Christ as being from 'both of Mary and of God', yet without clarifying how this occurs. Schoedel's observation that Ignatius 'emphasized the historical side of Christ's being here in opposition to what he regarded as

---

74. Hurtado, *Lord Jesus Christ*, 639.

the heart of the false teaching of the opponents – namely doceticism'[75] correctly places the comment in the context of the controversy it is addressing.

In another carefully structured sequence of affirmations, Jesus is described as being 'conceived by Mary according to the plan of God' (*Eph.* 18.2). This again presents the physical reality of the incarnation, even if this statement is not used in a context which is explicitly polemical.[76] The final reference to Mary in *Ephesians* occurs as part of a triad of cosmological events that remained hidden from the 'ruler of this age'. The first two elements in the triad refer to Mary: 'the virginity of Mary and her giving birth eluded the ruler of this age' (*Eph.* 19.1). These affirmations form the introduction to the so-called 'Hymn of the Star' that follows, which Ignatius employs to illustrate the salvific implications of the incarnation at a cosmic level. The outlook here is markedly different from that of Rev. 12.13–17, where the dragon is fully cognizant of the woman and her male child and actively seeks to destroy both of them. According to Grant, here 'Ignatius is amplifying a Pauline statement [1 Cor. 2.8] by relating it specifically to Jesus' birth and death'.[77] While Ignatius' knowledge of 1 Corinthians makes this possible, it is not necessarily the most likely explanation.

Both of the remaining two references to Mary again affirm the reality of incarnation. The first states, 'Jesus Christ, of the family of David, of Mary, who was truly born, both ate and drank, was truly persecuted under Pontius Pilate, was truly crucified and died' (*Trall.* 9.1). Schoedel describes this as a 'quasi-credal form'[78] and notes that it is formulated to counter the teachings of the false teachers. Finally, although not directly mentioned by name, Jesus is described in a further series of affirmations concerning the reality of his fleshly existence as 'truly born of a virgin' (*Smyr.* 1.1). With the possible exception of the cosmological triad in *Eph.* 19.1, Mary forms an important part of Ignatius' theological understanding of the incarnation. There is no interest exhibited in her apart from the support that her role provides in declaring the physical reality of the birth of Christ from a human woman, albeit through a miraculous virginal conception. Ignatius does not show any knowledge of the ideas of the perpetual virginity of Mary, nor does he see her as an object of piety and devotion. Such concepts were to emerge at a later stage.

---

75. Schoedel, *Ignatius of Antioch*, 61.
76. This formulation is seen as being traditional by Schoedel 'since the verb (κυοφορεῖν) does not appear elsewhere in Ignatius': *Ignatius of Antioch*, 84–5.
77. Grant, *Ignatius of Antioch*, 103.
78. Schoedel, *Ignatius of Antioch*, 152.

(iv) *Martyrdom*

Was Ignatius a stoic believer facing death in the full confidence of his own faith, or was he a somewhat twisted individual seeking his own destruction and exhibiting all the classic signs of a martyr complex? Either formulation is loaded with the presuppositions one brings to the text, but there can be little doubt that the prospect of death in Rome shaped Ignatius' thinking and the rhetoric he employed throughout all seven epistles. However, it is in the *Epistle to the Romans* that Ignatius provides his fullest reflection on martyrdom. Perhaps the reason for this stems from the fact that he was not concerned to refute opponents in that letter, nor to establish episcopal authority; rather, as he turns his face to Rome in writing, he has space to consider the significance of the events that await him.[79]

In *Romans* Ignatius provides his readers with the location, Smyrna, and the date of writing, the 24th of August,[80] but unfortunately no year is given. Some of the language used by Ignatius to describe his impending martyrdom echoes that supposedly employed by Paul in 2 Timothy. Ignatius refers to his death as being 'poured out as a libation [σπονδισθῆναι] for God' (*Rom.* 2.1), which may intentionally pick up the phrase 'for I am already being poured out as a drink-offering [σπένδομαι]' (2 Tim. 4.6). Thus, for Ignatius there may be a certain resonance between the fate he is about to face and that endured by prominent Christians before him, although he is careful to distinguish certain differences. He writes, 'I am not enjoining you as Peter and Paul did. They were apostles, I am condemned; they were free, until now I have been a slave' (*Rom.* 4.3). The final phrase illustrates that Ignatius saw his impending death as the means by which he would attain true freedom.

Frend, however, is correct when he observes that Ignatius' letters 'display a state of exultation bordering on mania'.[81] The images he uses to anticipate his martyrdom have a certain morbidity: for example, 'I am the wheat of God and am ground by the teeth of the wild beasts' (*Rom.* 4.1); 'coax the wild beasts, that they may become a tomb for me and leave no part of my body behind' (*Rom.* 4.2). But while such an outlook may sound somewhat discordant with modern sensitivities, it finds its antecedents in the New Testament, although many of the images of death have been domesticated to such a degree that they are not recognized for what they are. Ignatius is doing no more than following Jesus' example of taking up his cross. In many ways, early Christianity, or at least certain strands in it,

79. See in particular *Romans* 4—5.

80. Here Ignatius employs the typical Roman system of dating, describing the day as 'the ninth day before the calends of September' (*Rom.* 10.3).

81. W.H.C. Frend, *Martyrdom and Persecution in the Early Church* (Oxford: Blackwell, 1965), 197.

may accurately be described as a martyr cult. Ignatius represents the belief in a reversal, or inversion, of worldly values and attachments. In his bondage he has become free; in his death he will be made alive. By 'learning to desire nothing while in chains' (*Rom.* 4.3) he is learning to desire Christ more completely. Thus he understands the destruction of the flesh as producing the perfection of the disciple:

> Fire and cross and packs of wild beasts, cuttings and limbs being torn apart, the grinding of the whole body, the evil torments of the devil – let them come upon me, only that I may attain to Jesus Christ. (*Rom.* 5.3)

Such an attitude, although unpalatable to certain minds,[82] reflects the countercultural attitudes exhibited in early Christianity, whereby acts of martyrdom became world-negating events that served to rob the Roman empire and the dominion of the Satan of their power, and in an uncompromising way demonstrated the victory of Christ over the world. Therefore Ignatius can say, 'it is better for me to die in Jesus Christ than to rule the ends of the earth' (*Rom.* 6.1). These divergent cosmological outlooks confronted each other in the imperial edicts that sought to make Christians conform to acts of socio-religious piety such as reverencing the emperor, and the stubborn refusal of followers of Jesus to comply. As a consequence, the arena was not viewed as a place of defeat for the fledging Christian faith; rather, it was seen as the venue where one attained to Christ and received true illumination.[83]

(v) *Ignatius' Use of the New Testament*

The ongoing debate concerning the emergence of the biblical canon has sought some clarification by consulting the practices of Ignatius in citing the writings that later became collected as the New Testament. Only one citation of scripture is prefaced with an introductory formula and that is from the Old Testament, when Ignatius draws upon Prov. 3.34, 'For it is written, "God opposes the haughty" ' (*Eph.* 5.3). The use of the New Testament is more problematic, and it needs to be remembered that as Ignatius composed his epistles during transportation to Rome it was extremely unlikely that he had direct access to written copies of documents that were later included in the canonical New Testament. Notwithstanding these physical circumstances, it is interesting to note the accuracy and range of texts cited by Ignatius while writing his seven epistles. A thorough analysis of this topic was undertaken in 1905 by W.R. Inge, who adopted a maximalist position, declaring even faint echoes to be evidence that Ignatius knew certain New Testament

---

82. See, for example, Grant, *Ignatius of Antioch*, 13.
83. See *Rom.* 5.3; 6.3.

writings.[84] Others have revisited this question, especially in relation to the use of the Gospels by Ignatius. Koester adopts an extremely hard line for proving the use of a Gospel by a later writer. He maintains that one must be able to demonstrate the clear use of redactional material to ensure that the actual Gospel in question is being quoted, and not just some Gospel-like tradition.[85] Hence he claims that at no point in the seven epistles is it demonstrable that Ignatius was citing material drawn from any of the four canonical Gospels. By contrast, Massaux finds clear and repeated evidence of the use of Matthew's Gospel in the writings of Ignatius.[86] In part, these divergent findings represent alternative methodological presuppositions. Koester avoids the problem of allowing a few shared words or the faintest echo to become the basis of asserting that an author knew a text that was later deemed canonical. However, when there appears to be a clear case of Ignatius citing a piece of redactional material from Matthew's Gospel, Koester finds a less likely explanation to exclude what appears to be the obvious conclusion, namely that Ignatius knew and cited the first Gospel.[87] The text in question is drawn from Matt. 3.15 and cited in *Smyr.* 1.1. Discussing Jesus' baptism Ignatius states that it was done 'in order to fulfil all righteousness', a comment made only by Matthew. It should be noted that Matthean scholars have long recognized the term 'righteousness' as being part of the preferred vocabulary of the first Gospel.[88] This is the clearest example for demonstrating Ignatius' use of Matthew; all other examples cited by scholars show far fewer points of contact, but they are of value for building a cumulative case for Ignatius' use of the first Gospel.[89]

While Matthew may be the only Gospel for which it is possible to suggest that Ignatius is citing the text, more fruitful results can be

84.   W.R. Inge, 'Ignatius', in Oxford Society of Historical Theology, *The New Testament in the Apostolic Fathers* (Oxford: Clarendon Press, 1905), 61–83.

85.   H. Koester, *Synoptische Überlieferung bei den Apostolischen Vätern*, TU 65 (Berlin: Akademie-Verlag, 1957), 24–61.

86.   É. Massaux, *The Influence of the Gospel of Saint Matthew on Christian Literature before Saint Irenaeus*, book 1, *The First Ecclesiastical Writers*, New Gospel Studies 5/1 (ET, Macon, Ga.: Mercer University Press, 1990), esp. 85–122.

87.   See Koester's discussion of *Smyr.* 1.1, in *Synoptische Überlieferung bei den Apostolischen Vätern*, 57–9.

88.   For instance, Davies and Allison note 'righteousness' as being a 'special favourite of our evangelist' and observe that Matthew uses the term seven times, whereas it is absent in Mark and only used once in Luke: W.D. Davies and D.C. Allison, *A Critical and Exegetical Commentary on the Gospel According to Saint Matthew*, vol. 1, *Introduction and Commentary on Matthew I—VII* (Edinburgh: T. & T. Clark, 1988), 325.

89.   Further on this see my recent discussion, 'The Use of the Writings that Later Formed the New Testament in the Epistles of Ignatius of Antioch', in A. Gregory and C.M. Tuckett (eds), *The Reception of the New Testament in the Apostolic Fathers* (Oxford: Oxford University Press, 2005), 159–86.

determined for the Pauline epistles. The wide-ranging use of 1 Corinthians is apparent at various points through the seven letters of Ignatius.[90] Inge was so impressed by the use of 1 Corinthians that he stated, 'Ignatius must have known this Epistle almost by heart.'[91] There is no reason to dissent from this assessment. If the case for Ignatius knowing and citing 1 Corinthians is beyond doubt, his use of the Pauline letter to the Ephesians is almost as certain. Again the comment made by Inge is apposite: 'Though the correspondences between Ignatius and this Epistle are not nearly so numerous as in the case of 1 Corinthians, it may be considered almost certain that they are not accidental.'[92] Perhaps the two most compelling examples are the parallels between Ignatius' introduction to his own epistle to the Ephesians and Eph. 1.3–14, as well as *Poly.* 5.1b and Eph. 5.25. Perhaps only two other epistles can be shown to be used by Ignatius with any certainty: 1 and 2 Timothy.[93] Interestingly, Ignatius makes a comment in his own writings concerning the scribal habits of the apostle Paul. He states, while addressing the Christian community in Ephesus, that 'you are fellow initiates with Paul . . . who mentions you in every epistle in Christ Jesus' (*Eph.* 12.2). The majority of commentators, if they have discussed the issue at all, have taken the statement that Paul remembers the Ephesians in every letter as mere 'hyperbole'.[94] Schoedel states, 'the whole passage is highly idealized and tends to make sweeping claims on the basis of a few instances'.[95] Similarly, Lightfoot mentions the various hermeneutical devices that have been attempted to remove the apparent difficulty, including the alteration by the person responsible for the Longer Recension, 'who always in his prayers makes mention of you' (ὃς πάντοτε ἐν ταῖς δεήσεσιν αὐτοῦ μνημονεύει ὑμῶν). Yet Lightfoot himself uses the term 'hyperbole' to describe Ignatius' claim.[96] The tension arises since Paul does not in fact mention the Ephesians 'in every letter', but only in four of the epistles that form the Pauline corpus.[97] These are

---

90. Some of the most obvious examples are: *Eph.* 16.1:1 Cor. 6.9–10; *Eph.* 18.1:1 Cor. 1.18, 20; *Mag.* 10.2:1 Cor. 5.7–8; *Rom.* 5.1:1 Cor. 4.4.

91. Inge, 'Ignatius', 67.

92. Inge, 'Ignatius', 69.

93. See my discussion in Foster, 'The Use of the New Testament in the Epistles of Ignatius', 185.

94. Schoedel, *Ignatius of Antioch*, 73 n. 7.

95. Schoedel, *Ignatius of Antioch*, 73.

96. Lightfoot, *The Apostolic Fathers*, part 2, *Ignatius and Polycarp*, vol. 2, 65–6.

97. Lightfoot sees references to the Ephesians contained also in Rom. 16.5, ἀσπάσασθε Ἐπαίνετον τὸν ἀγαπητόν μου, ὅς ἐστιν ἀπαρχὴ τῆς Ἀσίας εἰς Χριστόν and 2 Cor. 1.8, Οὐ γὰρ θέλομεν ὑμᾶς ἀγνοεῖν, ἀδελφοί, ὑπὲρ τῆς θλίψεως ἡμῶν τῆς γενομένης ἐν τῇ Ἀσίᾳ: Lightfoot, *Ignatius and Polycarp*, vol. 2, 65. These references to 'Asia' obviously do not explicitly mention the Ephesians, although, as Revelation 1—3 makes clear, Ephesus was undoubtedly considered part of the Roman province of Asia by Christian writers.

1 Corinthians,[98] Ephesians,[99] 1 Timothy[100] and 2 Timothy.[101] What has not been considered until recently is the possibility that Ignatius' rhetoric at this point was not hyperbolic, but was in fact accurate, at least as far as he knew the facts.[102] An examination of the text of the seven letters appears to support the hypothesis that Ignatius knew the very four Pauline letters which explicitly make mention of the Ephesians. Thus to reiterate a statement I have made elsewhere,

> One must, therefore be content with the conclusion that a strong case can be mounted for Ignatius' knowledge of four Pauline epistles and the Gospel of Matthew. An interesting 'canon' for those who wish to draw wider implications from these findings![103]

5. *Conclusions*

When one opens the pages of the seven epistles of Ignatius one is struck by the force of the author's personality, perhaps more so than by any other writer in the corpus of the Apostolic Fathers. Thus, his death in Rome was surely not the only way in which Ignatius imitated his apostolic hero Paul. His certainty in the face of approaching martyrdom may be described in the epistles in somewhat mawkish terms, but it has also acted as an inspiration to countless members of the band of martyrs throughout the centuries. Yet when one sets admiration of this early church figure to one side and critically assesses the epistles, one is confronted by a plethora of contested and controversial issues.

In summary the positions espoused in this chapter are as follows. The seven epistles known as the Middle Recension are authentically Ignatian. The dating suggested by Eusebius in his *Ecclesiastical History* and *Chronicon* is extremely tenuous and may represent little more than his own guess at when the martyrdom of Ignatius took place. The theological tendencies in the epistles appear to make better sense if ascribed to the

---

98. In 1 Corinthians Ephesus is mentioned twice towards the end of the epistle: in 15.32, where Paul mentions fighting with wild beasts; and in 16.8, in the disclosure of the plan to remain in Ephesus until Pentecost.

99. In Ephesians, Ephesus in mentioned in the majority of manuscripts in the opening verse, τοῖς ἁγίοις τοῖς οὖσιν ἐν Ἐφέσῳ; significantly, however, the words ἐν Ἐφέσῳ are omitted in the three earliest manuscripts which are extant for Eph. 1.1: P[46], ℵ* and B, although later scribes inserted the reference to Ephesus into both ℵ[2] and B[2]. Moreover, the *subscriptio* which is included after 6.24 in many manuscripts, including the original hand of both ℵ and B, describes the epistle as being πρός Ἐφέσιους.

100. 1 Tim. 1.3, Timothy being urged to remain in Ephesus.

101. 2 Tim. 1.18; 4.12; and some forms of the *subscriptio* that occurs after 4.22.

102. See Foster, 'The Use of the New Testament in the Epistles of Ignatius', 162–4.

103. Foster, 'The Use of the New Testament in the Epistles of Ignatius', 186.

second quarter of the second century, and this may be a more appropriate period to which to date the epistles. Ignatius' support of a system of centralized episcopal leadership appears to be a significant innovation which was being opposed by those who favoured a more traditional charismatic structure within the Christian communities of Asia Minor. In his epistles Ignatius tackles two groups of opponents, those with proclivities towards Jewish practices – although not requiring circumcision, and another group who deny the reality of Christ's physical incarnation, suffering and redemption. This latter group may be labelled 'docetic' in the wide sense, as long as it is acknowledged that this term encompasses a spectrum of beliefs and can be evidenced among later groups who also marry docetism with Gnostic speculations.[104] For Ignatius it is not even appropriate to call such people Christians. Ignatius shows a limited knowledge of some of the writings that were later accepted into the New Testament canon. It can only be determined with certainty that he knew the Gospel of Matthew and four Pauline epistles: 1 Corinthians, Ephesians and 1 and 2 Timothy.

Regardless of whether Ignatius is viewed as the suppressor of diversity or the upholder of Christian truth, the instigator of a rigid hierarchy or an advocate of ordered communities, a self-interested power-hungry individual or a self-sacrificing humble servant of his master, he remains the most significant figure in the Christian movement from the first half of the second century and without grappling with the issues raised in his writings one can never fully understand the development in theology and ecclesial thinking that helped localized charismatic communities transform themselves into a universal church with a vision of their own significance and permanence.

Chapter 10

POLYCARP OF SMYRNA, *EPISTLE TO THE PHILIPPIANS*

Michael Holmes

The *Epistle to the Philippians* penned by Polycarp of Smyrna is sometimes dismissed as an example of a proof-texting moralism, indicative of the post-apostolic church's fall from the heights of Pauline Christianity. Read on its own terms, this complex exhortatory letter reveals a vigorous, pastorally sensitive effort to integrate both behavioural and theological aspects of 'righteousness' as Polycarp seeks to maintain the stability and integrity of the Philippian congregation.[1]

1. *Polycarp*

Polycarp of Smyrna may well have been the most important Christian leader in Asia Minor in the first half of the second century CE. Probably born about the time of the fall of Jerusalem in 70 CE, Polycarp was already Bishop of Smyrna when his older friend and mentor, Ignatius of Antioch, visited him and later sent him a letter of encouragement and advice as Ignatius, already condemned to the arena, made his way to Rome (possibly as early as 110–20). Several decades later, at age 86 (*c.* 155–60[2]), Polycarp died a martyr's death, condemned to the flames for his refusal to deny Christ and sacrifice to the emperor. Details of Polycarp's arrest, trial and execution were recorded by a member of his congregation in a letter now known as the *Martyrdom of Polycarp*. It portrays (in sometimes touching detail) both his steadfast commitment to his Lord (9.3, 'For eighty-six years I have been his servant, and he has done me no wrong. How can I blaspheme my King who saved me?') and his heroic valour as an 'apostolic and prophetic' 'teacher of all Asia' (16.2, 12.2) who fearlessly exemplfied 'a martyrdom in accord with the Gospel' (1.1).

1. The following is a substantially expanded version of the introduction to this document in M.W. Holmes, *The Apostolic Fathers in English*, 3rd edn (Grand Rapids: Baker Academic, forthcoming). For the Greek text consult M.W. Holmes, *The Apostolic Fathers: Greek Texts with English Translations* (Baker, Book House, 1999), 202–21.
2. Cf. Holmes, *The Apostolic Fathers: Greek Texts with English Translations*, 223.

Irenaeus (who as a young man met and was instructed by Polycarp) preserves a number of details and anecdotes about him. He reports that Polycarp's colleagues included both Papias (*AH* 5.33.4) and Florinus (Eusebius, *HE* 5.20.4–8), and mentions a trip to Rome in the early 150s, at which time Polycarp (a staunch Quartodeciman) debated the proper date for observing Easter with Anicetus, Bishop of Rome (neither, apparently, persuaded the other).[3] He also recalls a testy confrontation between Polycarp and Marcion, an occasion when Polycarp dismissed Marcion as the 'first-born of Satan'.[4]

Polycarp's life and ministry spanned the time between the end of the apostolic era and the emergence of catholic Christianity, and as a proto-orthodox leader he was deeply involved in the central issues and challenges of this critical era. These included the increasing possibility of conflict with the Roman state, the challenge of the emerging 'Gnostic' movement and its charismatic leaders (such as Cerinthus and Marcion), the development and expansion of the monepiscopal form of ecclesiastical organization, and the beginnings of the formation of a canon of early Christian writings. Irenaeus and Eusebius both considered him to be a significant link in the chain of apostolic tradition (a concept of increasing importance throughout the second century). Conservative and traditional, Polycarp exercised influence far beyond Asia as he sought to protect and maintain the proto-orthodox strand of the early Christian movement.

2. *Polycarp as Author*

Tradition portrays Polycarp as a prolific writer. Irenaeus speaks of him as the author of several 'letters which he sent either to the neighbouring churches, strengthening them, or to some of the brethren, exhorting and warning them'.[5] The anonymous author of the (historically worthless) *Life of Polycarp* is even more extravagant, attributing to Polycarp 'many treatises and sermons and letters'.[6] Also, a canon list attributes a *Didaskalia* to Polycarp.[7]

Of all these many writings attributed to Polycarp, however, only a single one survives under his name[8]: a letter he wrote to the Christian

---

3. Irenaeus, *AH* 3.3.4; Eusebius, *HE* 5.24; 4.14.1–5.
4. Irenaeus, *AH* 3.3.4; Eusebius, *HE* 4.14.7.
5. Irenaeus, *Letter to Florinus*, in Eusebius, *HE* 5.20.8.
6. *Vit. Poly.* 12, in J.B. Lightfoot, *The Apostolic Fathers*, part 2, *Ignatius and Polycarp*, 3 vols (London: Macmillan, 1885, 2nd edn 1889–90), vol. 3, 494.
7. Lightfoot, *The Apostolic Fathers,* part 2, *Ignatius and Polycarp*, vol. 1, 447, 351 n. 1.
8. The *Life of Polycarp* 'explains away' the loss of many documents by attributing their destruction to the same pagans who instigated Polycarp's martyrdom: 'He wrote also many treatises and sermons and letters, but in the persecution which arose on his account, when he

community in the Macedonian town of Philippi. Irenaeus offers the earliest testimony to this document: 'There is also a letter of Polycarp written to the Philippians, a most powerful one, from which those who so desire and are concerned about their own salvation can learn both the character of his faith and the message of the truth' (*AH* 3.3.4; cf. Eusebius, *HE* 4.14.8).

Has anything by Polycarp survived without his name attached? Victor of Capua attributes some extant comments on Gospel passages to Polycarp, but 'parts of these are manifestly spurious and the remainder are discredited by this base companionship'.[9] Hans von Campenhausen's claim that Polycarp also authored the Pastoral Epistles has rightly met with little acceptance.[10] More promising is the intriguing proposal (now the subject of a major monograph by Charles Hill) that Polycarp is the author of the anonymous apology known as the *Epistle to Diognetus*.[11] More probable is the prospect that some of Polycarp's oral teachings may be embedded in Irenaeus' writings. In *Against Heresies* (4.27.1–4.32.1), Irenaeus apparently passes on from memory the teaching of a presbyter, one who was, according to Irenaeus, 'a disciple of apostles, who heard and saw apostles and their disciples' (4.27.1). A number of scholars have now argued that this anonymous elder is, in fact, Polycarp of Smyrna[12] – who may also be, in Hill's opinion, the source for the 'catalogue of heresies' in *AH* 4.23—27.[13]

3. *The* Epistle to the Philippians

Brief, direct, and stylistically unpretentious, Polycarp's *Epistle to the Philippians* is a good example of what Stowers terms a 'letter of exhortation and advice', one that combines aspects of a paraenetic

---

9. Lightfoot, *Ignatius and Polycarp*, vol. 1, 473.

10. H. von Campenhausen, 'Polykarp und die Pastoralen', repr. In H. von Campenhausen, *Aus der Frühzeit des Christentums* (Tübingen: Mohr-Siebeck, 1963), 197–252.

11. P.F. Beatrice, 'Der Presbyter des Irenäus, Polykarp von Smyrna und der Brief an Diognet', in E. Romero-Pose (ed.), *Pléroma Salus Carnis: Homenaje a Antonio Orbe, S.J.* (Santiago de Compostela: Imprenta Aldecoa, 1990), 179–202; C.E. Hill, *From the Lost Teaching of Polycarp: Identifying Irenaeus' Apostolic Presbyter and the Author of* Ad Diognetum (Tübingen: Mohr-Siebeck, 2006).

12. F.D. Gilliard, 'The Apostolicity of Gallic Churches', *HTR* 68 (1975), 29 n. 30; Beatrice, 'Der Presbyter des Irenäus, Polykarp von Smyrna und der Brief an Diognet'; Hill, *From the Lost Teaching of Polycarp*, 7–24.

13. Hill, *From the Lost Teaching of Polycarp*, 24–31.

(exhortatory) letter, a letter of advice, and a letter of admonition.[14] Specific aspects of a paraenetic letter (the writer is the recipients' friend or moral superior, who recommends habits of behaviour and actions that conform to a certain model of character, in a letter typically directed 'at those who had already been initiated into a social group and needed to habituate the initial learning'[15]) are clearly evident in *Philippians*, especially chaps 2—10. The Philippians apparently have approached Polycarp as their social and ecclesiastical superior (his demurral in 3.1–2 notwithstanding), and he responds appropriately. Moreover, much of what he writes seeks to reinforce existing behaviour or affirm things already known.[16]

In chapter 11, characteristics of letters of advice (συμβουλευτικαι)[17] and admonition (νουθετήτικαι)[18] are evident as Polycarp combines traditional maxims (e.g. 'avoid love of money', 11.2) with his own opinion regarding how the Philippians should treat Valens ('be reasonable', 11.4) in an effort to restore the congregation's sense of σωφροσύνη ('self-control' or 'moderation').

Another style of discourse, the 'word of exhortation' (λόγος παρακλήσεως),[19] seems also to have influenced the document, especially in chaps 2—10. The basic pattern of this widely occurring form consists of (1) presentation of *exempla*, i.e. authoritative sayings (often scriptural) or examples, (2) a conclusion based upon the *exempla* indicating their relevance or significance for those addressed, and (3) an exhortation based upon that conclusion (which may also anticipate *exempla* and conclusions to follow).[20] This basic pattern occurs frequently in *Philippians*.[21]

With respect to its rhetorical features, the body of the letter may be

---

14. S.K. Stowers, *Letter Writing in Greco-Roman Antiquity* (Philadelphia: Westminster Press, 1986), 91–6.

15. Stowers, *Letter Writing in Greco-Roman Antiquity*, 96, 95.

16. Reinforcement of existing behaviour: 'you believe', 1.3; 'continue in the faith', 4.3; 'if we continue to believe', 5.2; 'persevering', 7.2; 'continue to hold steadfastly and unceasingly', 8.1; 'continue to stand fast', 10.1, 'maintaining', 10.2; 'self-control in which you live', 10.3. Affirmation of things known: 'knowing', 1.3, 4.1, 5.1; 'remembering', 2.3, 12.1; Paul taught and wrote them, 3.2; 'return to the word delivered to us from the beginning', 7.2; 'what we have believed', 8.2; 'which you saw', 9.1; 'do we not know', 11.2; 'you are all well trained', 12.1.

17. Stowers, *Letter Writing in Greco-Roman Antiquity*, 107–8.

18. Stowers, *Letter Writing in Greco-Roman Antiquity*, 125–7.

19. See L. Wills, 'The Form of the Sermon in Hellenistic Judaism and Early Christianity', *HTR* 77 (1984), 277–99, as refined and developed by C.C. Black II, 'The Rhetorical Form of the Hellenistic Jewish and Early Christian Sermon: A Response to Lawrence Wills', *HTR* 81 (1988), 1–18.

20. Wills, 'The Form of the Sermon in Hellenistic Judaism and Early Christianity', 279, 281–2, 284–5.

21. *Poly. Phil.* 1.3—2.1; 4.1; 5.1—2; 8.1—9.1a; 9.1b—10.3.

characterized as epideictic rhetoric, a type whose goals included enhance-
ment of an audience's existing beliefs.[22] This confirms what the epistolary
features suggest: that maintainance of the community, with respect to
both its beliefs and behaviour, was a key goal of the author.[23]

In short, the letter is a complex hortatory letter that employs a homiletic
style of discourse, and which also displays throughout an awareness of
Hellenistic epistolary conventions and rhetorical theory.

For many of his *exempla* Polycarp draws upon the scriptures, in the
form of the Septuagint. Schoedel suggests that he makes use of Psalms,
Proverbs, Isaiah, Jeremiah, Ezekiel and Tobit,[24] a list which, if revised,
might require reduction.[25] At the same time, the frequency with which
Polycarp's language and vocabulary are illumined by the Septuagint
suggests that his acquaintance with it may run deeper than his references
or allusions indicate.[26]

Polycarp also makes considerable use of early Christian writings. He is
quite familiar with 1 Peter and *1 Clement*, and also uses 1 Corinthians and
Ephesians. He probably made use of 1 and 2 Timothy and 1 John, and
perhaps Romans, Galatians and Philippians.[27] While none of these
documents are cited as 'scripture' (the reference to Ephesians in 12.1 being
a possible exception), the way in which Polycarp refers to them indicates
that he considered them authoritative writings. He also cites, as equally
authoritative, at least one saying found nowhere else in early Christian
sources.[28]

---

22.   Black, 'The Rhetorical Form of the Hellenistic Jewish and Early Christian Sermon',
5, summarizing the discussions of Aristotle, Cicero and Quintilian on this point; cf. G.A.
Kennedy, *New Testament Interpretation through Rhetorical Criticism* (Chapel Hill, NC and
London: University of North Carolina Press, 1984, 19: epideictic 'seeks to persuade [the
audience] to hold or reaffirm some point of view in the present'.

23.   Cf. H.O. Maier, 'Purity and Danger in Polycarp's Epistle to the Philippians: The Sin
of Valens in Social Perspective', *JECS* 1 (1993), 229–47, esp. 244–7.

24.   W.R. Schoedel, *Polycarp, Martyrdom of Polycarp, Fragments of Papias* (Camden,
NJ: Thomas Nelson and Sons, 1967), 5; cf. the earlier work by Daniel Völter, *Polykarp und
Ignatius und die ihnen zugeschriebenen Briefe* (Leiden: Brill, 1910), 29–30.

25.   Apparent allusions to the three major prophets may all be indirect or mediated.

26.   A.E. Barnett, *Paul Becomes a Literary Influence* (Chicago: University of Chicago
Press, 1941), 170, aptly notes that Polycarp displays a 'freedom of rendering as though he
were quoting from memory. Instead of making his references direct and formal, he usually
works the ideas and expressions into statements of his own.'

27.   M.W. Holmes, 'Polycarp's *Letter to the Philippians* and the Writings that Later
Formed the New Testament', in A. Gregory and C.M. Tuckett (eds), *The Reception of the
New Testament in the Apostolic Fathers* (Oxford: Oxford University Press, 2005), 187–227.
There are possible allusions to other documents (e.g. the four canonical Gospels, Acts, 2
Corinthians, Colossians, 2 Thessalonians, Hebrews and 2 John), but insufficient evidence to
demonstrate their use. This does not mean that Polycarp was unacquainted with these, only
that he does not appear to have made use of them in this particular letter.

28.   *Phil.* 6.1; cf. Holmes, 'Polycarp's *Letter to the Philippians*', 188–9.

It is worthwhile to observe how Polycarp utilizes his resources. The letter is often dismissed as little more than an unreflective pastiche of quotations and allusions.[29] But Polycarp is no mere 'seedpicker' (cf. Acts 17.18–21) mechanically stringing things together: he not only abridges or alters his sources in the process of incorporating them into his letter, but in so doing often changes the meaning or point to serve his own purposes.[30] In short, his heavy use of traditional materials is not without evidence of thought and originality – indeed, it likely reflects a strategic decision on his part.

4. *Occasion and Central Concerns*

Philippians was penned by Polycarp in response to a letter from Philippi (cf. 3.1; 13.1). On the basis of his response, it seems probable that the Philippians mentioned their reception of Ignatius (cf. 1.1); it is certain that they asked Polycarp to discuss the subject of righteousness (3.1), to assist their participation in the embassy to Antioch (13.1), and to send them a copy of Ignatius' letters (13.2). They may have raised the matter of Valens (an avaricious presbyter) on their own initiative as well (alternatively, however, it is possible that Polycarp learned of this matter via the letter carrier[31]). In the absence of further evidence, we can only speculate about why the Philippians wrote to Polycarp rather than someone else (though his repeated commendation of Crescens in chap. 14 implies some prior relationship[32]), what else they may have said in their letter, what circumstances prompted them to write, and whether they saw any link between their request for a discussion of 'righteousness' and the matter of Valens.

Whether or not the Philippians saw a connection between their request for a discussion of righteousness and the matter of Valens, it is quite possible that Polycarp did. Indeed, a major interpretive question is the relationship (or lack thereof) between these two main issues and the extensive exhortation.

---

29. See for details B. Dehandschutter, 'Polycarp's Epistle to the Philippians: An Early Example of "Reception"', in J.M. Sevrin (ed.), *The New Testament in Early Christianity* (Leuven: Leuven University Press and Peeters, 1989), 275; also K. Berding, *Polycarp and Paul: An Analysis of their Literary and Theological Relationship in Light of Polycarp's Use of Biblical and Extra-Biblical Literature* (Leiden: Brill, 2002), 4–6; P. Hartog, *Polycarp and the New Testament: The Occasion, Rhetoric, Theme, and Unity of the Epistle to the Philippians and its Allusions to New Testament Literature* (Tübingen: Mohr-Siebeck, 2002).

30. See e.g. his use of Ephesians and 1 Peter in *Phil.* 1.3—2.1.

31. Cf. in this respect 1 Cor. 1.11; and 7.1.

32. See the discussion in P. Oakes, 'Leadership and Suffering in the Letters of Polycarp and Paul to the Philippians', in A. Gregory and C.M. Tuckett (eds), *Trajectories through the New Testament and the Apostolic Fathers* (Oxford: Oxford University Press, 2005), 370–3.

P.N. Harrison exemplifies a traditional approach, which generally (1) sees no connection between the two issues, and (2) thinks that the problem of 'heresy' (which Harrison argues was sparked by Marcion) is the major problem.[33] Schoedel, who similarly sees no intrinsic link between 'love of money' and 'heresy',[34] nonetheless reads the letter as an interconnected whole by viewing the two issues as equally symptomatic of a profound moral failing in Philippi, to which Polycarp responds by scrutinizing both issues through the lens of (what he considers to be) a proper understanding of 'righteousness'.[35]

One of the first to argue in a thoroughgoing way for a connection between the two issues was Meinhold. Reading chaps 11—12 in light of chaps 3 and 7, and convinced that Marcion (whose teachings he thinks sparked a 'debate' about righteousness in Philippi) was the target of Polycarp's comments in chaps 2—10, he finds a link with chaps 11—12 by suggesting that Valens' sin was the acceptance of a monetary gift from Marcion.[36]

Steinmetz, reading chaps 2—10 in light of 11—12, achieves a unified reading of the letter by reducing the central issues to just one (the mention of 'heresy' in 7.1 being, in his estimation, almost entirely *pro forma*, of little significance with respect to the occasion of the letter): the case of Valens, who is symptomatic of a problem infecting the whole congregation. The substantial paraenetic emphasis reflects Polycarp's belief that virtue is the flip side of the coin of 'righteousness'.[37]

Maier's sociologically oriented analysis (which takes for granted the existence of two problems) combines a reversal of Harrison's evaluation of the relative importance of the two issues with Steinmetz's view that chaps 11—12 offer the key to the situation: 'While Polycarp was anxious about the spread and reception of false teaching, his ethical exhortation reveals a more profound concern with group solidarity and purity, phenomena compromised by Valens' abuse of wealth.' For Maier 'righteousness' is primarily a moral rather than a theological term, and 'the main focus of the letter is the protection of the purity of the Philippian church'.[38]

---

33.   P.N. Harrison, *Polycarp's Two Epistles to the Philippians* (Cambridge: Cambridge University Press, 1936), 169, 129–30.

34.   Schoedel, *Polycarp*, 17, 31.

35.   W.R. Schoedel, 'Polycarp of Smyrna and Ignatius of Antioch', *ANRW* 2.27.1 (1993), 282.

36.   P. Meinhold, 'Polykarpos', *Pauly–Wissowa Realencyclopädie der classichen Attertumswissenschaft* 21 (1952), 1686–7. (When Marcion joined the church in Rome, he is reported to have given it a gift of 200,000 sesterces: so Tertullian, *Praescr.* 30.2.)

37.   P. Steinmetz, 'Polykarp von Smyrna über die Gerechtigkeit', *Hermes* 100 (1972), 63–75.

38.   Maier, 'Purity and Danger in Polycarp's Epistle to the Philippians', 246, 246 n. 67.

Maier's rich sociological analysis reveals the shortcomings of purely theological readings (which stress the 'anti-heretical' aspects at the expense of other elements, and thereby fail to do justice to the paraenetic aspects of the letter); at the same time, it is unable adequately to account for the historical particularities of the situation. Furthermore, recent investigations, despite their shared belief that the letter exhibits a thematic unity, have differed regarding the nature or identity of that unity.

Steinmetz and Maier point us in a fruitful direction in two respects. First, they remind us of the need to take seriously the paraenetic character of the document. Second, they rightly downplay the role or importance of 7.1 in the letter. (Indeed, I would argue not only that 7.1 plays a minimal role in the document, but also that whatever role it does play reflects Polycarp's situation in Smyrna rather than circumstances in Philippi, and that Marcion is nowhere in view.[39]) *Contra* Steinmetz and Maier, however, I am not convinced that chaps 11—12 hold the key to the letter. One topic that we *know* the Philippians raised in their letter, and to which Polycarp devotes by far the greatest portion of his letter, is the subject of righteousness. This observation should therefore be given substantial weight in any assessment of the letter.

The observed inability to find a connection between the two sections of the document in the occasion of the letter suggests that it may lie elsewhere, perhaps in Polycarp's goals or his own theological perspective. The letter's epistolary and rhetorical features,[40] its sociological aspects, and key aspects of the historical context suggested above (namely, that the 'anti-heretical' elements likely reflect the situation in Smyrna and that Marcion is not in view) lead one to suggest that Polycarp's own theological understanding may provide the key to the letter's unity. That is, Polycarp believed that wrong behaviours were *prima facie* evidence of wrong beliefs, and that wrong beliefs inevitably produced wrong behaviours. Further, wrong beliefs and/or behaviours are characteristic

39. On the generic, non-particular character of the polemic in 7.1 (note, for example, the repeated ὅς ἄν, 'whoever'), cf. N. Dahl, 'Der Erstgeborene Satans und der Vater des Teufels', in N. Dahl, *Apophoreta* (Berlin: Töpelmann, 1964), 70–84, and Steinmetz, 'Polykarp von Smyrna', 73. In favour of Smyrna rather than Philippi, the following can be said: in view of (1) Ign. *Smyrn.* 4.1—5.3 (cf. 2.1, 6.1—7.2), where Ignatius specifically identifies in Smyrna 'certain people' whose teaching bears a very close resemblance to that proscribed by Polycarp, and (2) the absence in *Philippians* of evidence of sectarianism in Philippi, it seems likely that the target(s) of Polycarp's remarks lived not in Philippi but in or around Smyrna; cf. W. Bauer, *Orthodoxy and Heresy in Earliest Christianity* (Philadelphia: Fortress Press, 1971), 69–70. Against Marcion as Polycarp's target, see e.g. Hartog, *Polycarp and the New Testament*, 89–108.

40. Stowers notes that such a letter usually offers a 'model of what it means to be a good person in a certain role' and 'attempts to persuade and move the audience to conform to that model and to elicit corresponding habits of behaviour': *Letter Writing in Greco-Roman Antiquity*, 94.

of outsiders, not insiders. Consequently Valens' problematic behaviour with regard to finances represents a major threat both to the Philippian community's stability (in that it blurs the boundary between insiders and outsiders) and its theological self-understanding (in that it leads to questions or uncertainty about the meaning of righteousness).

This understanding of the letter makes sense of the way Polycarp stresses so strongly the behavioural aspects of what is usually viewed as a purely 'theological' concept, i.e. 'righteousness'.[41] For him, orthopraxy is the other side of the coin of orthodoxy; if the community is behaving properly, it is also likely believing properly. This position may explain the vigour with which he reinforces (what he thinks should be) the community's sense of behavioural norms and standards throughout the letter. His key goal was to maintain and protect the integrity of the community in terms of both its beliefs and behaviours. Thus throughout the letter he displays a primary, overriding concern: that the Philippian congregation continue to 'follow the example of the Lord, firm and immovable in faith, . . . cherishing one another, united in truth, . . . despising no one' (10.1), and thereby maintain a proper boundary between themselves and the Gentiles among whom they live.

5. *Key Theological Themes*

On the basis of such a short and so clearly occasional letter it is unwise to attempt to say anything of a comprehensive nature about Polycarp's theology. But because he does devote a substantial part of his letter to the topic of 'righteousness' – and because the preceding paragraph has already raised the question of what he means by that term – it seems appropriate to attempt a sketch of his views on some selected topics (to the extent that they are revealed in the letter).

(i) *Salvation*

Before turning to 'righteousness' it will first be helpful, in order to create a suitable context, to summarize Polycarp's views about salvation. Salvation for Polycarp is first and foremost something that God has accomplished through Jesus Christ: it is a matter of 'grace' – that is, 'by the will of God through Jesus Christ' – not 'works' (1.3). It involves 'faith' or 'trust' (1.3; 5.2) – itself a gift (3.2) – in the God who has raised from the dead (1.2; 2.1.2; 9.2; 12.2) Jesus Christ, who 'endured for our sins' (1.2),

---

41. It also takes account of the fact that in both sections of the letter Polycarp's primary concern is with the community: even in chaps 11—12 he devotes considerably more attention to the community than he does to Valens and his wife.

that is, 'who bore our sins in his own body upon the tree' (8.1), 'who died on our behalf' (9.2).

Furthermore, while salvation is to some extent a present experience ('you have been saved', 1.3), it definitely is eschatological in character and orientation, with resurrection the primary focus: the God who raised Jesus from the dead 'will raise us also' (2.2; cf. 5.2, 'we will receive the world to come as well, inasmuch as he promised to raise us from the dead and . . . we will also reign with him'; see also 5.3; 8.1; 12.2), and the Jesus who died for us will return as the eschatological Judge (2.1; 6.2).

But if salvation is a divine gift and promise, it is at the same time a matter of human achievement. For whether the past divine act on our behalf will in fact become actualized in the future depends a great deal, in Polycarp's understanding, on how humans respond in the present. God will raise up believers from the dead '*if*' they 'do his will' (2.2), '*if*', that is, they 'please him in this present world' and 'prove to be citizens worthy of him' (5.2; cf. 5.3; 8.1; 10.2). But response is not just a matter of behaviour; it also entails the acceptance of certain beliefs about God and especially Jesus (cf. 7.1).

In short, Polycarp works with a synergistic understanding of salvation; salvation (especially with reference to resurrection) is for Polycarp both a gift and an achievement.[42] It is a gift because it is the result of God's will and grace as manifested in the sacrificial actions of Jesus; it is an achievement in that its attainment at the eschatological judgement requires a response of faithful obedience, of acknowledging certain facts about Jesus, of endurance under trial, of keeping the divine commandments in accordance with God's will.[43] For Polycarp, as for 1 Peter, 'faith

42.   For the language of this last phrase and much of the next sentence I am indebted to F. Young, *The Theology of the Pastoral Letters* (Cambridge: Cambridge University Press, 1994), 58.

43.   This equal emphasis on both gift and achievement stands *contra* some who think that human achievement has become more decisive than the divine gift in Polycarp's theology, an alleged development which is then seen as revealing either 'a real failure . . . to apprehend the death of Christ' and 'to grasp the meaning of grace' (T.F. Torrance, *The Doctrine of Grace in the Apostolic Fathers* (Edinburgh and London: Oliver and Boyd, 1948), 93, 96), or a serious departure from the New Testament, especially Paul, in that faith is not so much a gift and therefore a presupposition (*Voraussetzung*) of resurrection, but has instead something of the character of a work and thus is a condition (*Bedingung*) of resurrection (A. Bovon-Thurneysen, 'Ethik und Eschatologie im Philipperbrief des Polycarp von Smyrna', *ThZ* 29 (1973), 256, 247–8, 250), or evidence of the Hellenization of the Gospel (H. Lohmann, *Drohung und Verheissung: Exegetische Untersuchungen zur Eschatologie bei den Apostolichen Vätern* (Berlin and New York: de Gruyter, 1989), 194; cf. Torrance, *The Doctrine of Grace in the Apostolic Fathers*, 97) – or perhaps all three at once.

Such formulations do not adequately represent Polycarp's understanding of human achievement or obedience, for at least three reasons: (1) they pay insufficient attention to the polemical context in which he writes, (2) they give insufficient consideration to Polycarp's

validates itself in action, to the extent that faith and action are indistinguishable'.[44]

(ii) *Righteousness*[45]

Whereas Paul uses 'righteousness' (δικαιοσύνη) in a distinctive eschatological sense, there is as well a broad stream of Jewish and early Christian tradition which understands the concept more in terms of behaviour conforming to God's will. Indeed, 'the use of the concept of *righteousness* in connection with the demand for authenticating deeds' is characteristic of 'a relatively broad early Christian tradition, in which δικαιοσύνη ['righteousness'], in contrast to its theological usage in Paul, becomes a major parenetic motif'.[46]

It is with this broad stream of early Christian tradition that Polycarp aligns himself with respect to his understanding of righteousness.[47] For Polycarp, the 'righteous' person is the one who, in response to the gracious divine initiative and acts, aligns both one's beliefs and behaviours with those proclaimed about, prescribed by, and exemplified by the one through whom God has both accomplished and made the offer of salvation, namely Jesus.[48]

Righteousness is thus a richly evocative and paraenetically useful term for Polycarp, one that primarily has to do not with divine activity on behalf of humans (as in Paul), but with how humans respond to divine activity and initiative on their behalf. It is a term that brings to mind for Polycarp a broad and probably clearly defined (though in this letter not fully stated) complex of beliefs and behaviours that ought to characterize authentic Christian existence.

This understanding of righteousness means that the term also plays an

---

initial statements about grace (cf. 1.3) and the persistent indicative–imperative dialectic throughout the letter (cf. 1.3—2.3; 5.2; 8.1–2), and (3) they impose upon the discussion a false either–or dichotomy that is often deeply shaped by later theological formulations or concerns (cf. esp. Torrance, who works with a narrow neo-orthodox understanding of Paul and charges any Apostolic Father who fails to repeat that precise understanding with a failure to understand the 'true' meaning of grace).

44.   J.R. Michaels, *1 Peter*, Word Biblical Commentary 49 (Waco, Tex.: Word Books, 1988), p. lxxiv.

45.   See also Steinmetz, 'Polykarp von Smyrna', 69–75, and R. Bultmann, *Theology of the New Testament*, vol. 2 (New York: Scribner, 1955), 171–3). Meinhold, 'Polykarpos', 1685–6, offers an interpretation in terms of an anti-Marcionite polemic.

46.   K. Kertelge, 'δικαιοσύνη', *EDNT*, vol. 1, 330.

47.   Similarly Steinmetz, 'Polykarp von Smyrna', 73.

48.   In emphasizing Jesus as saviour, teacher and model, Polycarp closely parallels 1 Peter, a document he apparently knows very well, and which represents, as Michaels notes, 'the work of one who, more than the Apostle Paul, made every effort to do justice equally to the teaching, the example, and the death and resurrection of Jesus Christ': Michaels, *1 Peter*, p. lxxv.

important 'diagnostic' function for Polycarp. For him, the presence of certain beliefs and behaviours – i.e. 'righteousness' – among the Philippians is a reassuring indicator that they are indeed 'enduring' (9.1) or 'bearing fruit' (1.2) or holding 'steadfastly and unceasingly to our hope and the guarantee of our righteousness', Christ Jesus (8.1),[49] and thus have hope of being raised up by God. Conversely, the absence of either certain beliefs (e.g. among the errorists in 7.1) or behaviours (cf. for example the quotation of 1 Cor. 6.9 in 5.3) indicates, to Polycarp, at least a strong probability of receiving a negative verdict when Jesus returns as eschatological Judge. Thus the concern for Valens: his present behaviour raises questions about his future fate. Such an understanding of righteousness in terms of present behaviour cannot easily be separated from the idea of a future judgement (a theme Polycarp stresses in 2.1–2; 5.2–3; 6.2; 11.2), and here may be the key to understanding the close link in Polycarp's mind between false teaching and wrong (i.e. 'unrighteous') behaviour in general, and the 'deniers' mentioned in 7.1 and Valens in particular. In short, Valens denies by his deeds what the 'heretics' deny by their words.

(iii) *Imitation*

Closely linked to and explicable in terms of his understanding of righteousness is Polycarp's use of the theme of 'imitation'(μίμησις). Apart from a passing mention in 2.2, the references to this topic are clustered in 8.2—10.1. While both Jesus' suffering and endurance are mentioned, it is the latter that receives the primary emphasis: endurance is the virtue urged upon the Philippians, while suffering is only a possibility. But Jesus is not the only one who exemplifies endurance: Ignatius, Zosimus, Rufus, 'others from your congregation', Paul, and the 'rest of the apostles' are also brought forward as examples of those who 'exercised unlimited endurance' (9.1) and therefore are to be imitated.

Because Polycarp grounds his call for endurance upon the sacrificial death of Jesus (8.1; 9.2), and thus sharply distinguishes Jesus from the other (merely human) examples, it is probable that Polycarp here is working with 'imitation' more in the sense of *Nachfolge* ('following after' as a response) than *Nachahmung* ('imitation' as an achievement), although it is not clear that he would distinguish the two so sharply.

What unites Jesus and the other examples is that they all have been 'raised by God' (9.2) – that is, all have experienced resurrection as the outcome of their endurance, and thus Ignatius, Paul and the others can

49. This is the only instance in *Philippians* in which 'righteousness' may bear something of the Pauline sense of the term (as noted by Bultmann, *Theology of the New Testament*, vol. 2, 172).

now be said to be 'with the Lord' (9.2). Thus the goal of 'imitation' is not so much to recapitulate the Lord's suffering (though in some cases that might happen), but similarly to experience resurrection, the goal towards which he urges the Philippians.[50]

(iv) *Holy Spirit*

A striking aspect of Polycarp's letter is the complete absence of any trace or mention of the Holy Spirit. While the term 'spirit' (πνεῦμα) does occur twice in Polycarp, at 5.3 and 7.2, in both instances it apparently refers to the human spirit rather than the Holy Spirit. But a discussion of the Holy Spirit in Polycarp's letter is not merely a matter of an argument from silence, since these are allusions to pneumatological activity using other terminology. For instance, in 8.1 there is a reference to 'guarantee' or 'pledge' (ἀρραβών), which in Paul is always the Holy Spirit (2 Cor. 1.22; 5.5; Eph. 1.14; cf. Rom. 8.23), is identified by Polycarp as 'Christ Jesus'. A consequence of this substantial difference is that whereas Paul under-stands Christian existence primarily in terms of divine empowerment, Polycarp apparently views it more as a matter of human effort or achievement.[51] That is, what for Paul are 'fruits of the Spirit' have for Polycarp more the character of virtues to be pursued. The differences between these two ways of understanding the dynamic of a life of faith are not inconsequential.

6. *When Was it Written? Has It Been Tampered With?*

As noted earlier, Polycarp probably died sometime between 155 and 160 CE. Thus his lifespan provides a window of some fifty or more years for the writing of Philippians, one that encompasses, in effect, the entire first half of the second century. Where the letter is placed within this range is dependent on the question of its integrity, because it has been suggested that *Philippians* as we now know it preserves two letters, not just one.

---

50.   On resurrection as the goal of imitation, cf. J. Liébaert, *Les enseignements moraux des Pères Apostoliques* (Gembloux: Duculot, 1970), 70–3.

51.   Cf. Schoedel, *Polycarp*, 9–10; also Bultmann, *Theology of the New Testament*, vol. 2, 171. On this issue Ignatius would seem to occupy a position somewhere between Paul and Polycarp. What Schoedel says with respect to the difference between Paul and Ignatius – 'this shift of emphasis has more to do with his [i.e. Ignatius'] conception of the way in which people are empowered to live godly lives than with his view of the way in which godly living is related to the final destiny of the believer' (N.R. Schoedel, *Ignatius of Antioch*, Hermeneia (Philadelphia: Fortress Press, 1985), 30) – would appear to be even more applicable to the difference between Paul and Polycarp.

(i) *Integrity*

The uncertainty regarding the document's integrity arises out of a feature intrinsic to the letter itself: the apparent tension between two of its references to Ignatius. In 9.1 (cf. 1.1), Polycarp seems to assume that Ignatius already has been martyred, whereas in 13.2 he appears to ask for information about his fate. These references have long been understood as indicating (1) that sufficient time had passed since Ignatius' final departure for Rome for Polycarp to assume that Ignatius had, by the time of writing, already been martyred, but (2) he had not yet received a confirmatory report.[52] Thus the letter is customarily dated not long after the time of Ignatius' death.

Some scholars, however, most notably Harrison, have proposed that *Philippians* is really two letters: chaps 13—14 are a brief cover note written to accompany a copy of the letters of Ignatius which Polycarp sent to Philippi very soon after Ignatius' departure from there but before his arrival in Rome, while chaps 1—12 comprise the substance of Polycarp's response to a later 'crisis letter' from Philippi, penned several years after Ignatius' martyrdom.[53]

The wide acceptance of Harrison's partition theory in the decades following its publication says more about a climate of opinion[54] than it does about the strength of his case, which effectively rests on a single assertion: that Polycarp could not have written chap. 9 prior to learning for certain that Ignatius had indeed been martyred. As Harrison puts it,

---

52.   Cf. similarly H. Paulsen, *Die Briefe des Ignatius von Antiochia und der Brief des Polykarp von Smyrna*, 2nd edn (Tübingen: Mohr-Siebeck, 1985), 112–13.

53.   Harrison, *Polycarp's Two Epistles*, 15–16, 225, 267–8. The suggestion that chap. 14 belongs with chaps 1—12 (so J.A. Kleist, *The Didache, The Epistle of Barnabas, The Epistles and the Martyrdom of St. Polycarp, The Fragments of Papias, The Epistle to Diognetus* (Westminster, Md.: Newman and London: Longmans, Green, 1948), 71, 82, 196 n. 100; and P. Vielhauer, *Geschichte der urchristlichen Literatur: Einleitung in das Neue Testament, die Apokryphen und die Apostolischen Väter* (Berlin and New York: de Gruyter, 1975), 559 – strongly; but cf. 154) is, on the basis of transcriptional considerations alone, extremely unlikely: cf. R. Joly, *Le dossier d'Ignace d'Antioche* (Brussels: Éditions de l'Université de Bruxelles, 1979), 23–8.

54.   In some quarters, it is thought that on the traditional (early) dating of the letter, certain features of its contents (such as its use of the term εὐαγγέλιον, 'gospel') are 'too early', and Harrison's partition thesis, which posits a considerably later date for the bulk of the letter, neatly 'resolves' the perceived difficulties. Cf., for example, A. Bellinzoni: 'The question of the use of Matthew (and Luke) in Polycarp's *Letter to the Philippians* is simplified by Harrison's thesis. It is not in the earlier letter (110–117) but in the later letter (135 or later) that we find clear use of Matthew, Luke, and *1 Clement*. The results, therefore, conform to our picture of the other early Apostolic Fathers, i.e. they reflect no use of our canonical gospels': 'The Gospel of Matthew in the Second Century', *SecCent* 9 (1992), 209. But as Everding observes, 'it seems rather too convenient to transport this data out of the earliest part of the century due to source critical arguments': H.E. Everding, Jr, 'A Response to Arthur J. Bellinzoni', *SecCent* 9 (1992), 261.

'Polycarp was much too experienced and much too sensible a person to shut his eyes to the inherent uncertainty of human affairs'; 'how could Polycarp dare to write such a thing without knowing whether or not it was true? . . . Must it not have occurred to any sensible man in Polycarp's place that to use language of this kind just then might be somewhat premature, indeed that he was running a risk of making himself ridiculous?'[55]

Those less certain than Harrison of our ability to 'know' what a figure such as Polycarp would or would not do have not found his rhetorical questions compelling – especially as Harrison, in attempting to eliminate one tension, created another. He suggested that the second letter was composed some twenty years or so after the first, but reviewers quickly recognized that the mention of Ignatius in 1.1 appears to reflect a *fresh* memory of Ignatius on the part of the Philippians. This new tension was resolved largely by dating the second letter *contra* Harrison to within a year or so of the first.[56]

But this proposal does not fully solve the problem: the Philippians, one may suggest, would have been far more likely to have mentioned Ignatius in their *first* letter to Polycarp after Ignatius' visit (which, on the two-letter hypothesis, would be the request for a copy of Ignatius' letters) than in the second. Furthermore, it eliminates the key reason Harrison's proposal proved so popular, namely that it permitted a 'late dating' of what on the traditional dating were perceived to be 'problematic' portions of *Philippians*.

A grammatical irregularity in 1.1–2a[57] suggests that if *Philippians* does consist of two letters, then the first one likely comprises the prescript plus 1.1 plus chaps 13—14, while the second consists of all of 1.2 (less the initial καί, 'and') through the end of chap. 12. On this scenario, (1) the longer second letter was shorn not just of its postscript (as in Harrison's proposal) but also of its prescript and a following aorist verb which would have opened the letter proper (equivalent to, if not identical with, the 'I rejoiced' which opens 1.1); (2) the prescript and opening lines of the short cover note (i.e. the prescript and 1.1 of the extant letter) were affixed to it

---

55.   Harrison, *Polycarp's Two Epistles*, 140, 151.

56.   See, for example, the reviews of Harrison by C.J. Cadoux, *JTS* 38 (1937), 267–70, of which an essay by L.W. Barnard, reads in many respects like an extended version (L.W. Barnard, 'The Problem of St. Polycarp's Epistle to the Philippians', in L.W. Barnard, *Studies in the Apostolic Fathers and their Background* (New York: Schocken and Oxford: Blackwell, 1966), 31–9); H.-C. Puech, *RHR* 119 (1939), 96–102; and H.D. Simonin, *RSPhTh* 27 (1938), 258–60.

57.   Namely, the non-parallel use first of a participial phrase (δεκαμένοι, 'you having welcomed') and then a ὅτι ('because') clause to express Polycarp's two 'reasons for joy'. For a full discussion (and a satisfying alternative explanation) see W.R. Schoedel, 'Polycarp's Witness to Ignatius of Antioch', *VC* 41 (1987), 1–10.

instead, and (c) the remainder of the cover note (chaps 13—14) was placed where it made the most sense, that is, after rather than before the body of the second letter.

But is any partition theory necessary? The only substantive basis for the various partition theories remains Harrison's claim that chap. 9 could not have been written at the same time as chap. 13 – that is, that Polycarp could not have expressed himself as he does in chap. 9 in advance of learning for certain of the fate of his friend. At least three considerations, however, strongly suggest otherwise.

First, as Harrison himself notes, Polycarp 'knew that Ignatius had been condemned by the Roman authorities in Antioch to be killed by wild beasts in the Flavian amphitheatre . . . common sense probably told him truly that the Romans could be trusted to take care that no one robbed Ignatius of his crown'.[58] However much allowance one might wish to make for the contingencies of human events, Polycarp had no reason to think that events might turn out differently than expected. Second, the emphasis in chap. 9 is more on Ignatius' *endurance* than his death. This aspect of Ignatius' life was as true and vivid before his death as it was after. Third, the example of Ignatius himself shows how it is possible for someone simultaneously to acknowledge the element of contingency in the future yet speak of it in advance in quite certain terms. There are clear expressions of contingency in Ign. *Rom.* 1.1 ('if it is his will'; cf. 3.2) and 1.2—4.1 (he appeals to the Roman Christians not to interfere), yet in 4.2 Ignatius can say, 'I *am* [εἰμί] God's wheat, and I *am being ground* [ἀλήθομαι] by the teeth of the wild beasts.' In short, so vivid is his vision of the future that he can speak of it as already present, his own uncertainties notwithstanding.

Therefore, the document is more likely a single unified letter[59] than it is a combination of two.[60]

(ii) *Date*

Chapter 13 was probably written within a month or two following 24 August (cf. Ign. *Rom.* 10.1–3) in the year in which Ignatius was apparently martyred. For those who accept the unity of *Philippians,* determining that

58. Harrison, *The Two Epistles of Polycarp,* 152.
59. Recent 'single letter' advocates include Schoedel, *Polycarp,* 4, 29, 37–8, with Schoedel, 'Polycarp of Smyrna', 277–83; Paulsen, *Die Briefe des Ignatius von Antiochia und der Brief des Polykarp von Smyrna,* 112; Dehandschutter, 'Polykarp's Epistle to the Philippians', 276–9; P. Nautin, 'Polycarp', in A. Di Berardino (ed.), *Encyclopedia of the Early Church,* vol. 2 (New York: Oxford University Press, 1994), 701; Hartog, *Polycarp and the New Testament,* 148–69.
60. Recent 'two letter' advocates include: Barnard, 'The Problem of St. Polycarp's Epistle to the Philippians', 31–9; Meinhold, 'Polykarpos', 1683–7; J.B. Bauer, *Die Polykarpbriefe* (Göttingen: Vandenhoeck and Ruprecht, 1995), 18–19; Berding, *Polycarp and Paul,* 15–24.

year will establish the date of the letter's composition. But as is evident from Paul Foster's discussion of this question in the previous chapter, determining that year is no easy matter.[61] Efforts to identify a specific year for his arrest and/or death rest upon hypothetical reconstructions or external testimony of uncertain reliability, and internal evidence is both sparse and vague. Perhaps the most that can be said with any degree of confidence is that Ignatius probably died sometime during the first third of the second century.[62]

On Harrison's division of the letter, which includes 1.1 as part of the second letter, the apparently fresh and still-vivid memory of Ignatius presupposed by 1.1 would almost require that it be dated within a year or so of Ignatius' death. On the preferable alternative partition hypothesis discussed (but not accepted) above, which joins the prescript plus 1.1 with chaps 13—14, the second letter (basically 1.2—12.3) could have been written any time between the death of Ignatius and the death of Polycarp. The absence of any identifiably Marcionite references in chap. 7 and the mention of Ignatius in chap. 9 suggest (but certainly do not require) a time closer to Ignatius' martyrdom than to Polycarp's.

(iii) *Authenticity*

Questions about the authenticity of *Philippians* – whether it has been forged, for example, or whether there are interpolations – arise from the circumstance that it offers the earliest testimony to the existence of the Ignatian correspondence (whose collection Polycarp apparently initiated; cf. *Phil.* 13.2). This means that anyone challenging the authenticity of Ignatius' letters must also argue that *Philippians* was either forged or expanded with interpolations by whoever forged the Ignatian corpus.[63] The challenge to the authenticity of *Philippians*, in other words, is really a corollary to the challenge to the authenticity of Ignatius' letters, and therefore properly belongs to the discussion of that vexed question.[64]

---

61.   See Chapter 9, sect. 2 above.

62.   The same point is made by Schoedel, 'Polycarp of Smyrna', 347–58, and C. Munier, 'Où en est la question d'Ignace d'Antioche? Bilan d'un siècle de recherches 1870–1988', *ANRW* 2.27.1, 380, 484.

63.   For recent examples cf. R.M. Hübner, 'Thesen zur Echtheit und Datierung der sieben Briefe des Ignatius Antiochien', *ZAC* 1 (1997), 44–72, and T. Lechner, *Ignatius adversus Valentinianos? Chronologische und theologiegeschichtliche Studien zu Briefen des Ignatius von Antiochien* (Leiden: Brill, 1999); for surveys of the question consult Harrison, *The Two Epistles of Polycarp*, 27–72, and Schoedel, 'Polycarp of Smyrna', 276–85; cf. also M.J. Edwards, 'Ignatius and the Second Century: An Answer to R. Hübner', *ZAC* 2 (1998), 214–26.

64.   On this question see now Foster's remarks in Chapter 9, sect. 2 above.

7. *Conclusion*

Polycarp's *Epistle to the Philippians* offers an important glimpse into the life of two churches and the mindset of an important Christian leader in the early second century, a tumultuous time of conflict, challenge and change. His concern for order, stability and tradition (an ethos which he shares with the Pastoral Epistles) as he seeks to maintain the stability and integrity of these two congregations is motivated throughout by a theologically informed faith and hope committed to 'love for God and Christ and for our neighbour' (*Phil.* 3.3). If this one surviving letter is at all typical of the man, it is possible to appreciate why many (pagans and believers alike, according to his martyrologist) esteemed him as a faithful and distinguished teacher (cf. *M. Pol.* 19.1).

Chapter 11

THE *MARTYRDOM OF POLYCARP*

Sara Parvis

The *Martyrdom of Polycarp* is probably the most readable of the works commonly grouped under the title 'Apostolic Fathers'.[1] It has a pace unmatched by *1* or *2 Clement*, an immediacy which is lacking in, say, *Barnabas* or *Hermas*, and a narrative flow not shared even by the *Didache* or the epistles of Ignatius. It does, however, share with most of these works their problems of date, unity or otherwise of composition, and even authenticity, as well as their quality of providing vital and illuminating snapshots of early Christianity in the making.

Nevertheless, in the case of the *Martyrdom of Polycarp*, the stakes are higher. It is worth considering in some detail the problems of the dating, composition and authenticity of the work, for the following reason: it is not too strong to say that the whole notion of an unbroken doctrinal tradition accessible to us now, for those who care about such a thing, depends on what we can securely say about Polycarp. If the Apostolic Fathers are generally thought of as the bridge between New Testament times and the emergence of the great Christian writers of the latter half of the second century such as Justin Martyr and Irenaeus, it is Polycarp who holds that bridge together, since he is uniquely claimed to have spanned the whole period with his own life, knowing the apostles in his youth and Irenaeus in his old age. In the case of the other sub-apostolic works, we are lucky if we have a credible named author, a definite geographical setting, or a single plausible date. In the case of the *Martyrdom*, we have a work set in a specific time and place, about a specific individual and a specific series of events, which seems to have been written less than a year

1. Translations from the work in this chapter are my own, generally following the text of the classic edition by J.B. Lightfoot, *The Apostolic Fathers*, part 2, *Ignatius and Polycarp*, vol. 3 (London: MacMillan, 1890), 363–403. Convenient editions with facing translation may be found in the Loeb Classical Library: K. Lake (ed. and tr.), *The Apostolic Fathers*, LCL 24 and 25, 2 vols (London: William Heinemann, 1913), vol. 2, 312–45, and its successor, B.D. Ehrman (ed. and tr.), *The Apostolic Fathers*, vol. 1, LCL 24 (Cambridge, Mass.: Harvard University Press, 2002), 366–401.

after they happened. It makes an enormous difference to our knowledge of the period if it can be said to be genuine.

Polycarp's biography, of course, does not depend on the *Martyrdom*; even if the work is a pious fiction, the information Irenaeus gives us about him could still be genuine, as could Polycarp's *Epistle to the Philippians*. But rejecting the authenticity of the *Martyrdom* would make Irenaeus' information, Polycarp's letter, and indeed the Ignatian corpus, with which *Philippians* is closely connected, look considerably less secure. The *Martyrdom* squares with Irenaeus in particular so well that it could easily be accused of having been written to authenticate Irenaeus' portrait: Polycarp's age is stressed (9.3), and he is called 'an apostolic and prophetic teacher, bishop of the catholic church in Smyrna' (16.2), a designation which matches Irenaeus' theology quite closely. If the *Martyrdom* is genuine, it provides a powerful underpinning for Irenaeus' claim of some authentic knowledge of what the apostles and their successors actually taught. If it is a pious fiction whose details do not add up, the best corroborative evidence for Irenaeus' portrait of an apostolic tradition disappears. The details, therefore, matter.

1. *The Date of the Account*

The text of the *Martyrdom* itself gives us precise information about the date of Polycarp's death, and also a clear indication of the date of the composition of the work. Chapter 21, a coda to the letter of the church of Smyrna which actually tells the story, informs us,

> And the blessed Polycarp bears witness at the beginning of the month of Xanthikus, on the second day, seven days before the calends of March, on a great Sabbath, at the eighth hour. And he was arrested by Herod in the time of the High Priest Philip of Tralles, Statius Quadratus being proconsul but our Lord Jesus Christ reigning for ever – to whom be glory, honour, majesty, an eternal throne from generation to generation. Amen.

Elsewhere (18.3), the text tells us that the community intends to celebrate 'the birthday of his martyrdom', using a future tense: ἔνθα . . . ὡς δυνατὸν ἡμῖν . . . παρέξει ὁ κύριος ('there [in the unnamed burial place], as we are able, the Lord will allow' the celebration). This would seem to imply that the account is being written less than a year after Polycarp's death.

The Roman historian W.H. Waddington identified Statius Quadratus as Lucius Statius Quadratus, Roman consul *ordinarius* in 142. Waddington argued on the basis of references to Quadratus in the *Sacred Tales* of Aelius Aristides that he must have been proconsul of Asia twelve years later, in the year 154/5 (the gubernatorial year ran from May to May).[2] J.B. Lightfoot championed Waddington's date and the arguments for it in his enormously influential commentary on the *Martyrdom*.[3] On their reckoning, Polycarp's death would therefore have taken place on 23 February (the second of Xanthikus) 155, which, neatly enough, fell on a Saturday.

Both reckoned that, according to the norms of the Antonine period, Quadratus would have been due to become proconsul of Africa or Asia, the two prize Roman provincial governorships, around thirteen years after the consulship. (The emperor Claudius had specified a five-year delay between the two offices a century earlier, but a backlog always built up because of the practice of appointing suffect consuls later in the year to share the honour of the office by taking over from the two *ordinarii* who had given the year their names.) Since they thought of the thirteen years as an average delay, a gap of twelve seemed to them perfectly plausible.

The date of 155 seemed set. It seemed also to fit in with the other traditions concerning Polycarp's life. Irenaeus claims that Polycarp went to Rome in the time of Anicetus, when they discussed the date of Easter together; Anicetus' period as a church leader there (Eusebius gives him eleven years[4]) is usually dated (partly on the basis of this meeting, it must be said) from about 154 to about 165. Polycarp claims in the text (9.3) to have served the Lord eighty-six years (it is not clear whether this means from his birth or from his boyhood); Irenaeus claims (*AH* 3.3.4; Eusebius, *HE* 5.24.16) that Polycarp knew John, 'the disciple of the Lord', and was appointed Bishop of Smyrna by 'the apostles'. If Polycarp was born in the year 70 or so, he could easily have known John (who is linked by tradition to nearby Ephesus), and being apparently fairly wealthy,[5] could well have been appointed to some kind of episcopal role in the community in Smyrna while there were still 'apostles' around (whatever the word *episkopos* is taken to mean at this stage, perhaps overseer of the community's financial affairs). Since his parents had presumably been Christians too (if Polycarp was Christian from his childhood), they might well have known some of the generation in the church at Ephesus who were brought in by Paul. Polycarp could then even take Irenaeus right back to the first generation of Asian Christians.

Waddington's date therefore looks more or less plausible, not to say exciting. Unfortunately, matters are not necessarily quite so simple,

---

2. W.H. Waddington, 'Mémoire sur la chronologie de la vie du rhéteur Aelius Aristide', *Mémoires de l'Institut Impérial de France, Académie des Inscriptions et Belles Lettres* 26 (1867), 203–68.

3. Lightfoot, *Ignatius and Polycarp*, vol. 1, 646–77.

4. Eusebius, *HE* 5.24.16.

5. Polycarp withdraws to two different farms outside the city (*M. Pol.* 5.1; 6.1), which are presumably his own, because he gives orders for food and drink to be brought to those who come to arrest him (7.2).

because Eusebius of Caesarea tells us that Polycarp's martyrdom took place in the reign of Marcus Aurelius, between 161 and 180.[6] This, often coupled with the view that the Phrygian voluntary martyr mentioned in chap. 4, Quintus, must be a Montanist, has led some scholars to posit a date of 166 for the martyrdom (if the 'great Sabbath' is a Saturday),[7] 167 (if it is a Sunday),[8] or even 177 (thus linking Polycarp's death with the persecution of the martyrs of Lyon and Vienne).[9] Others, however, have pointed out that Eusebius' own date can hardly be relied on, since he also dates the martyrdom of Pionius (which took place under Decius in the mid-third century) to the same period.[10] Quintus' Phrygian origins, meanwhile, by no means necessarily constitute a reference to the 'Phrygian heresy', as what later came to be called Montanism was then known to its detractors. They could easily be a matter of mere banal historical fact.

Timothy Barnes, while agreeing with Waddington and Lightfoot that the text's own proconsular date rather than Eusebius' imperial one should be the basis of any serious attempt to pin down the year of Polycarp's death, has pointed out that there is a real difficulty with a date of 154/5 for the proconsulship of Statius Quadratus. Despite Lightfoot's talk of thirteen years between the consulship and the senior proconsulships as an 'average' gap, there are no instances at all of a consul in the Antonine period who became proconsul of Asia or Africa as few as twelve years later. Even a thirteen-year gap was in fact very rare, fourteen or fifteen being more common. The year 154/5 ought therefore to be ruled out. 155/6 remains possible, while 156/7 or 157/8 would be rather more likely in the normal course of events.[11]

Barnes raises further difficulties also. Philip of Tralles the high priest ('Philip the Asiarch' in the main body of the letter, 12.2) held that office (a state religious office of the province of Asia) on or before the year 149/50, since he is attested as Asiarch on an inscription of that year (the designation 'Asiarch' was kept after the year-long office of high priest was

---

6. Eusebius, *HE* 4.14.10—4.15.1. In Eusebius' earlier *Chronicon*, the martyrdom is assigned to 167, though the abandonment of the exact date in the *History* shows that it had been merely a guess forced by the need to enter the event under a specific year.

7. E. Griffe, 'A propos de la date du martyre de S. Polycarpe', *Bulletin de Littérature Ecclésiastique* 52 (1951), 170–7.

8. P. Brind'amour, 'La date du martyre de Saint Polycarpe (le 23 février 167)', *Analecta Bollandiana* 98 (1980), 456–62.

9. H. Gregoire, 'La véritable date du martyre de S. Polycarpe (23 février 177), et le "Corpus Polycarpianum"', *Analecta Bollandiana* 69 (1951), 1–38.

10. Eusebius, *HE* 4.15.46–7.

11. T.D. Barnes, 'A Note on Polycarp', *JTS* n.s. 18 (1967), 433–7, and 'Pre-Decian *Acta Martyrum*', *JTS* n.s. 19 (1968), 510–14.

demitted).[12] Barnes argues that he held the office no more than once.[13] It is possible that the claim in chap. 21 that Philip was high priest at the time Polycarp died is merely a false extrapolation on the basis of the title Asiarch in the text of the letter by whoever composed the coda (caused, presumably, by the irresistible pull of the Gospel parallel), but the two dates cannot otherwise be reconciled.

In the light of Barnes' rejection of 155, meanwhile, Aelius Aristides also turns from being part of the solution to being part of the problem. Aristides notes, in reminiscing about the course of his seventeen-year illness, that his friend Quadratus succeeded a certain Severus as proconsul of Asia.[14] Severus was proconsul in the tenth year of the illness, while a certain Julianus (epigraphically datable as proconsul in 144/5 or 145/6) had been proconsul in the second year of the illness (or no earlier). This would make Severus proconsul in 152/3 or 153/4; if he was succeeded by L. Statius Quadratus, this would have to be no later than 154/5, the year already ruled out as too soon after Quadratus' consulship. Aristides may be misremembering, or we may be dealing with a different Quadratus,[15] but in any case, Waddington's package no longer looks quite so neat. Barnes himself, however, it is worth taking into account, remains firmly in favour of a date in the late 150s, and sees these difficulties as no real hindrance to it.

The 'great Sabbath' (μέγα σάββατον) is a final complication: there has still never been a fully satisfactory explanation of what it actually means, or how the two terms fit together. 'Sabbaton' ought to mean Saturday, because Polycarp is said in the text to have been arrested on a Friday (ἡ παρασκευή, 'the Preparation', 7.1). Polycarp's death could have occurred on a Saturday in 156 as well as 155, it should be noted, because 156 was a leap year.[16] It has been pointed out, nonetheless, that by the fourth century, τὸ μέγα σάββατον can mean Sunday. This might allow Eusebius' date of 167 to be correct, it has been argued, though twenty-four hours would then seem to have been lost in the middle of the narrative.[17]

12.   So Barnes, 'A Note on Polycarp', 434.

13.   Barnes, 'A Note on Polycarp', 434, 437.

14.   Aelius Aristides, *Sacred Tales* 4.63–7. The work is analysed and translated in C.A. Behr, *Aelius Aristides and the Sacred Tales* (Amsterdam: Adolf M. Hakkert, 1968); for 4.63–7, see 267–8.

15.   Behr argues (speculatively) that the Quadratus of 4.63–7 is in fact not the Statius Quadratus of the *Martyrdom*, but rather C. Julius Quadratus Bassus, suffect consul in 139: *Aelius Aristides and the Sacred Tales*, 84 n. 84.

16.   On this point, see Barnes, 'Pre-Decian *Acta Martyrum*', 513–14, and the still-valuable discussion of C.H. Turner, 'The Day and Year of St. Polycarp's Martyrdom', in *Studia Biblica et Ecclesiastica*, vol. 2 (Oxford: Clarendon Press, 1890), 120–4.

17.   Brind'amour, 'La date du martyre de Saint Polycarpe', a view rejected by J. den Boeft and J. Bremmer, 'Notiunculae Martyrologicae 4', *VC* 45 (1991), 108, because of the reference to ἡ παρασκευή.

Μέγα has often been taken to indicate a major Jewish feast: Lightfoot proposed the festival of Purim,[18] because of the time of year, though there seems nothing in particular to link the term with this feast. Eduard Schwartz suggested that the occasion intended was the Sabbath preceding Passover, which the Jewish communities of Asia Minor of the time celebrated unusually early because the month of Xanthikos came earlier in the Asian calendar than in the Syrian/Macedonian one.[19] The Jewish calendrical scholar Sacha Stern has recently vigorously rejected this view.[20]

On the other hand, the games in progress suggest a pagan festival of some sort rather than a Jewish one, perhaps a local Smyrnean yearly holiday.[21] Pionius, a mid-third-century martyr of Smyrna, is said to have been martyred on Polycarp's anniversary (also designated a 'great Sabbath'), which would fit well with the picture of an annual civic celebration, presumably coinciding with the provincial governor's yearly visit to the city (and hence with the execution of the local criminals). Such a festival might reasonably attract the adjective 'great', but the day of the week would then be irrelevant, since it has no place in a civic calendar.

For some scholars, the parallel with the Gospel accounts of the death of Jesus is sufficient explanation for the term, particularly the parallel with the phrase 'For that Sabbath was a high day [μεγάλη ἡ ἡμέρα]' (John 19.31).[22] But in the Gospel accounts, Jesus dies on the day of preparation itself, not on the Sabbath; the origin of the phrase must therefore be something more than mere imitation. Perhaps, as happens several times in the *Martyrdom of Polycarp*, the author is merely fashioning a Gospel parallel by glossing with language redolent of the passion narratives some fairly mundane facts: the fact that Polycarp died on a Saturday, and the fact that there was a pagan feast in progress at the time.

When all of the above points have been fully considered, the year 156 emerges as the best date for the death of Polycarp, in my view. If the case for it is far from watertight, the alternative dates are even less satisfactory:

18. Lightfoot, *Ignatius and Polycarp*, vol. 1, 711–13.

19. E. Schwartz, *Christliche und jüdische Ostertafeln*, Abhandlungen der Königlichen Gesellschaft der Wissenschaften zu Göttingen, Philologisch-Historische Klasse, n.f., 8, 6 (Berlin: Weidmannsche Buchhaudlung, 1905). Schwartz's argument is based on a list of dates for the Jewish observance of sixteen consecutive Passovers attached to an Easter table that was submitted to the Eastern Council of Serdica in 343.

20. S. Stern, *Calendar and Community: A History of the Jewish Calendar Second Century BCE–Tenth Century CE* (Oxford: Oxford University Press, 2001), 79–80.

21. W. Rordorf, 'Zum Problem des "Grossen Sabbats" im Polykarp- und Pioniusmartyrium', in E. Dassmann and K.S. Frank (eds), *Pietas*, Jahrbuch für Antike und Christentum Ergänzungsband 8 (Münster: Aschendorff, 1980), 245–9, suggests the Roman feast of Terminalia, but that celebration, as den Boeft and Bremmer pointed out, is 'not attested outside Rome itself': 'Notiunculae Martyrologicae 4', 108.

22. Stern makes this suggestion: *Calendar and Community*, 80.

Eusebius clearly has no real information, and whatever the difficulties with the Aelius Aristides evidence and the role of Philip of Tralles, they still make far more sense in the context of the 150s than later. But as with so much that concerns the *Martyrdom of Polycarp*, though one's doubts can on the whole be satisfied on the grounds that the alternative theories are even more problematic, niggling questions remain.

2. *The Composition of the Text*

The main body of the *Martyrdom of Polycarp* purports to be a letter, now divided into twenty modern chapters, from the church of Smyrna to the church of Philomelium, recounting the death of their bishop Polycarp. This begins with a fairly standard opening ('The Assembly of God which is dwelling in Smyrna, to the Assembly of God which is dwelling in Philomelium, and to all the dwellings in every place of the holy and worldwide assembly'[23]), and finishes with a standard greeting: 'Greet all the saints. Those with us greet you, and also Evaristos, who wrote this, with his whole household.' It is followed by a coda of two chapters: chap. 21 (quoted above in full), which puts a date to Polycarp's death and ends with an Amen, and chap. 22, which also ends with an Amen, and runs as follows:

> (22.1) We pray that you are well, brethren, walking in line with the gospel word of Jesus Christ, with whom be glory to God, both Father and Holy Spirit, for the salvation of the holy elect – as the blessed Polycarp attested. May it be that we be found in his footsteps in the kingdom of Jesus Christ!
> (22.2) Gaius transcribed these things from the copy of Irenaeus, the disciple of Polycarp – and Gaius lived with Irenaeus. And I, Socrates, wrote it out in Corinth from the copy of Gaius. Grace be with you all!
> (22.3) And again I, Pionius, wrote from the aforementioned copy, after seeking it out, in accordance with the revelation of the blessed Polycarp, who manifested it to me, as I will explain in what follows. I gathered it up when it was now nearly worn out by age, that the Lord Jesus Christ might also gather me up with his elect into his heavenly kingdom – to whom be glory with the Father and the Holy Spirit for ever and ever. Amen.[24]

23. ἁγία καὶ καθολικὴ ἐκκλησία can, of course, be translated 'Holy and Catholic Church', but a non-technical translation has been preferred so as not to prejudge questions of church order at this period.

24. One of the manuscripts, Moscow 390, presents chap. 22 in quite a different form. The contents are generally the same, but there has been substantial rewriting, apparently on the basis of the biographical information Irenaeus gives about Polycarp. It is possible to argue the toss, but my view is that the Moscow recension is a secondary reworking of the text form that I have translated above.

This plethora of conclusions reminds one of two people unable to end a telephone conversation. It purports to be an authenticating tradition of its own: the chain of scribes is traced back to Irenaeus, and forward to Pionius, the third-century Smyrnean martyr with a problematic martyrdom account of his own which has a whole series of parallels to the *Martyrdom of Polycarp*. This has made more than one scholar suspicious: miraculous revelation of the whereabouts of a hidden 'ancient' manuscript is a well-known device for authenticating a newly written one, and the connection with Pionius seems a little too neat. On the other hand, the connection with Irenaeus is plausible enough: it is easy to imagine him wanting a copy of such a document if he knew of its existence, and Corinth is a likely enough place for him to have stopped off on his way to the West, allowing the unknown Gaius to take a copy of the inspirational document in his turn.

Some scholars, most notably in recent times Hans von Campenhausen, have seen this list as evidence, not merely of a number of scribes, but of a number of redactors who have all added material to an original historical core.[25] von Campenhausen noted, as others had before him, that there are a number of differences between the text cited by Eusebius of Caesarea in his *Ecclesiastical History* and the rest of the manuscript tradition of the *Martyrdom*: above all, that the Eusebian account does not contain most of the parallels with the passion narratives of the Gospels. He developed these observations into a theory of a series of redactions of the text both before and after Eusebius. Pre-Eusebian additions would include material concerning the cult of martyrs in chaps 17—18 (which von Campenhausen saw as anachronistic), the Quintus story (chap. 4), and some miraculous material (for example, the voice from heaven that tells Polycarp to 'be strong' as he enters the stadium, 9.1); post-Eusebian would be the Gospel parallels, more miraculous material (particularly the dove which emerges from Polycarp's death-wound, 16.1), and the dating in the proconsulship of Statius Quadratus, with which Eusebius' dating disagrees.

It is certainly true that the text of the *Martyrdom* given in Eusebius' *Ecclesiastical History* 4.15 does differ in a number of places from the manuscript tradition of the *Martyrdom* as it has survived elsewhere.[26]

---

25. H. von Campenhausen, *Bearbeitungen und Interpolationen des Polykarpmartyriums*, Sitzungsberichte der Heidelberger Akademie der Wissenschaften, Philosophisch-Historische Klasse, 1957, 3 (Heidelberg: Winter, 1957), reprinted in H. von Campenhausen, *Aus der Frühzeit des Christentums: Studien zur Kirchengeschichte des ersten und zweiten Jahrhunderts* (Tübingen: Mohr-Siebeck, 1963), 253–301 (citations in this chapter from the latter).

26. The two versions are printed side by side with the divergences underlined in G. Buschmann, *Das Martyrium des Polykarp*, KAV 6 (Göttingen: Vandenhoeck and Ruprecht, 1998), 19–34 (following Dehandschutter). There is a good summary of the manuscript tradition in B. Dehandschutter, 'The Martyrium Polycarpi: A Century of Research', *ANRW* 2.27.1, 486–7. There are seven manuscripts in all. Five were known from the time of

Nonetheless, the most important of these differences can be accounted for by the fact that Eusebius is clearly summarizing the first section (chaps 1—7) rather than giving it word for word, in order to concentrate on the martyrdom itself, which is what really interests him. The minor differences in the second half (8.1—19.1) are, as various scholars including Lightfoot have pointed out, not greater than those generally found in texts cited by Eusebius. There are few significant differences from the section which Eusebius purports to be quoting verbatim (κατὰ λέξιν) rather than summarizing: his omission, from *M.Pol.* 15.2, of the comparison of Polycarp's body to baking bread, in favour of a concentration on the alternative comparison with gold and silver being refined in the furnace; and the ömission from 16.1 of the dove which was said to have come out of Polycarp's body after it was stabbed by a professional death-blow dealer (κομφέκτωρ).[27] These details are, surely, more likely to have been present in Eusebius' exemplar and censored by him on grounds of implausibility than to have been the only significant additions to this section (nearly half the work) by a putative post-Eusebian redactor. A further slight change in the same verse makes this even more likely: the weapon used to dispatch Polycarp is a ξιφίδιον (dagger) in the non-Eusebian tradition, but in Eusebius' account becomes a ξίφος (sword). It is easy to imagine Eusebius changing the first to the second in the interests of plausibility (though both demand that the fire be pretty definitively dying out at this stage, to allow the dispatcher to approach); it is very difficult to imagine a rationale for a post-Eusebian change in the other direction.

It is also true, however, that the text itself does come across as dislocated at certain points. von Campenhausen, indeed, might be accused of not going far enough: Conzelmann's still more radical account addresses these dislocations rather better.[28] As he points out, Polycarp's arrest, interrogation and execution are described in great detail, but the story of the others who were martyred at the same time is told briefly and allusively, with no discussion of how they were taken, and little of their individual deaths. Polycarp is said to be the twelfth martyr in Smyrna

---

Lightfoot; a sixth (in Istanbul) was added in the early twentieth century; and a seventh was described and collated by B. Dehandschutter, 'A "New" Text of the Martyrdom of Polycarp', *Ephemerides Theologicae Lovanienses* 66 (1990), 391–4. All are collections containing various readings for saints' days in February, and all belong to the same family (labelled g), except Moscow 390 (M), noted above, which differs significantly in having (among other things) a longer final coda.

27. On the κομφέκτωρ (professional dispatcher of beasts), see Lightfoot, *Ignatius and Polycarp*, vol. 3, 390.

28. H. Conzelmann, *Bermerkungen zum Martyrium Polycarps*, Nachrichten der Akademie der Wissenschaften in Göttingen, Philologisch-Historische Klasse, 1978, 2 (Göttingen: Vandenhoeck and Ruprecht, 1978).

together with those from Philadelphia (19.1), which leads us to expect the story of all twelve, but we only learn the name of one other, the 'most noble Germanicus', who encourages those who are facing the beasts with him (3.1). The account describes in general terms the cruel tortures the (unnamed) others underwent, but a narrative is only really established as Germanicus pulls a beast violently towards him to hasten his death, and the crowd calls for Polycarp. The odd paragraph concerning the Phrygian Quintus is then introduced (chap. 4), interrupting the flow, describing how he first forced himself and others to come forward, and then was persuaded to sacrifice. A brief moral is added ('It is because of this, brothers, that we do not praise those who hand themselves over'), and then the narrative returns to the call for Polycarp's death, recounting Polycarp's hearing of it, his withdrawal on the advice of friends, and his pursuit and capture by the city authorities.

It is therefore easy to wonder about this section of the narrative in particular – to be tempted to see the Phrygian story as a later interpolation, or to imagine that there was originally more to the tale of Germanicus and the others, or that the style of the whole was originally as allusive and undetailed as this part of it, and was worked over at a later date. But von Campenhausen's theory well demonstrates the major problem with most 'multiple redactor' theories: assigning a plausible motive to the various putative redactors, especially when there are a number of these. Why should this text, in particular, have been worked over so many times over the space of a mere couple of centuries, when there is no obvious need to bring it up to date? Why suddenly add in a reference to a heavenly voice which addresses Polycarp, or decide out of nowhere to have Polycarp placed on a donkey (and this before the other Gospel parallels are added)? It is not as though we are dealing with oral formulaic poetry.

In the case of Conzelmann's more thoroughgoing proposals, perhaps more plausible in themselves than von Campenhausen's because they do not begin from the desire to excise certain passages for theological reasons, but rather from the observation of some oddities in the narrative structure, we should still seek alternative explanations before accepting a radical dismantling of the text. There may well be other plausible ways of accounting for the interest in Polycarp and the glossing over of the other martyrs: perhaps the narrator did not know the other people involved, or did not like some of them, or perhaps the details of their lives, arrests or deaths included uncomfortable or unedifying matters which the narrator did not wish to dwell on (there is a dark allusion to 'all the things which had happened before' Polycarp's death (1.1), as though the addressees are likely to know what these were). At the very least, it appears from the narrative that the whole episode of persecution has been precipitated by some acts of voluntary martyrdom; it is not surprising that the narrator should want to refrain from direct praise of those involved, when their actions pose a danger to the whole community (cf. 1.2), or that the narrative should seem to skirt rather awkwardly around the subject.

As the trend for source criticism and for dismembering texts has receded, so has acceptance of von Campenhausen's analysis, once very influential: recent studies have, on the whole, preferred to see the work as a unity.[29] One serious problem with von Campenhausen's theory is that the omissions with textual support from Eusebius – the Gospel parallels and the presence of Christ by the side of the martyrs – are precisely those which are least theologically problematic in a second-century context. Eusebius, in other words, gives us no real warrant to begin to take the text apart. von Campenhausen's other proposals must stand or fall on their own merits, which may not look particularly strong to those who believe voluntary martyrdom and the cult of the martyrs to be perfectly plausible in a mid-second-century context.[30]

von Campenhausen's theory, in other words, may appeal to one's suspicions about the text, but it does not prove what it sets out to prove, and it is hard to see how any similar theory could do so either, rather than seeming simply arbitrary. Meanwhile, a more wholesale theory of the *Martyrdom* as a composite text, such as Conzelmann's, ends up paring off almost the whole account and leaving nothing in the middle; it becomes for practical purposes a theory of inauthenticity rather than multi-layered composition. The suspicions caused by the scribal chain of chap. 22 may remain, but without a more sophisticated mechanism for identifying the work of redactors than has so far been proposed, it seems to make more sense to concentrate one's enquiries on the authenticity of the text as a whole, rather than to peel off putative editorial layers. After all, if enough of it is impugned, we have more or less lost the text as a witness to the sub-apostolic period in any case.

3. *Authenticity*

The question of the authenticity of the *Martyrdom* has been very much intertwined with the questions of the date and integrity of the text discussed above. If these can be successfully challenged, the account cannot be trusted. But there are also a number of other reasons to wonder

---

29.   On this drift away from complex source theories for the *Martyrdom*, see Buschmann, *Das Martyrium des Polykarp*, 37–8, and B. Dehandschutter, 'The New Testament and the *Martyrdom of Polycarp*', in A.P. Gregory and C.M. Tuckett (eds), *Trajectories through the New Testament and the Apostolic Fathers* (Oxford: Oxford University Press, 2005), 398–9.

30.   Voluntary martyrdom is clearly attested in Justin's *Second Apology* in around 155 (*2 Apology* 2.20), and the cult of the martyrs probably by implication in Eusebius' account of the martyrs of Lyon and Vienne in *c.* 177 (*HE* 5.1.57–63).

about the veracity of the text, and some of them are difficult to explain away.

Traditionally, as has been touched on above, the most obvious reason for scepticism about the work's authenticity has been considered to be the number of its parallels with the Gospels in general, and with the passion of Christ in particular.[31] Polycarp withdraws with some friends, and spends time in prayer (5.1). He knows and predicts that he is going to be captured, and how he is going to die (5.2). The eirenarch ('peace chief', in charge of city peacekeeping) is called Herod (6.2), and his father is also involved in Polycarp's arrest (8.2). Those arresting Polycarp go armed with weapons, as against a robber. They come for him in the evening, and he could have escaped but does not (7.1). Polycarp is brought back to Smyrna on a donkey (8.1). He has a dialogue with the Roman governor, who also has one eye on the crowd (9.2—12.1). The crowd call for his death (12.2–3). 'The Jews' are involved in his death (13.1). His followers try to get his body (17.1). None of these things is actually implausible in itself, however: 'Herod' is a perfectly plausible name for an aristocratic Jew (Smyrna had long had a large and distinguished Jewish community), or even for a good pagan;[32] the association of Christians with donkeys for satirical purposes is well documented;[33] and in this period it would hardly be sensible to attempt an arrest of someone on his own property without weapons. Many of the parallels are in fact less close than one might expect if they were invented: the claim that Polycarp was 'betrayed by those of his own household' (6.1) merely because one of his slaves gave away his whereabouts under torture is only a parallel with Judas in interpretation, not really in fact.[34] The narrator makes every possible connection with the Gospels, certainly, but that does not prove that none of these things happened.

Then there are the miraculous occurrences. As already noted, Polycarp predicts his own death (5.2). A voice comes 'from heaven' urging Polycarp to 'Be strong and be a man!' (9.1). The fire does not consume him, but billows out like a sail, surrounding him like a wall. His body looks like baking bread, and smells like sweet perfume (15.2). When his body is stabbed, there comes out a dove and a great quantity of blood which extinguishes the fire (16.1). Again, though, none of these things (even the last, if one leaves room for interpretation) is inherently implausible. His

---

31. The debate is summarized in Dehandschutter, 'The Martyrium Polycarpi', 503–7.

32. An example is Polycarp's contemporary, the fabulously wealthy Herodes Atticus, an Athenian and a Roman consul.

33. See, for example, the well-known graffito of a crucified man with an ass's head from the Palatine in Rome, reproduced in G.F. Snyder, *Ante-Pacem: Archaeological Evidence of Church Life before Constantine*, revd edn (Macon, Ga.: Mercer University Press, 2003), 60, and discussed on 61–2.

34. Lightfoot makes this point well: *Ignatius and Polycarp*, vol. 1, 610–14.

arrest was not unexpected, fire was a common means of execution, and it is not unheard of for people to predict their own deaths in times of war or persecution. The fact that 'no one saw the one who had spoken' to Polycarp hardly rules out a human origin for the voice. Executions in which the victim is actually baked or roasted rather than being burned are well documented.[35] One would have to know how the fire was constructed (it was built in haste for an ad hoc execution) to ascertain fully the likelihood of its behaving as described, but given that the incident is supposed to have taken place in a coastal city on a late afternoon in February in the middle of a U-shaped stadium which was open at the west (seaward) end (though partially protected by the hill of Pagos), the strong and swirling wind that would be needed to produce the effect depicted seems plausible enough.[36] The fire must have been nearly out already by the time Polycarp was stabbed by the κομφέκτωρ, or it would not have been safe for him to approach. Even the dove need be no more than a bird flying up from the direction of the fire, assuming the witnesses would have been some distance from the events and unable to ascertain where it had actually come from (or perhaps a Christian onlooker bought one while the wood-collecting was going on and brought it to release symbolically at the appropriate moment).[37]

The most difficult part of the narrative to explain is not in fact any of the miraculous details, but the Roman legal proceedings. It is frankly astonishing to find Polycarp apparently on trial for his life before one of the leading magistrates of the empire on a public holiday in the middle of a sports stadium, with no use of the tribunal, no formal accusation, and, strangest of all, no sentence.[38]

Polycarp would have expected to be tried, as Christians generally were, under *cognitio extra ordinem* – the Roman governor's power to hear any

35.   Patrick Hamilton died in St Andrews in 1528 in such a manner. It may be considered the mark of a botched execution, where the fire has not been constructed properly, quite likely in the present instance because it seems not to have been planned. One may hope that Polycarp died of suffocation relatively quickly.

36.   On the archaeology of the Smyrna stadium, see Louis Robert, *Le Martyre de Pionios, prêtre de Smyrne*, ed. G.W. Bowersock and C.P. Jones (Washington, DC: Dumbarton Oaks Research Library and Collection, 1994), 114–15.

37.   Lightfoot offers the splendid parallel of the vulture which the satirist Lucian of Samosata has rise from the flames as Peregrinus commits suicide at the Olympic Games (*Peregrinus* 39), as well as the eagle which was released from the funeral pyre of dead emperors (*Ignatius and Polycarp*, vol. 3, 390–1).

38.   This point is made surprisingly seldom in discussions of the *Martyrdom*, though it is raised by Gary Bisbee in his study of pre-Decian martyr *acta*: 'The setting that is given for Polycarp's trial should give us pause, for it is not a magistrate's tribunal or any other such municipal setting . . . . The stadium is an improbable place for a trial': G.A. Bisbee, *Pre-Decian Acts of Martyrs and Commentarii*, Harvard Dissertations in Religion 22 (Philadephia: Fortress Press, 1988), 121–2. Cadoux also raises the point: 'From the point of view of the

local case brought before him which he thought fit, and give sentence on it.[39] The proconsul had power to execute justice, including capital punishment, to a considerable extent as he pleased, though with some reference to whether or not the accused was a Roman citizen. Nonetheless, although the judicial decisions of a governor might seem arbitrary (he could dismiss the case or hear evidence concerning it for as long as he wanted, and then release the accused or sentence him or her to hard labour, corporal punishment or death, as seemed good to him at the time), the forms were not. The forms used in all other trials in authentic martyr *acta* (and those which want to sound authentic) are clearly recognizable, either expressly or by implication. The Christians are brought by their accusers before the tribunal (βῆμα), the judgement seat; the governor may consult with his *consilium*, and the sentence (κρίσις) is given formally by him, often being read out from a tablet. At least one of these features (accusers, judgement seat, or sentence) appears in all four Gospel accounts of the trial of Jesus.[40]

In Polycarp's case, however, all of these are lacking. He is arrested in the middle of a public holiday, and apparently taken directly to the governor as the latter attends the games, with no intervening hearing in a suitable place, such as the forum, or the governor's palace. Nonetheless, the proconsul does go through some of the motions of a trial analogous to that faced by other Christians of the period: he asks Polycarp his name, and then proceeds with the stock lines of magistrates at Christian trials: 'Respect your age', 'Curse Christ', 'Swear by the genius of Caesar' (9.2–3). When Polycarp refuses, he apparently simply turns him over to the crowd, and allows them to order his execution as they see fit. Can we really accept these proceedings as historical?

It is worth looking at the account in some detail, because the narrative gives us many little touches which address the strangeness of the proceedings in an interesting way. We are invited to view Statius Quadratus as acting inappropriately, I would argue, with disdain for the traditions of Roman justice, Roman piety and Roman ethics. Quadratus is shown up as being neither a pious philosopher nor a just ruler – very much the terms which concern Justin Martyr in writing his *Apologies* at more or less the same time.

Polycarp is brought forward (within speaking distance of the governor, 9.2). The proconsul proceeds to what purports to be a trial, which must be

customary forms of proconsular justice, the proceedings were unusual': C.J. Cadoux, *Ancient Smyrna: A History of the City from the Earliest Times to 324 A.D.* (Oxford: Basil Blackwell, 1938), 359.

39. On *cognitio extra ordinem*, see A.N. Sherwin-White, *Roman Society and Roman Law in the New Testament* (Oxford: Clarendon Press, 1963), 17–18.

40. Mark 15.3–4 (accusers); Matt. 27.12, 19 (accusers, βῆμα); Luke 23.24 (κρίσις); John 19.13 (βῆμα).

a mark of contempt in the context, given the setting. The narrative presents Polycarp throughout as responding to the proconsul's games-playing with dignity and gentlemanly openness (παρρησία, 10.1).

Polycarp's first act, once he has answered to his name, is to look round 'with dignity in his face' at all the crowd of 'lawless' Gentiles in the stadium, and gesture towards them (ἐπισείσας) with his hand (9.2). The meaning of this gesture is not spelled out – it is connected in the narrative with the governor's demand that Polycarp say 'Away with the atheists,' and is usually taken as a rather insolent indication that he means to say 'Away with the atheists' to the crowd. But, though he does indeed say the words after this gesture, he says them immediately after groaning and looking up to heaven – so his reply is not an insolent but an ambiguous one (as his third reply, μετὰ παρρησίας ἄκουε (10.1), 'hear it openly', makes clear). The gesture is, in fact, as much to the stadium as to the crowd, and may be taken to mean 'Do you really intend to try me *here*?'

The governor presses on, saying 'Swear, and I release you; curse Christ.' Polycarp gives another dignified but still slightly covert answer, the famous 'For eighty-six years I have served him, and he has done me no injustice [ἀδικεῖν]; how can I slander my King who has preserved me?' (9.3). The mention of injustice is one of a series of such subtle references to the questionable nature of the governor's procedure in this section.

The governor presses Polycarp again to swear by the genius of Caesar, and this time Polycarp changes tack: he is explicit in his reply, openly criticizing the governor for his actions and making his own position plain: 'If you emptily think [κενοδοξεῖς] that I should swear by the genius of Caesar, as you say, and are pretending that you do not know who I am, hear it with boldness: I am a Christian. And if you want to learn the rationale [λόγος] of Christianity, fix a day and hear [the case]' (10.1). Polycarp here essentially accuses the proconsul of using legal formulae in an empty manner, asking Polycarp's name and telling him to swear when he is not in a suitable setting for a trial. Polycarp challenges the governor's cynical behaviour by making the clear confession appropriate to a trial and asking the governor in return to follow the normal procedure of naming a day and hearing the case properly.[41] But the proconsul, continuing his contemptuous treatment, tells Polycarp instead to persuade the people (δῆμος, but in the shape of the stadium crowd). It is unlikely that he fears a riot – his unusual action in hearing the case outside a formal setting is more likely to cause one than to prevent one. Polycarp continues his dignified practice of recalling the governor to his own

41. A Roman governor would arrange in advance to hear a case in a given city on the assize circuit during his formal assize sessions there, sometimes on a given day, sometimes not. See the discussion in G.P. Burton, 'Proconsuls, Assizes and the Administration of Justice under the Empire', *Journal of Roman Studies* 65 (1975), 101.

position: 'You I would have held worthy of an account, for we have been taught to allot honour which is proper and does not harm us to rulers and authorities appointed by God. But these I do not hold as fitting for a defence to be made to them' (10.2).[42] Polycarp is very clear what constitutes a proper authority and what does not; he is presented as being more on the side of Roman justice than the proconsul is.

The governor seems to have in mind a sadistic game of making Polycarp plead with the crowd. When Polycarp refuses to play, he begins to threaten him, first with wild beasts, then with fire. Polycarp, in his reply, implicitly accuses the proconsul of being a bad philosopher and of being impious (and hence a bad representative of the emperor Antoninus Pius and his philosopher sons).[43] He first invokes a philosophical commonplace with a sting in the tale: 'Change of mind from better to worse is not a possible change for us, but it is good to make a change from harsh proceedings to just ones [ἀπὸ τῶν χαλεπῶν ἐπὶ τὰ δίκαια]' (11.1).[44] He then brings out the stock Christian answer to the threat of fire ('You threaten a fire that burns for an hour and then is quickly quenched'), but adds, 'you do not know the fire of the coming judgement and eternal punishment which awaits the impious [τοῖς ἀσεβέσι]'. The sentiments are close to those of Justin Martyr. Polycarp, having made his point, then cuts the proceedings off: 'But why are you delaying? Do what you want to' (11.2).

In normal circumstances, Polycarp's bold speeches to such a prestigious figure might be dismissed as simple invention – a normal technique for speeches in any ancient narrative, historical or otherwise. They may well be such in any case: the narrative says that Polycarp said 'these and many other sayings' (12.1), and attributes to the proconsul 'the other things which follow, as they are accustomed to say' (9.2). But if we accept that the proconsul was acting against normal custom, and was enjoying himself playing with Polycarp for the crowd's benefit, then some response such as Polycarp's begins to sound plausible.

What the narrative is keen above all to stress is that Polycarp kept his dignity and the governor lost his. Polycarp's 'face was filled with grace' and did not fall at the things said to him, whereas the proconsul was 'beside himself' (12.1). This may well be an exaggeration, but if we accept that Statius Quadratus did hold a trial in such undignified circumstances

42. This passage is often taken as demonstrating a desire on the proconsul's part to give Polycarp a chance (cf. e.g. Lightfoot, who is agnostic on the point: *Ignatius and Polycarp*, vol. 3, 381). Polycarp might then be thought to be merely stubborn in passing up the opportunity. But it is the proconsul himself who has made the decision to hear the case then and there in the stadium, instead of putting it off until a regular assize session, which he could easily have done. In making this decision his intention cannot be benign.

43. For this theme, see Justin, *1 Apology* 1; *2 Apology* 2.16 and 15.5.

44. Cf. Plato, *Republic*, 381b–c (2, 20).

for the benefit of the stadium crowds, he did indeed compromise to some degree his standing as the representative of justice and good order.

The course of the execution itself is not easy to reconstruct. No sentence is pronounced on Polycarp,[45] and it is very difficult to work out who actually gives the order for him to be executed. The proconsul sends his herald into the middle of the stadium to proclaim three times 'Polycarp has confessed that he is a Christian!' (or perhaps 'Polycarp has confessed three times that he is a Christian!'[46]) (12.1). The crowd then ask Philip the Asiarch (who seems to be in charge of at least the mock-hunting section of the games) to set a lion on Polycarp, but he refuses on the grounds that it is not permissible (ἐξόν), since he has now completed the hunting (12.2). This is a very interesting comment. On the one hand, it may signify that he has now fulfilled his expensive duty of animal provision and has no intention of spending any more money unnecessarily. On the other, he may be signalling a certain disapproval of the casual attitude to legal form shown by the proconsul, and washing his hands of the affair. He may even be seeking to draw a line under the quasi-trial (since no actual sentence has been passed) by interpreting the crowd's request, not as a demand to execute Polycarp as a criminal, but as one to enlist him as a professional beast-fighter.[47] Either way, his mention of impermissibility may well be a tacit rebuke to the proconsul, who has already threatened Polycarp both with wild beasts and with execution by fire.

---

45.   The giving of sentence was, in fact, the most carefully prescribed and closely defined part of *cognitio* procedure, and a sentence could be invalidated if it was not given properly: see T. Mommsen, *Le droit pénal romain*, vol. 2, tr. J. Duquesne, Manuel des antiquités romaines 18 (Paris: Albert Fontemoing, 1902), 128–30, with 30 n. 5.

46.   The Greek can be read either way. For a discussion, see J. den Boeft and J. Bremmer, 'Notiunculae Martyrologicae III: Some Observations on the Martyria of Polycarp and Pionius', *Ephemerides Theologicae Lovanienses* 39 (1985), 111–13.

47.   The word for 'hunt' is κυνηγεσία = Latin *venatio*. In the arena, exotic and/or dangerous species would be pitted against (free or slave) *bestiarii* ('beast-fighters'), made to fight each other, or used to execute criminals who had been condemned *ad bestias*. κυνηγεσία could be used in a wider sense of any of these activities: see the discussion in the classic work of Louis Robert, *Les gladiateurs dans l'Orient grec* (Paris: Edouard Champion, 1940), 310–12. But normally the various forms of hunt were separated from the execution of the condemned, though *bestiarii* might feature in both parts of the programme – in the former as protagonists, in the latter as stagehands, as it were, managing the animals. Reliefs and mosaics sometimes show scenes of armed *bestiarii* fighting beasts and scenes of criminals being devoured by them in the same panel (an example is the gruesome border of a floor mosaic from the villa of Dar Buc Amméra in Tunisia, reproduced in K.W. Coleman, 'Fatal Charades: Roman Executions Staged as Mythological Enactments', *Journal of Roman Studies* 80 (1990), 55, plate II), but proximity in representation does not necessarily imply simultaneity of occurrence. Criminals were sometimes sentenced to serve as *bestiarii* (see Justinian's *Digest* 48.19.11), but that was not – directly – a sentence of death. So Philip may be saying both that his part of the proceedings is over and that executions are not his responsibility anyway. It is noticeable that he does *not* say that there are no lions left.

What happens next is not very clear (the narrative claims, with a ring of authenticity, that it all happened very quickly). The crowd cry out that Philip should have Polycarp burned (12.3): the narrator uses the phrase ἔδοξεν αὐτοῖς (it seemed good to them), surely an ironic reference to the usual formula for giving a legal decision.[48] The narrative does not tell us how Philip responded, or how the proconsul reacted, but it is not unlikely that Philip said there was no wood, because the next thing that happens is that the crowd go off and bring wood from nearby stockpiles in (their own?) bathhouses and workshops (13.1), presumably passing them down to the men who have been orchestrating the games. Someone must have given the nod for the pyre to be built and Polycarp to be placed on it, whether Philip or the proconsul or Herod the eirenarch, though the authority by which it was done was of course ultimately the proconsul's, the only official present with the right to execute. The narrative speaks only of 'they' and 'the men of the fire' who were going to nail him but desisted at his request (13.3), who gave him time to pray (14), and who finally lit the fire (15.1).

At length 'the lawless ones', seeing that the fire was not going to consume his body, 'commanded' (ἐκέλευσαν) a *confector* to go up to him and stick a dagger into him (16.1; exactly whose authority is behind this is once again unclear). After this action, administrative practice more or less returns to normal. It is the pronconsul who has the right to release the body for burial or not; Herod's father Niketas persuades him not to hand it over (17.2), so 'the centurion' (under the proconsul's command, and mentioned for the first time) takes the body and burns it on a pyre, after which the Christians are able to collect and remove the bones, 'more refined than gold', and preserve them (18.2).

So the text itself does address, up to a point, the strangeness of the legal proceedings it describes. They are subtly presented, both by Polycarp and by the narrator, as out of step with normal Roman legal practice, but within a system which, from a Christian point of view, is fairly arbitrary anyway. Paradoxically, their strangeness probably makes them more likely to be historically accurate. Polycarp's trial with no sentence in a stadium on a public holiday could only have been invented for one of three reasons: out of ignorance of Roman judicial practice, out of lack of interest in it, or out of a desire to characterize the Roman authorities as arbitrary and incompetent. Since Eusebius' *Ecclesiastical History* is the *terminus ante quem* for the work, its date of composition must be a time when normal Roman capital trial procedure is all too well known to

48. The argument has sometimes been put forward that in the second century acclamations of the δῆμος of the cities of Asia Minor had some sort of juridical force; for a convincing critique, see S. Ronchey, *Indagine sul Martirio di san Policarpo*, Nuovi Studi Storici 6 (Rome: Istituto Storico Italiano per il Medio Evo, 1990), 133–45.

Christians. A work of fiction as fantastical as the late-second-century *Acts of Paul and Thecla*, in which Thecla is saved from her execution pyre by a timely shower of hail, from wild beasts by perfume, and from man-eating seals by an opportune flash of lighting, still takes the trouble to include the details of a proper trial, including the βῆμα, the *consilium*, and the κρίσις (*Acts of Paul and Thecla* 20, 21, 27). And it seems odd that a work so keen to follow the Gospels in other matters does not follow them in this. Yet on the other hand, not enough is made of the governor's departure from normal practice to argue that the piece is a deliberate crude attack on Roman arbitrariness. And ultimately, there was nothing to stop the proconsul of Asia acting in this way, especially with a group such as the Christians, who were not in a position to seek redress.

Some final points might be made in favour of authenticity. There are, despite the difficulties with the proconsul's actions, some persuasive touches in this narrative. Polycarp's death ends the persecution (1.1): this would make sense if the proconsul came to recognize after the event that his actions had not been conducive to respect for law and order. Polycarp's plea, in answer to the demand to curse Christ, 'For eighty-six years I have served him, and he has done me no injustice: how can I blaspheme my King who saved me?', does sound like something he might actually have said (perhaps in discussion beforehand). When Polycarp undresses for the fire, he has trouble, at his age, taking his shoes off, because members of the community always used to fight over the privilege of doing it for him (13.2). The over-theologizing of Polycarp's death, concentrating on his noble mien, his appearance as of baking bread and the sweet smell as of incense, is characteristic of the usual contemporary Christian reluctance simply to report the horrors of persecution without some formula which presents the pain as not entirely real, not entirely there, because of God's grace or the presence of Christ: the same can be found in the account of the martyrs of Lyons, the *Martyrdom of Pionius* and the various accounts given by Eusebius of Caesarea. The striking blend of horror and admiration with which Polycarp's end is watched is perhaps the strongest argument for the work's authenticity.

The theology of the work is also persuasive as coming from the middle of the second century. Polycarp is described as a bishop, and is very keen on catholicity, but the narrative itself is much more interested in him as a true disciple of Christ than as a church leader. Non-Christians, who would later be called 'Greeks' or 'those outside', are here described as 'the nations' (τὰ ἔθνη, 9.2; 12.2; 19.1), the usual Jewish term for non-Jews. The Christian community is still in something of a ghetto: the code-words of Roman education and philosophy, which Justin is bandying about in Rome so enthusiastically at this time, are largely absent here. The crowd, both pagans and Jews, are still entirely hostile. Nonetheless, Polycarp is well enough known in Smyrna as a church leader to be shouted for by name; and though the greatest response the narrator can envisage from the people to his witness is astonishment or wonder, not sympathy or real interest, the narrative ends with Polycarp being talked about in every place, 'even by the nations' (19.1).

4. *Conclusion*

The date, unity and authenticity of the *Martyrdom of Polycarp* continue to be argued over and puzzled over by scholars. To a considerable extent, this reflects the interest of the piece, and the preciousness of the glimpse it offers us of the mid-second-century Asian church. We find in it a frail old man, faithful unto death, accepting a cruel and humiliating public execution rather than deny 'my King who saved me'. Too edifying for some, perhaps, and too good to be true for others. But ultimately, the *Martyrdom of Polycarp* is most interesting if it is true, if it is the authentic record of how someone in the church of Smyrna made sense of Polycarp's death. For if we look behind the text, if we read between the lines, we can see a community which is all too human: where some step forward in bravado and catapult others into the centre of a horrific and deadly public entertainment; where the community can remember some members with loving pride and brush aside even the names of others; where Christians and Jews regard one another with bitter hatred; where having property and slaves is all part of Polycarp's holy persona. At the same time, we can be impressed, perhaps, by Polycarp's care for little and great, by his dignity in the face of a system carefully designed to strip dignity entirely away, by the community's enormous respect for him, by the narrator's concern for the terrible sufferings of the other martyrs, and distress that they should have been exposed out of some people's bravado, by the determination of the community to carry on, as well as by the narrator's obvious love of and knowledge of the Gospels.

But there is, ultimately, no better place for the *Martyrdom of Polycarp* than the mid-150s, as I have tried to show. Philip of Tralles and Statius Quadratus fit nowhere else; the Justin parallels fit nowhere better; the ghetto mentality fits nowhere later so well. The Gospel parallels seem too forced to be invented; the proconsul's actions seem too unusual for polemic. The level of narrative artistry concerning such a recent atrocity may give us pause, but it is an effective means of distancing the narrator from the horror of what is being described.

In addition, none of the alternative theories really work. Composite narrative theories are unnecessary (since Eusebius' omissions are not difficult to explain away) and often arbitrary, or else so far-reaching as to be virtually arguments for inauthenticity. But arguments for inauthenticity stumble over this one fact above all: there is nothing in the text that cannot belong to the mid-second century.

When these two conclusions, positive and negative, are put together, they must outweigh whatever suspicions remain. *The Martyrdom of Polycarp* is in some ways a strange text, strangely distanced from its subject and strangely manicured. It shares its strangeness with many of the other writings described by the term 'Apostolic Fathers'. But it simply does not fit anywhere else than where it is.

Chapter 12

THE *EPISTLE TO DIOGNETUS*

Paul Foster

No text and no context. These circumstances confront the investigator of
the document known as the *Epistle to Diognetus*. The single medieval copy
of the manuscript that preserved the text was destroyed by fire in 1870,
and the contents of that text gave no firm indications about where or
when it was written. Moreover, its placement among the admittedly
arbitrary corpus known as the Apostolic Fathers is somewhat dubious.
This situation, however, is not quite as bleak as it may sound, since a
number of transcriptions of the manuscript had been made prior to its
loss, and while the context for its composition remains a contested issue,
generic comparisons may cast some light on both the purpose and origin
of the document.

1. *The Text*

The text that has become known as the *Epistle to Diognetus* is not referred
to in any of the extant patristic writings, and only became known through
a single manuscript, the history of which can perhaps be traced back to
the fifteenth century. Marrou, in his commentary on *Diognetus*, describes
the discovery of the manuscript in Constantinople around 1436 by a
young Latin cleric, Thomas d'Arezzo, in a fishmonger's shop, among a
pile of wrapping papers.[1] According to this story, d'Arezzo purchased the
manuscript at little cost, then before he set out on a mission to the
Muslims the codex was passed on to the future cardinal Jean Stojkovic de
Raguse. The document remained in Stojkovic's possession until his death
in 1443, when his library was left to the Dominicans and Carthusians in
the town of Basle. Although some elements of this reconstructed history
are speculative, it is based on the personal writings of Stojkovic (known

---

1. H.I. Marrou, *A Diognète: Introduction, édition critique, traduction et commentaire*
(Paris: Éditions du Cerf, 1951), 6.

by that stage as Cardinal Giovanni da Ragusa).[2] But it is not until the beginning of the sixteenth century that it becomes possible to speak with certainty about the history of the manuscript. Within the codex, at the rear of the volume, there was a note in Johannes Reuchlin's (d. 1522) hand stating 'that the MS. had been in his custody and that he had bought it from the Carthusian brotherhood in his native town'.[3]

During the last quarter of the sixteenth century three transcriptions were made of the manuscript. The first, made around 1580 by B. Haus, was lost for three hundred years until it was rediscovered in 1880 in the University Library at Tübingen, where it is still housed. Second, J.J. Beurer of Freiburg copied the text around 1590, and although this transcription was subsequently lost, a number of its readings have been preserved in an appendix to the edition published by Stephanus (Henri Estienne). The *editio princeps* published by Stephanus was based on a transcription he himself had made in 1586. Further, as Ehrman notes, 'two careful collations of the manuscript were made in the nineteenth century for Otto's edition of the text, one by E. Cunitz and the other by E. Reuss in 1861'.[4] However, in 1870 during the Franco–Prussian War,[5] the library in Strasbourg where the manuscript had arrived at some point between 1793 and 1795 caught fire,[6] and the manuscript, which up until that point had survived the vagaries of history, was destroyed.

2. *The Genre and Content of the Epistle*

The opening lines of the epistle are reminiscent of the prologue to Luke's Gospel addressed to Theophilus. The unnamed author speaks to the recipient in the following terms:

> Since I see, most excellent Diognetus, that you are exceedingly zealous to learn the religion of the Christians and are making very clear and careful enquiry about them . . . I welcome this eager desire in you, and I ask God . . . that it may be given to me so to speak that you may gain as

2.   Marrou, *A Diognète*, 6 n. 1, and G. Mercati, 'da incunaboli a codici, 1. Di dua ou tre rari codici greci del cardinale Giovanni da Regusa (d. 1443)', in L. Donati (ed.), *Miscellanea bibliografica in memoria di don Tommaso Accurti*, Storia e Letteratura 15 (Rome: Edizioni di 'Storia e Letteratura', 1947), 3–26.

3.   See H.G. Meecham, *The Epistle to Diognetus* (Manchester: Manchester University Press, 1949), 68.

4.   B.D. Ehrman, *The Apostolic Fathers*, vol. 2, LCL 25 (Cambridge, Mass. and London: Harvard University Press, 2003), 128.

5.   For a description of the wider events that led up the ourbreak of the Franco–Prussian War and a description of its extent, see M. Foot, 'The Origins of the Franco-Prussian War', in J.P.T. Bury, *The New Cambridge Modern History*, vol. 10, *The Zenith of European Power 1830–1870* (Cambridge: Cambridge University Press, 1960), 577–602.

6.   Meecham, *The Epistle to Diognetus*, 68.

much benefit as possible by your hearing, and to you so to hear that the
speaker may not be put to grief. (*Diog.* 1)

Common features, such as the form of address 'excellent', a very similar
opening word in both accounts (Luke: Ἐπειδήπερ; *Diog.*: Ἐπειδή), and
the reference to careful enquiry in both prologues, may suggest that the
author of *Diognetus* has consciously modelled his introduction on that of
the third Gospel. Alternatively, the similarities may be due to wider
rhetorical conventions. However, after the opening, the similarity with the
Gospel genre ceases.

The literary form is that of a letter, addressed to a certain Diognetus by
an unnamed and unknown author.[7] This is a literary letter, rather than a
personal note. In terms of generic categories it is closer to the New
Testament epistle to the Hebrews, with its self-conscious literary flour-
ishes, than it is to Philemon, which is written with a specific situation in
mind and addressed to a single individual, with the apostle Paul
presumably seeing no further applicability in that brief piece of correspondence than its original intent of softening Onesimus to grant his
request. By contrast, the *Epistle to Diognetus*, though addressed to a
named person (although this could be a literary device), has an
intentionally generalized style without 'the inclusion of any homely
personal touches'.[8] Classification of the genre is further complicated by
the observation that the present form of the letter has a 'literary seam'
separating chaps 1—10 from 11—12. These different sections appear to
represent two distinct sources that have been combined during the process
of transmission. The identification of this seam is supported by a marginal
note that existed in the manuscript at the end of chap. 10, and which reads
'and here the copy has a break'.[9] Furthermore, another marginal note
described a lacuna found at 7.6 in the manuscript from which the scribe
was copying. As Ehrman comments, 'there is no way to know how much
of the intervening text has been lost, whether just a few words or a page or
more'.[10]

While the text is in the form of a letter, it has an obvious pedagogical
and apologetic function. The Christian apologists were active in the
second half of the second century, and their purpose was 'explication of
Christian beliefs, practices and morals, and of course the explication

---

7. For the suggestion that Polycarp was the author of the *Epistle to Diognetus*, see C.E.
Hill, *From the Lost Teaching of Polycarp: Identifying Irenaeus' Apostolic Presbyter and the
Author of* Ad Diognetum (Tübingen: Mohr-Siebeck, 2006), 24–31.

8. Meecham, *The Epistle to Diognetus*, 8.

9. Ehrman, *The Apostolic Fathers*, 124.

10. Ehrman, *The Apostolic Fathers*, 124.

tended to grow imperceptibly into defence'.[11] Chief among these writers
was Justin Martyr,[12] who tried to convince his interlocutors that
Christianity had affinities with philosophy and reason rather than with
mythology and popular religion.[13] In a similar vein the *Epistle to
Diognetus* seeks to encourage its readers 'to put aside prejudice and
acknowledge the superiority of Christians' understanding and service of
God to that of Jews'.[14] The connection with the apologists is further
strengthened by consideration of the codex in which the manuscript of
Diognetus was bound. Marrou lists the 22 works that this 260-page
manuscript contained.[15] The first five were works attributed to Justin, of
which the *Epistle to Diognetus* was the fifth and bore the Greek title τοῦ
αὐτοῦ πρὸς Διόγνετον ('of him to Diognetus'), with the pronoun αὐτοῦ
('him') referring back to the title at the head of this collection of five works
by Justin, τοῦ ἁγίου Ἰουστίνου φιλοσόφου καὶ μάρτυρος ('of St. Justin,
philosopher and martyr'). The two parts of the epistle mean that it is
probably necessary to identify two authors of this now-composite work.
Most scholars have rejected the claim of the codex that Justin was the
author, even of chaps 1—10, the apologetic section. Presumably this is on
the basis of stylistic variation and an awareness of the tendency to
attribute unknown works to prominent figures. Regardless of the specific
author, the epistle appears to be most satisfactorily dated in the period of
the apologists in the second half of the second century, although a later
date is not impossible.

In the epistle a number of themes and topics are addressed, but there is
some progression of thought. The contents can be tabulated in the
following manner:

1	Prologue
2.1–10	Futility of paganism
3.1—4.6	Futility of Judaism
5.1—6.10	The character and religion of Christians
7.1–9	God's purpose and the nature of his envoy
8.1—9.6	God's Son: revealer and saviour
10.1–8	Imitation of God
11	Ministry of the Word
12	Unity of knowledge and life

11. R.A. Norris Jr, 'The Apologists', in F. Young, L. Ayres and A. Louth (eds), *The
Cambridge History of Early Christian Literature* (Cambridge: Cambridge University Press,
2004), 36.

12. Other apologists include Tatian, Aristides, Quadratus, Melito, Athenagoras, and, as
a late flowering of the phenomenon, Origen in his *Contra Celsum*.

13. Norris, 'The Apologists', 37.

14. Norris, 'The Apologists', 43–4.

15. Marrou, *A Diognète*, 10–17.

It can be seen that whereas the first ten chapters have an apologetic focus, the final two have internal ecclesial concerns.

3. *The Teaching of the Epistle*

In discussing the religious practices of pagans, the author draws on a strand of polemic that can be traced back at least as far as the prophetic book of Isaiah. Criticising the physical objects before which adherents offer devotion to their gods, the author mockingly writes,

> Is not one a stone, like that which we tread on, another bronze, no better than the implements which have been forged for our use, another wood already decayed, another silver, which needs a man to guard it lest it be stolen . . .? (2.2)

This sarcastic polemic may well be based upon a similar critique in Isa. 44.12–17, which, while not demonstrating the author was ethnically Jewish, does demonstrate a willingness to appropriate Jewish teaching against idolatry. The author identifies the non-participation in idol worship by Christians as the reason for their persecution (2.6). In fact, it is the refusal of Christians to reverence inanimate objects that, according to the author, highlights pagan 'bondage to such gods' (2.10).

Although the author is happy to draw upon Jewish antecedents to criticize pagans, this does not prevent him from subjecting Jews to equally withering criticism. In this regard he appears to observe a category distinction that is prominent in Christian thought between the biblical Israelites, who are classed as proto-Christians, and the contemporary Jews, who are classed as recalcitrants and rejecters of the claim that Jesus is the Messiah. The fundamental argument in chap. 3 revolves around the offerings presented by Jews. While they do not present their gifts to 'images void of sense', the author, nonetheless, accuses the Jews of assuming that God 'were in need of them' (3.3). In this sense the author turns the Jewish critique of paganism against the Jews themselves. Thus, as Jefford describes the train of thought, 'it is claimed that the Jews also have turned the one, true God into an image of idolatry'.[16] The argument continues by suggesting that Jewish 'faddiness' or 'fussiness', to employ Blakeney's terms,[17] is inconsistent since they accept some of God's created gifts for their use while rejecting others, in what the author characterizes as a totally arbitrary fashion (4.2).

Having swept aside the religious practices of both pagans and Jews, the author next presents the positive virtues of the Christian faith. Adherents

16. C.N. Jefford, *Reading the Apostolic Fathers: An Introduction* (Peabody, Mass.: Hendrickson, 1996), 163.
17. E.H. Blakeney, *The Epistle to Diognetus* (London: SPCK, 1943), 42–3.

of this faith are good citizens in that they do not separate themselves from the rest of society (5.1–2), which is surely a thinly veiled criticism of Judaism. They live moral lives and perform good works, yet while presenting these positive aspects the author also describes the reality of the persecution they endure:

> When doing good they are punished as evildoers; suffering punishment,
> they rejoice as quickened into life. By the Jews they are warred against
> as foreigners, and are hunted down by the Greeks. Yet those who hate
> them cannot state the cause of their hostility. (5.16–17)

In chap. 6 the author develops the metaphor that Christians are the 'soul of the world', living as the incorruptible element among corruptible objects. This worldview, with its description of the invisible soul and the contrast between the corruptible and incorruptible, has clear parallels with Platonic thought, and may reflect the way in which Christian apologists tried to appropriate the concepts of Hellenistic philosophers for their own polemical purposes.

Although both Meecham[18] and Jefford[19] group chap. 7 with the previous two chapters, this section has little in common with describing the nature of Christians and their religion, the purpose of the preceding material. In fact chap. 7 is much more closely connected with the two chapters that follow. The focus is upon the Almighty God's choosing not to act through some inferior intermediary, but instead sending as his envoy 'the very Artificer and Maker of the universe himself, by whom he created the heavens' (7.2). The term 'Logos' appears once in chap. 7 (7.2), but not as a title for the one who is referred to as the 'Artificer and Maker'. Nevertheless, this passage may well have a Logos Christology informing its reflection concerning the divine envoy. Cosmological reflection on the role of the Logos was a key aspect among apologists in the development of their Christologies (see e.g. Justin, *Dial.* 129.3–4). Commenting on the development of Logos Christology, especially in the Eastern, or Greek-speaking, church, Dunn states,

> it afforded the better link with the philosophical speculation of the day
> and enabled Christians to contribute their own distinctive claims to the
> then dominant concern of wider religion and philosophy to understand
> and conceptualize the relation between God and the cosmos.[20]

This Christological outlook adds further weight to the case for dating *Diognetus* to the second half of the second century, when the apologists were most active.

18. Meecham, *The Epistle to Diognetus*, 6.
19. Jefford, *Reading the Apostolic Fathers*, 167.
20. J.D.G. Dunn, *Christology in the Making: A New Testament Inquiry into the Doctrine of the Incarnation*, 2nd edn (London: SCM Press, 1989), 214.

In the remaining three chapters of the first section of the letter, the author speaks about the inability to know God apart from divine self-disclosure. This, it is claimed, has occurred, being communicated by God through his παῖς ('servant; child'). Chapter 9 elucidates the salvific dimension of what God brought about through the work of his Son in making righteous those who were formerly wicked (9.3–5). Finally, this is seen as placing a responsibility on those whom God has loved (10.1), which requires them to emulate the goodness of God.

The additional two chapters show a marked change in style, rhetoric and content. In chap. 11 the favoured Christological title 'Logos' occurs six times in this short piece of text. On the basis of the apparent 'progressive development from the status of λόγος to that of υἱός or παῖς',[21] Connolly suggests, on the basis in turn of parallel ideas in *Contra Noetum*, that Hippolytus is also the author of the epistle's two appended chapters.[22] Scholars have not been quick to take up this suggestion. In chap. 12 the author presents an allegorical reading of the two trees that stood in the Garden of Eden (Genesis 2—3). Those who adhere to the divine truth are described as 'a Paradise of delight, who raise up in themselves a fruitful and flourishing tree, and are laden with various fruits' (12.1). However, the author subverts the original Genesis story by supporting the partaking of the fruit from the tree of knowledge. He argues that 'the tree of knowledge does not kill; disobedience kills' (12.2). This creative retelling of the biblical narrative may be motivated by a desire to demonstrate that Christianity is not antithetical to knowledge. In fact, those to whom this allegory is addressed are encouraged to eat from the tree of knowledge: 'if you bear this tree and pluck its fruit, you will always gather what God desires' (12.8). The passage continues by reversing the negative picture of Eve. In contrast to the way the New Testament refers to her as the archetypal transgressor and deceiver (2 Cor. 11.3; 1 Tim. 2.14), *Diognetus* declares, 'Eve is not corrupted, but believed on as a virgin' (12.8). It is likely that an allegorical interpretation is being presented, with Mary portrayed as the second Eve in the new Paradise formed by those who are obedient to the Logos of God. Such symbolism is evident from the mid-second century onwards, and as Meecham observes, 'The parallel between the Eve of Genesis and the Virgin Mary is familiar'.[23] Justin provides a more explicit parallelism between these two women (Justin, *Dial.* 100), as do Irenaeus (*AH* 3.22.4) and Tertullian (*De Carn. Christi* 17). The epistle concludes with a panegyric, eulogizing the salvific plan, the knowledge of the apostles and the providence of God. In

21. Meecham, *The Epistle to Diognetus*, 145.
22. R.H. Connolly, 'Ad Diognetum', *JTS* 37 (1936), 2ff.
23. Meecham, *The Epistle to Diognetus*, 145.

contrast to the argued defence of Christianity in the first ten chapters, this homily is definitely produced for internal consumption.

4. *The Theology of Diognetus*

The theological ideas put forward in this letter vary from the conventional to the creative, and from the mundane to the mature. Its reflections on a number of issues both place it within the wider context of late-second-century thought, and show that the author was capable of innovative and fresh thinking. The anti-pagan and anti-Jewish rhetoric continues a tradition of Christian hostility towards those religions. However, the author creatively uses Jewish polemic against idolatry as the basis for his critique of Judaism: 'The Jews offer God worship in the same fashion as the Greeks; Jewish sacrifices are as foolish as pagan offerings.'[24] The doctrine of deification prominent in Eastern Orthodoxy also appears to be present in the thinking of *Diognetus*, at least in embryonic form.[25] In the final chapter of the first section the epistle states that through practical acts of charity directed to neighbours one may 'become a god to those who receive them, this one is an imitator of God' (10.6). Marrou notes how this doctrine emerges out of the concept of the 'heroic person' in Hellenistic thought.[26] However, by linking this process with acts of charity *Diognetus* grounds the notion of deification in concrete acts which are incumbent upon all Christians.

The ideas about God that are presented in this epistle are not developed in a systematic manner, but rather emerge in an *ad hoc* fashion in the discussion of other topics. God is affirmed as the creator (7.2) and the maker of the universe (8.7). Yet this needs to be held in tension with the presentation of the agent through whom 'he created the heavens' (7.2). Such ideas may be influenced by the Platonic desire to distance the supreme God from the taint of the material realm. The reference to an intermediary may also stem from a more functional concern to attribute a role in creation to the pre-existent Logos. Although the author concedes that it may have been supposed that God had 'no concern or care for us' (8.10), this has been shown to be a misjudgement, because, by the communication of his purpose through his child, God 'proved himself not only a lover of mankind but also long-suffering' (8.7). Thus, through such reasoning the author of *Diognetus* presents a God who is both

24.   Meecham, *The Epistle to Diognetus*, 35.
25.   For a comprehensive treatment of the doctrine of deification see R. Norman, *The Doctrine of Deification in the Greek Patristic Tradition* (Oxford: Oxford University Press, 2005).
26.   Marrou, *A Diognète*, 216.

fundamentally benign and also providential in his planning for the redemption of humanity and the revelation of his love.

Christology is another key theological topic implicit in the thinking of *Diognetus*. Logos Christology is most prominent in the two appended chapters, but it also appears to inform the train of thought in chap. 7. The more prominent titles employed in the first ten chapters are 'child'/ 'servant' (παῖς, 8.9; 9.1), various titles involving the term 'son' ('son of God', 9.4; 'his own son', 9.2; 'only-begotten son', 10.2), 'saviour' (9.6), 'Lord' (7.7) and 'Artificer and Maker of the universe' (7.2). The concentration of these titles in chaps 7—10 is not surprising when one takes into account the progression of thought in the epistle, which turns to the nature of God's envoy only after tackling other issues. Meecham characterizes the Christology as 'simple and unscholastic',[27] and also suggests that 'the author thinks of the Son as not only pre-existent, but subordinate to the Father'.[28] It would, however, be anachronistic to accuse the author of subordinationism. While the divinity of the Son may appear to be derivative on that of the Father, since the plan of redemption needs to be 'communicated to his child', the author does not offer a treatise on the relationship between the first and second persons of the Trinity, and even if he had attempted this it is doubtful whether during the second century the conceptual development had taken place that would have allowed writers to avoid the charge of subordinationism.

Ecclesiology is not a prominent concern in *Diognetus*. The author does refer to believers collectively, and thus shows an awareness of the communal nature of Christianity, but he offers little insight into the governance of that community. The Church is mentioned twice in chap. 11, but this section may date to a period later than that of the preceding material. In chap. 11 the Church is described as the recipient of grace and revelation through the work of the Son, and its role is to ensure that 'the pledges of faith are not broken nor the decrees of the fathers transgressed' (11.5). This position of safeguarding the deposit of faith is articulated again in the following verse: 'the faith of the Gospels is established, and the tradition of the apostles is guarded, and buoyant is the grace of the Church' (11.6). It is interesting to note the plural reference to the 'Gospels'. Stanton observes that 'the fourfold Gospel emerged in the *second half* of the second century and that the Muratorian Fragment and Irenaeus are our primary witnesses'.[29] It may well be that *Diognetus* should be added to this list of primary witnesses to a multiple Gospel canon, although this is not necessarily quite the same thing as a 'fourfold

27. Meecham, *The Epistle to Diognetus*, 26.
28. Meecham, *The Epistle to Diognetus*, 26.
29. G.N. Stanton, *Jesus and Gospel* (Cambridge: Cambridge University Press, 2004), 63, italics in original.

canon'. Papias also bears witness to multiple Gospels, but not necessarily to a corpus of four Gospels.[30]

4. *Conclusions*

Although no manuscript of the *Epistle to Diognetus* is extant, the transcriptions of the text still allow access to the thought-world of the author of the text. Although there are no direct indications of the date of composition or the geographical location of its writer, generic comparisons do assist in situating the document. One must also bear in mind that the epistle is a composite document, and while it may be possible to identify plausible dates for the component parts, it is impossible to suggest when or by whom these components were united. The concerns and style of the first ten chapters have many points of contact with the apologists. This suggests a date after 150 CE. Its plural reference to the 'Gospels' may push this date forward, into the last quarter of the century, but caution is required since the plural form is evidence of some degree of multiplicity without demonstrating an awareness of a fourfold Gospel canon. The dating of the final two chapters are equally problematic, but they give a feel (albeit no more) of being later, and a possible date may be the first half of the third century.

Diognetus gives a robust defence of the Christian faith, and exudes a confidence in the superiority of that form of belief to that of its main competitors, paganism and Judaism. Persecution remains a reality for the author, and to this end he tries to convince his readers that Christianity is no threat, but actually surpasses the best expressions of reason and philosophy. These arguments are an attempt to convince those outside the community that Christianity is a rigorous and attractive faith, worthy to be pursued by all who cherish reason and despise superstition. The vagaries that preserved this letter down through the generations from the late second century to the fifteenth century are unknown, and the fact that it is nowhere cited in patristic or medieval sources is puzzling. However, its rediscovery provides a vivid snapshot of an early attempt to present rationally the integrity of Christianity to a society that was both pluralistic and hostile.

---

30.   Though see the discussion by Hill in Chapter 5, sect. 3 above.

INDEX

Ignatius *Epistle to the Romans* 23, 81, 82, 89, 99, 102, 103
Ignatius *Epistle to the Smyrneans* 81, 89, 90, 95, 96, 98, 100, 101, 104
Ignatius *Epistle to the Trallians* 81, 89, 94, 95, 100, 101
three recensions 82–4
use of the New Testament 103–6, 107
eschatology 9, 10, 12, 19–20, 45, 49–51, 117
eucharist 3, 4, 8, 14, 17–18, 93–8
Eusebius *Historia Eccesiastica* 1n. 2, 6n. 18, 23, 33, 42, 43, 44, 46, 47, 52, 53–5, 57, 61–2, 84–5, 106, 109, 110, 128, 130, 133, 134, 143, 145
Eve 153
4 Ezra 60

Fragments of Papias 42–51, 57
Franco-Prussian War 148

Gaius 133
Gentiles 15
Gnosticism 11, 48, 91
   Basilides 48–9
Gospel of Peter 9n. 29
Gospel of Thomas 3, 5, 9, 40
gospel traditions 45–7, 70, 155, 156

Hadrian 48, 55–6, 75, 89
Harnack, Adolf von 13–14, 18
Holy Spirit 18, 66, 120
hospitality 11

Ignatius 10, 23, 39, 108, 113, 119, 121–3
incarnation 39
Irenaeus 23, 37, 43, 44, 49, 50, 58–9, 109, 110, 126, 127, 128, 153

Jerome 56, 72–3
Jerusalem 19, 108
Jesus 2, 3, 19, 30, 39, 99, 117, 151
Jewish-Christianity 15, 16, 50, 71, 80
Johannine secessionists 90
Judaism 7, 77–80, 90–2, 144, 150, 151, 154, 156
Jupiter Capitolinus 75
Justin Martyr 35, 45, 50, 61, 80n. 46, 126, 139, 141n. 43, 144, 150, 152

Lord's prayer 8, 18

Marcion 108, 114, 115, 124
Marcus Aurelius 6, 61
martyrdom 10, 81, 102–3, 106, 108, 123, 134–6, 138–45
Martyrdom of Polycarp 81, 108, 125 **126–46**
   authenticity 136–45
   composition of text 132–6
   dating 127–32, 146
Mary, Mother of Jesus 89, 100–1, 153
Melito of Sardis 34
Minucius Fundanus 6
monarchical episcopacy 11, 24, 87, 97
Montanism 67, 129
Muratorian Cannon 1, 64

Nerva 74

Origen 24, 61, 72–3, 85

paganism 151, 156
Palestine 3
Papyrus Egerton 2, 9n. 29
Paul 2, 3, 4, 10, 11, 16, 30, 70, 80, 98, 102, 106, 108, 118–19, 128
penance 66
persecution 28, 36, 38, 64, 66, 68–70, 155
Peter 23, 46, 103
Pharisees 18
Philo 75, 80n. 46
Photius 31
Pionius 129, 131, 132, 133
Pliny the Younger 6, 11
Polycarp 11, 81, 95, 108, 126–46
Polycarp's *Epistle to the Philippians* 1, 22, 29, 73, 81, 89, **108–25**, 127
   authenticity 124
   date 123–4
   imitation 119–20
   partition theory 120–3
   righteousness 113, 115, 116, 118–19
presbyter 29, 35, 93–4
prophet 19
proto-orthodox 109
Pseudo-Clementine Recognitions 23, 24
Purim 131

Q 2, 3, 9, 17, 45
Quadratus, apologist 55–6
Quadratus, bishop of Athens 55–6